Mary Gilliatt's
NEW GUIDE TO
DECORATING

Mary Gilliatt's
NEW GUIDE TO
DECORATING

conran
OCTOPUS

—Conran Octopus—Mary Gillatt's New Guide to Decorating—MP

First published in 1988 by
Conran Octopus Limited
2-4 Heron Quays
London E14 4JP
www.conran-octopus.co.uk
First published in paperback in 1992

Reprinted 1994 (twice), 1998 (twice)

This paperback edition published in 1998

Repinted 1998, 2001

British Library Cataloguing in Publication Data
Gilliatt, Mary
      Mary Gilliatt's new guide to decorating.
      I. Residences. Interiors. Decorating
Amateurs' manuals
      I. Title
      643'.7

ISBN 1 85029 979 X

Author of part 4   Elizabeth Wilhide

Project Editor   Polly Powell
Editor   Paul Barnett
Technical Editors   John McGowan   Roger DuBern
                       Christine Parsons
Editorial Assistant   Jane Harcus
Visualizer   Jean Morley

Art Editor   Karen Bowen
Design Assistant   Alison Shackleton
Picture Research   Shona Wood
Production   Michel Blake
Illustrators   Hayward Art Group Vanessa Luff
                       Cherrill Parris   Maggie Raynor
                       Chris Welch   Roy White

Typeset by Tradespools
Printed in China

Where terminology differs, the British word is followed
by the American equivalent in brackets.

CONTENTS

Part 4: *Successful Decorating*

INTRODUCTION

This book is not only a comprehensive and practical guide to decorating, it is also a very personal work. It is personal because it is an updated distillation of my own experiences as an interior designer, experiences which I think have universal application.

As a design writer I am fortunate enough to see not only other people's design and decoration, but also all that is new and interesting in decorating techniques, lighting, furniture, fabrics, and wall and floor coverings. But as an interior decorator who has had to learn the hard way for myself, I have to think how best to use this wealth of merchandise and techniques, and where. On a daily basis I have to cope with the reality of juggling with these elements to create a satisfying whole. I have to deal with the problems that so often occur to upset the best laid plans. I know the compromises one has to make before a room, or an apartment, or a house can be finished to one's satisfaction. I understand the difficulties so many people have in reaching a decision, making choices, and the frustrations this can cause. But equally I know the pure delight of achievement, of seeing ideas and schemes translated into rooms that really do give pleasure and enjoyment. And this is worth a very great deal.

Although I have written other guides to decorating in the past, the fact is that I never stop learning, never stop experiencing. And it is with this ever-increasing number of experiences fresh in my mind that I write now. I hope that this book will help people to recognize the pitfalls that can exist and how to avoid them, offer them formulae that I know work well and guide them through the whole process of decorating a home. Above all, I want people to experience for themselves the very real delight and pleasure that good interior decorating can bring.

Part 1

Getting the Framework Right

The Professional Approach

Good interior design is as much about practicality, comfort and detail as it is about style and aesthetics. Any competent designer asked either to improve a home or to plan one from scratch would first try to find out exactly how the occupants live, how they would like to live if they were sufficiently wealthy, and how much they can actually afford to spend. Starting with the ideal and working backwards towards a realistic budget is as good a way as any of sorting out the genuine priorities.

First Questions The most useful thing that the designer can do at first is to draw people out in order to establish their tastes and the factors in their home that make them feel most at ease. This done, the designer can use the information as a basis for his or her design solutions. Obviously, if you are acting as your own designer, it makes sense to ask yourself the same kind of salient questions, however elementary they might seem, and to take a hard objective look, in the light of the money available for the project, at each room you want to decorate. The most successful decoration is the result of effective elimination. And working slowly within a clearly defined framework gives you more time to think problems through, to experiment and to learn.

The questions that a designer would ask clients generally come under three categories: the *practical*, the *aesthetic* (on questions of taste and style preferences) and the *budgetary*. The following are typical examples of questions a designer would be likely to ask you, and which you should therefore ask yourself.

Practical
- How long do you expect to stay in your present home?
- Are there, or are there likely to be, children in the household?
- What is the maximum number of rooms you think you will need? Can these be found from existing space? Could you, for example, use roof or attic space?
- Do any elderly relatives live with you, or are they frequent house-guests? Do you, for example, need extra lighting or hand-grip rails?
- Are there any pets in the household? (This, of course, affects the types of finishes and surfaces used.)
- Where does the family feel most comfortable eating – in the kitchen, living room, family room or dining room?
- Almost certainly some of your rooms will have multiple uses (for example, the children may do their homework in the dining room); if so, are the needs of the various users likely to conflict?
- How often do you entertain, and how? How many people do you generally entertain at once?
- Where do you entertain? The living room? The dining room? The kitchen?
- Is sleeping accommodation cramped for the family?
- Are the washing/bathing/toilet facilities inconvenient? Are there problems at peak times (for example, in the mornings)?
- Is your overall storage space insufficient? If so, is it capable of being expanded?
- What are the regular leisure-time activities of the members of the household? Watching TV or video, or using a computer?
- Do any of the family have any specialist activities or hobbies, requiring rooms to be set aside as workrooms? Should there be rooms reserved for equipment such as the washing machine and dryer, or the freezer?

Aesthetic
- Would you say you and your partner share similar tastes or do you have decidedly different tastes? Have you agreed to have your own way in different rooms?
- When it comes to colour schemes, do you feel quite sure of what you want? Are you confused and uncertain, or are you open-minded?
- With what particular colours are you happiest? Are there any colours you really dislike?
- Would you say your taste in decorating and furnishing is eclectic? Traditional? Modern? Romantic? Idiosyncratic? Minimalist? Do your views depend on the house or room in question? And what styles do you admire? Country style (from whatever country)? Sophisticated townhouse? Oriental? Indoor–outdoor? American Colonial? Empire? Regency? Victorian? Neoclassical? Post-Modern? Edwardian? Art Nouveau? Art Deco? 1950s retrospective?
- Do you possess any particular painting, fabric, rug or similar item which would make a good starting point for your basic colour scheme?

Budgetary
- What do you feel is the maximum you can spend on your project (bearing in mind that you should always keep a contingency sum in reserve for emergencies)?
- Do you think this budget will be restrictive? Reasonable? More than adequate? Is your opinion on this based on research into current prices for merchandise and services, or is it just guesswork? (If the latter, it is essential that you research all prices *first*. You will find that almost everything is more expensive than you think.)
- If you could list (ignoring costs) the ten luxuries that would make your home seem more attractive to you, what would they be?
- Is any member of the household good with their hands? (This can make a big difference to the overall budget.) Skilful at carpentry? Painting?
- Even if your budgeted plans are reasonably modest, will you have to borrow money from somewhere, such as the bank? Would it make sense, in terms of the value of the house or your desire for a better lifestyle, to be more ambitious in your plans and arrange a large loan?

STRUCTURE AND SERVICES	REMARKS
Roof	Slight dip. Tiles missing. Gutter air brick broken.
External Walls	Rendering cracked, patches missing. Damp patch by front window.
Internal Walls	Crack in hall/kitchen wall. Stain on bathroom wall.
Floors	Stairs creak, handrail loose. Dining room floor needs stripping.
Windows	Living room and bedroom one, windows need replacing. How much?
Insulation	Check insulation in attic. Front windows on main road need double glazing.
Woodwork	Get in specialist to check for woodworm.
Ceilings	Cracks in main bedroom and dining room.
Doors	Front door rattles. Back door needs new lock. Dining room door sticks.
Electricity	Does system need rewiring?
Gas	None - any possibility?
Heating	Check boiler - looks old. Check cost of replacement - wall hung boiler?
Ventilation	Ask about an extractor fan in bathroom. Will landing window open?

Assessing Alterations   Once you have a rough idea of what you need, want and think you can afford, list the rooms you want to reorganize, noting for each of them any repairs needed and any alterations that you would like to make. Ask yourself some more questions:

● How will you treat the walls, woodwork, ceilings and windows? Would it be an improvement to add French doors anywhere?

● How new is the wiring in the house? Is it up to the standard required by the law, and is it adequate for your needs? What sort of lighting will you need and how will you achieve it? Do you have enough sockets (outlets), and are they in the right places?

● If you have air conditioning, are the units unsightly? If so, can they be improved? Could you remove them from the windows and resite them in the walls?

● Is the heating adequate? How old is the system? How much would it cost to have it replaced? If you have unsightly ducts for hot-air heating, how much would it cost to replace the system with hot-water pipes?

● What about means of escape in the event of fire? Are there laws in your area governing such things as fire doors and fire escapes? Should you consult an expert on this?

● What about the plumbing? Can you fit in another bathroom, shower room, or lavatory? And how much would this cost? Do existing fixtures need replacing or can they be resurfaced? How (and how well) do all the toilets flush?

● What about the flooring? Are there handsome floorboards under the existing flooring? Can they be scraped and sanded? Do they need repairing or replacing? If you would like a different kind of floor (for example, quarry tiles or marble), is that feasible and, if so, what is the cost? If the price is too high, what about painting the floor, or doing interesting things with linoleum or vinyl tiles? Where do you need carpeting, and what is that going to cost?

● Do you need to put in burglar, fire and smoke alarms? How much will these cost?

● Is the house fully insulated? If not, is it important to you that it should be? Again, how much will this cost? (If it proves extremely expensive, it may make more financial sense not to insulate – but this is unusual.)

● In what condition is the existing hardware – door handles, locks, fingerplates, window catches, light switches, dimmers and taps (faucets)? Do they need replacing, replating or rebrassing? What will this do to your budget? (These are just the sort of details that can all too easily be forgotten.)

Structure and Services   All the questions noted above might seem elementary, but in the enthusiasm or the confusion of the moment it is easy to forget the basics: far too many people embark on ambitious decorating and furnishing projects before they deal with basic structural matters. Moreover, unless you know the answers to all these questions – and the likely costs in each case – you cannot really form a realistic budget. If you own your home, it is vital that you get the framework into good, solid workable order before you embark on the more glamorous cosmetics, such as wall, window and floor coverings, the furnishings and the other various accessories. It is a waste of time, effort and money to start to decorate before the structure is put in order.

So that you do not miss defects that you will later have to remedy, whatever the cost, it helps to make a preliminary checklist. The two main headings are 'Structure' and 'Services'. By each subheading under these main headings, note the basic state of affairs: if a service is in good working order or if improvements or repairs are needed. A typical example of such a list, with the comments written in, is shown here.

Rented homes are, of course, another matter. It is to be hoped that the landlord will have taken care of any structural faults. Nevertheless it certainly helps to be aware, before you sign the lease, of the external condition of the property and the state of its amenities – heating, air conditioning, wiring, plumbing, windows, drainage, roof, and so on. If they seem not to be in good order and the landlord is unwilling to attend to them, think very seriously before you take on the lease, especially if it is for a reasonable period of time and you want to embark on your own decorating.

Getting the Framework Right

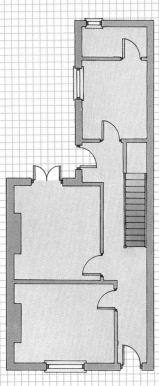

Making the Most of Space

Alterations to the structure and fittings of your home can radically affect internal space – and the way you use it. Some types of building work may cost less than you think, but remember that structural changes will almost certainly cause major disruption.

You could:

1 Unblock fireplaces
2 Knock through an internal arch
3 Install French doors
4 Build a conservatory or back porch
5 Relocate external or internal doors
6 Install larger windows
7 Replace the wall between the kitchen and the dining room with a counter
8 Install an additional washroom

Structural Assessment

Faced with an empty room or rooms which you want to change, what is your first step? Most people are generally so relieved to have found somewhere to live that is reasonably affordable, reasonably convenient and reasonably cheap to heat, cool and light, that they just accept and adapt to whatever space they have, however awkward it might be, without too much question. All too often they start on the basic decoration and furnishing without pausing to consider seriously the shape of the space and how it could be manipulated to its best advantage. Yet rooms can often be rethought, changed around and vastly improved at a surprisingly low cost.

Spatial Solutions Do not be afraid of taking down partition walls. This costs very little by comparison with building new ones, and usually makes a profound difference. However, even if you are certain that you are dealing with a non-load-bearing partition wall, check with an expert before you risk starting to demolish it. You should, of course, be wary of walls that contain water or gas pipes, electrical conduits, and so on. Professional house or apartment plans may show whether things like these are present but, if you have come new to a home and have no means of knowing, common sense and a little detective work reveal their whereabouts. For example, be cautious of walls with electric switches and sockets (outlets), walls below or next door to a bathroom or lavatory or to the sink or appliance wall of a kitchen, and obviously walls with radiators, ducts, vents or air-conditioning units.

Walls can have an archway cut through them, or be cut halfway down or at either side so that they form divisions rather than solid masses. Or if you have totally removed a partition wall, you can form your own flexible room dividers using bookcases, shelving units, screens or screen-like structures. A particularly graceful effect can be achieved using pillars, or pillars and pilasters; these can be picked up either from places selling architectural remnants and details or from one of the many companies who are now reproducing such architectural merchandise.

Do you need all the hall, gallery or corridor space you have at present? It may well be that you can slice off bits of these to add to your living areas, or to make a kitchen big enough to eat in.

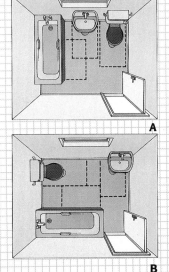

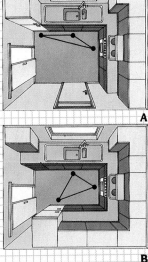

Planning Your Bathroom
An important factor to consider when planning your bathroom is the individual 'activity' space needed around each piece of equipment. Some overlap may be acceptable (A), but ideally each space should be self-contained (B)

Planning Your Kitchen
An L-shaped plan (A) is ideal for kitchens with limited wall space and for combined cooking and dining areas. A U-shaped plan (B) can be used for small spaces, but it can be awkward if more than one person uses the kitchen at the same time.

You might consider making internal 'windows' or openings in a dividing wall to provide more light and airiness. These could be conventionally square or oblong, arched, or in the shape of long slits, like clerestory windows, so that the adjoining space (and its light) shows through and gives more perspective to the room. New doorways, too, can be situated in more convenient positions, and old ones can be closed up in order to provide more wall space. If you find old or antique doors which you would like to work into your scheme you can make the openings to fit them. However, always consult an expert before knocking through a wall; you can never be too cautious when it comes to altering structural elements.

New windows can often be added to rooms. These make an enormous difference to the feeling of light and space, especially if French doors or long windows can be added (or substituted for smaller varieties). There is a large choice of ready-made windows in all shapes and sizes, including storm windows with flyscreens for the summer, and you can have infinitely more varieties made. But it is, of course, important always to think of what the windows will look like from the outside of the building before you enthusiastically cut out new apertures. Moreover, new windows should match existing windows as closely as possible, and should comply with any local building or planning regulations. Putting in new windows is difficult structural work, however, and certainly you should not tackle it without expert advice.

Getting the Framework Right
STRUCTURAL ASSESSMENT

Making the most of a small space demands careful planning and organization. Here two basic rooms have been converted into a studio apartment.

1 The main dividing wall was removed

2 Partition walls were built to create a bathroom, lobby and shower room

3 Major plumbing work had to be carried out to install the bathroom and kitchen

4 The door into the smaller room was blocked up

5 A section of wall was built to enclose the entrance and to support a built-in desk and some storage space

6 The kitchen units were extended across the room to act as a space divider and storage area

7 The chimney breast and fireplace were removed to make space for a sofa bed

8 A cupboard (closet) was constructed for storing clothes

If you definitely need more rooms in your house, think carefully about reorganizing the space you already have. Could you, for example, make a large kitchen–dining room out of the basement in order to free valuable space on the ground or first floor? Or, if the attic is big enough, what about making a pair of bedrooms and another bathroom up there? Again, you could think of converting the attic into a playroom, studio, games room, family room or media room/den. Built-in (integral) garages are often successfully converted into additional rooms. If you are fortunate enough to live in a detached house, you may be able to make more sense and space out of a house simply by reorienting it, so that the main entrance is on another side.

If it is not possible to conjure more rooms from the existing space you will have to think of adding on an extension. This means you will certainly have to hire an architect (see page 24) in order to achieve the best possible blend, but first you must find out the cost of building per square foot in your area and make sure that you can get from any relevant authorities the permission to go ahead and build. Also, look up the costs of adding

on a prefabricated building, such as a conservatory or sun room, before you make a final decision to build an extension from scratch. Remember that, if a prefabricated building contains the kind of space that will suit you, it may be possible to effectively disguise its origins by putting some sort of fence around its foundations, painting it to match the main structure and growing climbing plants up the side. Whatever the alterations you decide to make, remember to first check with your local authorities.

One-Room Living In a small studio or one-room apartment you can help create the feeling of space by building in multifunctional furniture. For example, you could build a platform big enough to put a mattress on and serve as a desk top with storage space underneath. Other options include a dining-table–desk, built-in bench-seating with lift-up seats and storage underneath, and window seats built along the same lines. Where no window seats exist, or if there is no natural place for them, a little ingenuity can help you out – providing extra seating that does not take up too much space,

5 4 6 3 2 1 8

while incidentally helping make a characterless room look much more interesting. You can frame a window down to the floor with lengths of timber (lumber) some 60cm/2ft deep which can be painted in with either the walls or the woodwork. You can then build a ledge across at seat height and make it comfortable with fabric-covered foam and with pillows or cushions at the back. Instead of draperies or curtains, use a shade of some sort which matches the window-seat cover.

Different levels, even if the differences are only very slight, can often segregate the various areas of a single room, whether it is too small and has to serve as both a living and a sleeping room or – as in the case of a loft or a renovated country barn – is too big. In a small studio apartment, differentiating, say, dining–working, sitting and sleeping areas, or even one step up at one end or around the perimeter of the room, can make an extraordinary difference to the way a given space looks and works. This might sound a complicated solution, but in fact it is not as expensive as it sounds. However, such alterations must be considered at the beginning of your decorating schedule.

Storage Ideas

● Hinged window seats provide extra storage space
● Shelving is cheap, easy to install and provides an excellent opportunity for display
● Use hooks and wire grids to hang kitchen utensils, tools and clothing
● Tailor-made beds raised off the floor can incorporate cupboards and drawers
● Simple drapes or curtains can turn a recess into a useful space for hanging clothes
● Brightly coloured stacking systems are ideal for children's rooms – but they are just as useful for storing tools and cleaning equipment
● Old chests and deep wooden boxes – either stripped or painted – make attractive side tables and provide extra storage

Space Savers

● Painting a room in plain, light colours can make it feel more airy and spacious
● Fold-up chairs and tables, which can be stored out of the way, are practical and convenient
● Mirrors, in the form of sheets or tiles, reflect light and can have the effect of doubling the apparent proportions of a room
● See-through furniture is unobtrusive in a room that is short of space
● Choose furniture for flexibility – a piece of furniture that can be moved around a room easily is invaluable
● Buy low-level furniture for small rooms. Towering units and bulky cupboards will overcrowd the space
● Use simple window dressings and keep windows clear of clutter

Drawing Up Plans

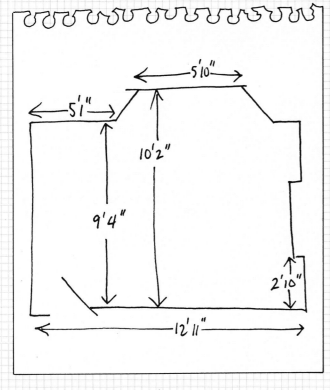

Assuming you own your house or apartment, you can take down internal partition walls, add new ones, block up old doors and make new openings in more convenient places. The visual and practical differences such changes will make are out of all proportion to the comparatively modest expense involved. If none exist already, it is certainly worth making a new set of plans of each room. Quite apart from their usefulness when you are working out any changes, they will also be invaluable for deciding on furniture arrangement later.

To make your preliminary plans you simply measure the room or rooms and draw the area out roughly to scale – not forgetting to add details of windows, doors, fireplaces, odd corners and indentations, fireplaces, supporting pillars and any other permanent fixtures. Then measure accurately the lengths of the walls, the proportions of the doors, windows and any other features, the thickness of partitions, and the distance between fittings. Measure also the positions of electrical

sockets (outlets), telephone sockets (jacks), radiators and other permanent heating appliances, and air conditioners. All these should be clearly marked on the sketch. This constitutes your preliminary survey. To draw up an accurate plan you must decide on the scale: a scale of 2cm to 1m (about ¼in to 1ft) is reasonable for general areas, such as living rooms and bedrooms, but a larger scale – perhaps twice this – is better for rooms such as kitchens, bathrooms and laundry rooms which have to take a number of fixtures.

Draw the sketch of the room to your chosen scale using a sharp pencil. It is essential to do this absolutely accurately. It may seem tiresome to keep stressing accuracy, but I have learned from bitter experience how the slightest inaccuracy can spoil an inspired idea. I once had to send back a complete set of kitchen units because the architect's measurements were out by a tiny amount – but just enough to ensure that there was no way in the world the cabinets could be fitted into their assigned niches. Because they had been custom-made I could not reclaim any money, so there was nothing for it but to pay all over again. The only consolation is that the architect is now known to be the most accurate measurer in the world!

Another point to bear in mind is that the correct measurement of windows, doors and staircases (especially at any turns) is particularly important when it comes to moving in furniture. Many a double bed, piano, large armchair or cabinet has had to be returned to the supplier when narrow doors and windows made access to a room impossible. By the same token, do not forget to measure the depth, width and height of elevators.

Once you have a reasonable plan or plans with which to work, you can juggle around the various possibilities for making the most of your space.

Plans also provide an excellent means of working out furniture layout: they can help you to arrange what you already have or to decide what you need to buy. The simplest way to assess the merits of different layouts is to draw the outlines of the furniture on a separate piece of paper, then cut out the shapes and move the pieces about on the plan until you discover the optimum arrangement. Remember that the furniture cut-outs should be constructed to the same scale as the basic room plan.

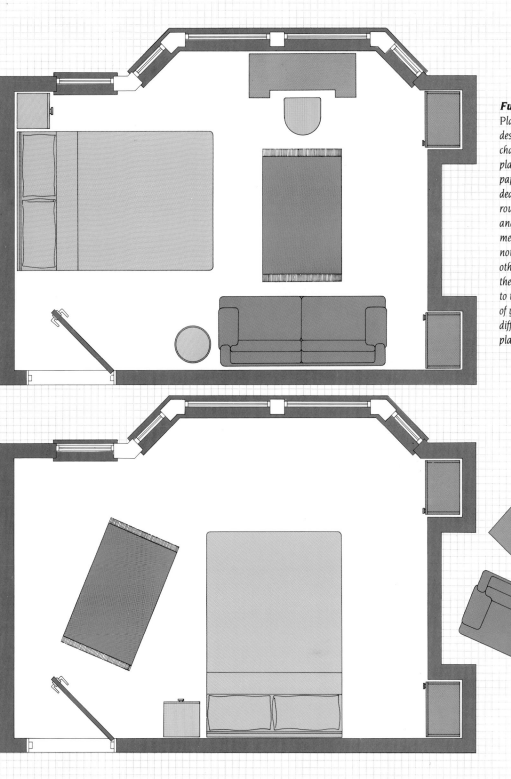

Furniture Arrangement

Plans are important tools in the design process. Even if you are just changing the furniture around, planning the new arrangement on paper first can save you a great deal of time and effort. Make a rough sketch of the area (far left) and mark on it accurate measurements of all dimensions, noting alcoves, doors, windows and other structural details. Draw up the plan on graph paper. Working to the same scale, cut out the shapes of your furniture and try out different arrangements on your plan (above left and below left).

Checking Out the Faults

Dampness, rot or wood infestation should be treated *before* you embark on any decorating. You would not be pleased if your newly painted walls began to crumble because of rot, or your wall treatments began to peel because of damp.

Dampness is a complex problem for which, often, there is no single cause and no single straightforward or cheap remedy. In order to cure a patch of dampness, it is, for example, often necessary to open up sections of walls, floors and so on; doing this can reveal other defects so that the cost of the project rises very rapidly. It is important, therefore, that proper advice is sought right from the beginning of your decorating schedule in order to avoid unnecessary expense.

Dampness is caused by several factors such as:
- excessive condensation
- penetration of water through cracked rendering, poorly constructed exterior cavity walls, bricks or tiles that need repointing
- a defective damp-proof course (vapor barrier), or no damp-proof course at all
- leaking pavements (in the case of town houses with basements)
- badly formed junctions of roofs to chimneys, or leaking or blocked gutters
- badly constructed flat roofs, or missing tiles

All of these factors can cause further defects such as dry rot, wet rot and efflorescence (in which soluble salts in the plaster or mortar, on contact with water, force their way to the surface and spoil decorations).

Applying cosmetic cures is rather like digging holes in wet sand. The only solution is to try to correct the basic constructional fault at the foot of the trouble. In Britain, for example, you can take advantage of certain proprietary systems designed for specific problems. A popular method of putting in a damp-proof course is to inject chemicals into the wall. Another method involves cutting out a course of mortar and putting in a damp-proof membrane. A less common means of eliminating dampness is the use of hygrovents. These are porous earthenware tubes inserted in walls to attract water, which is then evaporated away through them. Finally, waterproof liquids are painted on to prevent penetrating damp; they have to be periodically renewed.

In the United States the problem of dampness is limited largely to basements and there is special damp-proofing paint available which can be applied to both external walls and the inside basement walls. This paint acts as a water-repellent shield against dampness and resists mildew.

Eliminating Rot Dry rot starts in moist wood and is usually found in old, damp buildings – although occasionally it is found in new ones – and it can lurk behind walls so that it is not immediately obvious. This type of rot is extremely dangerous because it can spread from wet wood to dry wood by means of airborne spores or through strands of fungal growth. It is essential to eradicate dry rot as quickly as possible after you have spotted the problem. You can detect dry rot by its musty, rotting mushroomy smell, and the excrescences it grows, which are of an orange to deep-brown colour. Affected wood is inclined to crack in squares.

If you find dry rot, your best plan is immediately to contact a firm that specializes in the treatment of dry rot. All defective wood will need to be replaced, and the new wood will have to be treated with preservative. Any adjoining brickwork or plasterwork should also be thoroughly sterilized.

Wet rot occurs only in conditions of constant dampness: if the cause of the dampness is arrested the rot dies. Decayed wood and the surrounding area should nevertheless be treated in the same way as for dry rot, because dry-rot spores may well be present and the drying-out process provides them with the perfect conditions for germinating.

Woodworm and Termites Ordinary woodworm is caused by the common furniture beetle, which has either flown in through the window or been escorted in, comfortably ensconced in an infected piece of furniture. Young beetles usually emerge in June or July; they lay their eggs in cracks and joints or in the rough backs of furniture. Early summer is thus the time to exterminate them: spray or brush unpainted and unvarnished wood (e.g., beams) with an insecticide, and inject insecticide into every third hole in painted and varnished wood.

Termites are a major problem in the United States and, in many states, a termite inspection report must be done. They should be exterminated as quickly as possible to avoid major damage.

Insulation·

Windows, doors, walls, fireplaces, letterboxes, floors and above all the roofs of old houses are all potential heat losers, and money spent on insulation will certainly be saved on fuel bills. Do not, however, make a house so draughtproof that *no* air can get in or out, because rooms will only get muggy, fires will not draw properly, the boiler or furnace (if any) will do less than its best (and become dangerous), and doors will not close. If you are going to the trouble of insulating internal walls, you may want to insulate for sound as well.

Windows   Double glazing, or the addition of storm windows, is not cheap, but it can make an enormous difference to heat loss. It is best installed in a house that is anyway undergoing extensive renovation, since existing windows may have to be removed – a process that will inevitably cause a mess. Another consideration is that the installation of double glazing may add to the value of your house. Remember, however, that you may have to seek permission from the relevant authority before going ahead.

Doors   Gaps under doors can be cured by fixing a draughtproofing strip bought from a hardware store. For outside doors, some manufacturers make bronze strips that are relatively unaffected by rain or damp and are guaranteed to last 10 years. Threshold fittings where one part is fixed to the floor and the other to the bottom so that the two parts are pressed against each other when the door is closed are very efficient, as are the ones that consist of a drop-flap made of rubber or vinyl, which is forced down against the floor when the door is closed to make a draughtproof seal. Small closed porches added to outside doors can make a difference to heat loss.

Roofs   Roofs are fairly easy to insulate. If you have a sloping one and use the space only, if at all, for storage, insulate the floor area with some loose-fill material like vermiculite granules poured between the joists and levelled off. If the area is draughty enough for the granules to be blown around, it would be best to use glassfibre blankets. If you intend to convert the space into an attic room, insulate the sloping rafters with fibreboard or with plasterboard (drywall) or wallboard with glassfibre blankets underneath.

Before Insulation

25%

10%

35%

15%

8%

15%

12%

5%

9%

9%

After Insulation

Keeping the Cold Out
Without insulation, heat will escape from your home via windows, doors, walls, the roof, the ground floor – even from fireplaces and letterboxes. Roof insulation, double glazing and draughtproofing will reduce heating bills.

Fireplaces   Always get throat controls fitted to fireplaces – otherwise you will be heating the outside air through the chimney to nobody's benefit except that of the fuel company!

Letterboxes and Pet Doors   These can be protected from howling gales and snow storms by a variety of flaps made of bronze, brass, stainless steel or other metal. Alternatively, you can tack a piece of leather or heavy fabric above a letterbox on the inside. Pet doors can be sealed shut at night.

Floors   Ground-level wood floors can be draughty because of the air flow coming through the air bricks in the house walls. Ventilation is vital to prevent the wood rotting so never block air bricks. Any good floor covering, especially carpet, will eliminate draughts. Before laying the material, seal gaps as described for sanding floors (page 168); lay hardboard (masonite), plywood or underlay – depending on chosen floor covering – and seal gaps below skirtings (baseboards) with beading.

Walls   Cavity walls can be filled with blown glassfibre or other mineral fibre injected by a specialist company. Solid brick walls can be lined with plasterboard (drywall) fixed onto a wood framework with a glassfibre blanket sandwiched in between.

21

Getting the Services in Order

Any alterations or improvements to services or utilities like electricity, gas, plumbing, heating, television, cable, telephone and air conditioning should definitely be done before any decoration is started. Having to add pipes and wires after the walls and floors are finished constitutes a disaster.

Electricity Anyone buying an old house or apartment should get a surveyor's (engineer's) report on both the structure and services. He or she will give you a reliable indication of what must be done to the building right away and what can wait. However, it is also important to inform the surveyor of any changes you might be planning to make in the electrical supplies (or, for that matter, in the plumbing or heating), since this might make a vital difference to his or her comments on the current adequacy of the service. If, for example, you want to install extra electric appliances – a new stove, perhaps, instead of an old gas one; air conditioning units; a dishwasher, washing machine and dryer; a waste extractor, or a low-voltage circuit to provide special lighting for art and low lighting for the garden – the existing electrical sockets (outlets) might be far from sufficient, especially in an old apartment block. The surveyor can tell you so only if he or she has been informed that this is what you want to do. Ignorant of your plans, the report may state that the electrical services are perfectly adequate.

It will certainly assist any electrician and help you to get an accurate idea of costs if you take a clean copy of your room plans (see page 18) and mark on them exactly where you want to add any new electric sockets and their purpose – for a table lamp, heater, air conditioner, towel heater or whatever. Then mark on the plans where you need any special lighting fixtures, like wallwashers, framing projectors, spots of every description and wall lights, as well as where you want light in every room, and where you want switches and dimmers. If you do not want centre lights you must say so at the outset, and make sure that you specify that you would like the switches for lamps and wall lights to be near the doors, or you will forever be crawling around in the darkness trying to find them.

If you can decide at this stage exactly the fixtures that you would like, it will be an even greater help to your budgetary planning (see page 26). Installing lights – especially sophisticated ones – in a number of rooms can add up to a surprising amount of money: totting up the prices for an ideal lighting scheme can definitely give you an 'electric shock'! Nevertheless, since good lighting more than pays for itself in the long run in terms of looks and comfort – not to mention safety, especially if there are elderly people around – making sure that the lighting scheme you install at least allows you much flexibility as possible for the future.

Gas Unless the building already has a mains gas supply or you are doing a great deal of renovation, usually it is not worth the trouble of getting it laid on – although 'bottled gas' (or propane gas) appliances can often be an attractive option, particularly if you live in a remote area. That said, if you already have a gas furnace or stove, it should be comparatively easy to run gas pipes to the fireplace for a gas-fuelled imitation coal or log fire: these can be surprisingly realistic.

The ease of installing mains gas supplies varies from country to country. In Britain it is not too terribly expensive and payment can be spread out over a long period. This is not necessarily the case in North America, where you would do best to stick to electrical supplies – unless, as I have noted, gas is already installed. Another factor worth considering, especially if your household contains very old or very young people, is that of safety.

Plumbing and Heating If you want to add on a new bathroom, shower room, kitchen, cloakroom or lavatory, it is always best to try to plan the addition around existing plumbing, or at least beside an outside wall so that waste pipes can be accommodated. Renovating an existing bathroom to make it more luxurious – even just changing the position of the various fixtures to get more storage space or to make the room seem larger – is a complicated, dusty job which should certainly be finished before any decorative work is started. Equally, remember that items of bathroom equipment like baths, jacuzzis, showers and double basins tend to be bulky, and so should be carefully measured to ensure that you will have no difficulties installing them.

It is likely that the house will already have an adequate heating system but, if not, you should call in

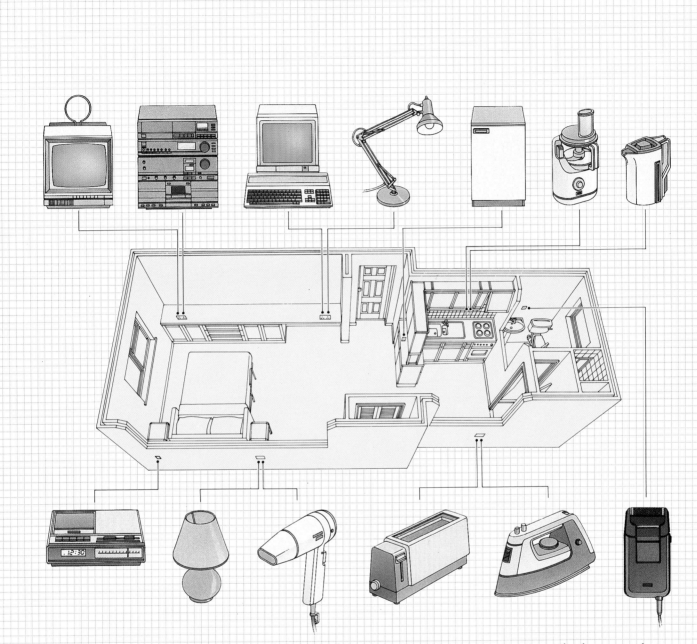

an expert to give you advice and an idea of price. Much will depend on the height of the ceilings and the general age, size and condition of the house. A great many people, however, need or want to change the heating method in their homes – from ducted warm-air heating to small-bore hot-water heating, for example, or from conventional radiators to skirting (baseboard) heating. Consult your chosen contractor on this, or talk to your local oil suppliers and heating engineers. In any event, all this should once again be planned and budgeted for in advance.

Air Conditioning, Telephone and Television   Air conditioning, if you want it, is another basic service that must be installed in advance, assuming you want the

Positioning outlets
Before you begin to decorate, it is essential to plan where all electrical appliances and equipment will go

to ensure that there are enough outlets and that they are correctly positioned. Trailing flexes (cords) are both unsightly and hazardous.

units to be fitted into a wall rather than stuck in a window where they will make any sort of window treatment difficult as well as obstruct the view.

Although telephone-service installers are usually tidy and rarely leave behind a tangled mess of cables, it is still a good idea to get them in before you start the final decorations, just as it is important to get the television aerial (antenna), cable equipment, wall-mounted stereo speakers and other fitted equipment installed before your wall decorations are too far advanced.

Finding the Right Help

Architects If your house or apartment is very dilapidated, very inconvenient, too small or too large, you may well find that you need to employ an architect. He or she should be able to make your life a lot easier by suggesting clever ways of getting around spatial problems, by preparing plans and working drawings, by finding out about any local permissions needed or possible legal snags that might obstruct proposed alterations, by estimating how much the structure will cost to renovate, run and maintain, by finding and supervising an appropriate builder or contractor, and generally by coordinating the whole operation to produce a better-looking and easier-to-run home. It is quite possible that the entire renovation, even including the architect's fees, will cost less than if you had gone ahead on your own.

Unless your budget is elastic, it is usually best to use young and local architects for a straightforward renovating job. However, charges may vary: in Britain the Royal Institute of British Architects (RIBA) publishes scales of recommended charges (mostly based on a percentage of the cost of the building work to be done), and most architects should stick to these scales. The American Institute of Architects (AIA) offers a similar service in the United States. Architects generally charge for time and expenses, on top of their normal commission. It is also possible, of course, to persuade an architect to render a 'partial service' which consists of preparing sketch plans (for an agreed set fee) to show how best to realize your home's potential, leaving you to do the rest.

If you do decide to hire an architect, how do you set about getting one? Personal recommendation is probably the best way; asking the advice of an architectural acquaintance is another. Alternatively, you could ask the architecture department of the local college or university, or get a recommendation from your local architectural organization, or write to the relevant national association for suggestions in your area; in Britain, the RIBA has a directory of architects showing which are likely to be suitable for various types of work. The AIA publishes a comprehensive directory of architects working in the United States.

Once you have got together a list of 'possibles', scrutinize some examples of their work. Satisfied clients will rarely mind their houses being looked over, and architects themselves will always be prepared to arrange appointments and provide photographs.

Interior Designers and Decorators The services of a good designer can often, like those of an architect, save money in the long run and should certainly save you time, confusion and strain. A good designer will look at your home with fresh but informed eyes and will suggest ways of making your rooms function more efficiently and schemes that may well cost less, and will definitely look better, than the kind of piecemeal effect which spoils so many homes. A designer will also find fabrics, papers, rugs and carpets that you would be lucky to find in retail establishments – or perhaps he or she might even design these things especially. In addition the designer might get curtains and draperies made up, plan beautiful upholstery and bed treatments, find exactly the right pieces of furniture, recommend and supervise good builders, contractors and crafts people, help you choose accessories, and take all the other time- and nerve-consuming chores off your hands.

Above all, good designers acknowledge that many if not most of their clients have excellent ideas of their own, and need only a good arbitration, editing and translating service – plus the experience and knowledge of resources that a good designer should have – in order to realize those ideas. Finally, a good designer will try very hard to keep to a realistic budget and will always warn you if something is likely to go over budget. In this latter case, the designer should present you with a cheaper option.

There is no cut-and-dried fee structure in the interior-designing profession. Some designers charge an initial consultation fee and, if the client wants to proceed, a full design fee plus a percentage calculated on the cost of all goods purchased. Others charge a consultation fee plus a much larger percentage of the costs of purchases and services. Others still charge an hourly fee for their work – this can really mount up. Whatever the fee structure, most designers take the precaution of asking for 50 per cent of the design fee up front, or a retainer fee based on the overall expense, plus a pool for purchases.

If you do decide to employ an interior designer you should first try to ascertain what kind of firm would suit you best. Obviously word-of-mouth recommendation and asking friends whose homes you admire for details of their designer is one way; as with architects, seeing work in a magazine or in a newspaper's design pages is another way of getting started. Clearly, if your taste is spare and minimalist you should go to someone who specializes in this sort of look and not to someone renowned for their eclecticism, and vice versa.

 Builders and Contractors As with architects and designers, the best way to choose a contractor is through a reliable recommendation; seek advice from friends who have recently been pleased with work completed on their homes. Helpful architects in your locality may be prepared to suggest contractors they know to be reliable. And managers of local hardware or paint stores or builders' suppliers, who probably cater for most of the contractors in the area, might be persuaded to give you their opinion on the subject.

·When a list of possible contractors has been drawn up and their financial stability checked as far as possible, ask three or four of the firms to inspect your home. Make sure each is given a copy of the general work and decorating schedule so that they can put in a competitive bid or estimate. This might seem a somewhat pedantic way of going about the task, but it could save you a great deal of money, time and worry in the long run since estimates often vary wildly between one contractor and another.

Once you have received all the estimates, study them in detail. First, do any of the bidders guarantee the number of weeks or months they will take? Have any of them given you their time schedule in writing? Do they take into account a similar quantity and quality of paint and the same number of coats? (If you prepared your specification properly all of the bidders certainly should.) And are all the estimates for exactly the same amount of work and materials? Pay attention at this early stage to the uncertain costs in the estimate, such as the materials whose expense the contractors cannot predict exactly because they have yet to be chosen.

Remember to read conditions on the back of the tender and make sure you thoroughly understand them. For example, there might be denials of obligation in the event of the contractor's employees causing damage or of materials going missing from the site.

If the bids are very similar, you should contract the person or firm who guarantees the earliest completion date (to which you can usually add in your mind at least a month or two, unless you are prepared to bully, cajole, and be on the contractor's tail throughout the job); the largest contractor (bigger contractors have less need to subcontract); or the contractor whose personality you like the best – if the firm is large, try to meet the overseer assigned to the job (a key figure, and someone whose personality might well affect your final choice).

 Getting the Best Service To ensure that bills are kept to a minimum, specify that all additional costs are quoted for in writing and are attached to the main estimate; otherwise your contractor is given the opportunity to increase the bill in no time at all, giving as an unanswerable excuse the fact that you kept asking for more things.

If the job is of any size (say, the renovation of a house as opposed to that of a few rooms) it is a good idea to fix up a site meeting at least once a week. Remember to take your master checklist (see page 28) and go over the repair work room by room with the contractor (or foreman), the carpenter, the electrician, the plumber – whoever is relevant and can be mustered. Make a note of anything that is discussed and arranged. Date and file these notes, making sure the contractor has two copies, one of which should be initialled and returned to you.

It is advisable to visit the site as often as possible (unless you are already 'camping' in the middle of the mess) just to ensure that the work is progressing and to sort out any problems or misunderstandings. It is wise not to say in advance when you are coming, unless you specifically want to meet with a particular tradesman, and to vary your times a little. You should not expect contractors to undertake any sort of design decisions for you unless you have complete faith in their taste – or no faith in your own.

Getting the Framework Right

Sofa and Chairs

Lighting

Rugs and Cushions

WORKING OUT THE COSTS

EXAMPLE A: COMPLETE REDECORATION

Structural repairs
Treatment of dry rot and damp
Treatment of infestation
Repair of floorboards, etc.
Contractor's fee

Services
Checking of electrical system
2 sockets (outlets) to be fitted in
  living room
Downlights to be installed in
  dining room
Electrician's fee
Installation of basin in second
  bathroom
Plumber's fee

Decorating
Hire of wallpaper stripper and
  stepladder
Paint and wallpaper
Tiles for bathroom and kitchen
Tools and equipment

Furnishings
Purchase of rug for living room
Hire of carpet cleaner
Fabric for loose covers
Tracks and trimmings
Brass door handles throughout

EXAMPLE B: INSTALLING A NEW LIGHTING SCHEME

Fittings:
  Two recessed downlights
  Picture light over mantelpiece
  New sockets (outlets) in
    alcoves
  Concealed lighting
Building of baffle/pelmet
  (cornice)
Materials
Replastering
Electrician's fee
Contractor's fee

Living Room Budget
*This breakdown of a moderate
budget for decorating and
furnishing a living room
demonstrates how money should be
allocated, with the major pieces of
furniture, such as sofas and
armchairs, together with light
fittings, accounting for the greater
proportion of money spent.*

Storage Units and Occasional Tables

Plants and Prints

Paint

Blinds

Successful Budgeting

Having found exactly what *should* be done in a home, what you would like to do in the way of alterations and improvements, what could be done, and what each operation, service and ingredient would actually cost, you will be in a better position to work out a realistic budget. Even if you are hoping to borrow the money for improvements, you will still have to give a summary of these improvements and their various prices to the bank, so it is as well to have your projected expenditure listed in order of priorities.

When you are decorating for the first time, it is difficult to know exactly when to save and when to spend on a home. As a rule of thumb, a large amount of your budget should be spent on items that will get the most wear and tear, and will have to last the longest. The corollary is that savings can be made on less-used furniture and on inessentials where substitutes will do just as well.

As we have seen all structural repairs come in the 'spending' category, as well as any rewiring, pest, damp and rot control, efficient heating, air conditioning if needed, and any insulation. (To this list could be added the matter of precautions against burglary.) These can be followed by necessary appliances and furnishings: kitchen and washing equipment (stove, refrigerator, freezer, washing machine, dryer and dishwasher), beds, at least two good comfortable chairs, the best lighting you can afford, generous closet and storage units, and good flooring. Local or national legislation may have an effect on your budget. It is your responsibility to find out if your plans conform to prescribed safety regulations, if the drainage will be officially regarded as adequate, and so on. The easiest thing to do is to pay an expert to find out all these things for you.

A good deal of furniture can come in the 'saving' category, especially dining tables (which can be cheaper, more adaptable and often a better size when made from a circle of wood fixed to a solid base and covered by a large cloth), conventional window treatments (which can use up vast quantities of expensive fabric), top-quality carpet (when there are all sorts of alternatives), and expensive glass, porcelain, cutlery and linen.

Once you have decided on the sort of budget that you can afford for your home, on how much money, if any, you can realistically borrow, and on what necessities will

have to be provided, the plan of action can be drawn up. However, it is important to be realistic about ideas and to cost them carefully. Most important of all, be clear about your designs, needs and ideas of comfort.

Another important point to bear in mind in relation to any improvements is that you do not *over*improve a property in the light of its surroundings. If an area or locality appears to be deteriorating, no amount of apparent luxury will help the resale value of your house. On the other hand, if you are hoping to sell a house within a certain period of time in order to 'trade up' in the property market, there are certain improvements that will be worth their weight in gold, or at least in terms of a quick and profitable sale. Most potential buyers are understandably beguiled by properties which have the sort of sound framework we have been discussing, for this leaves them free to spend their money on decoration that will suit their personal tastes and needs. Good, well fitted kitchens and bathrooms are always a sales plus, as are good entertaining space and a handsome master bedroom, while a well planted terrace or climbers growing up a house can add thousands to the price. You cannot give your house or apartment scenic views out of the window if it is in the middle of a city, or bright summer light if all the windows face in the wrong direction, but you can substitute warmth and cheerfulness for light and particularly interesting colour schemes for a view.

CAN YOU AFFORD IT?

● Have you taken into account all contractors' fees?
● Have you set aside a sum of money for unforeseen expenditure – for example, eliminating rot?
● Do you have a comprehensive insurance policy?
● Have you been over-ambitious in estimating how much work you can take on yourself?
● Have you considered the cost of hiring equipment?

● Will your alterations affect the day-to-day running costs of your home?
● Are your employment prospects and long-term plans stable?
● Will your spending power be restricted or your standard of living affected by the amount of money you intend to spend on redecorating?
● Have you left yourself enough money to buy essential furnishings and fittings?

Planning
Finalize design scheme
Draw up room plans to scale
Check structural changes with local authorities

Preparation
Calculate quantity of paint, wallpaper or tiles needed and buy
Measure up for soft furnishings, and order fabric and materials
Move all furniture out of room or cover with dust sheets

Inform neighbours
Check budget

Roll up rugs, cover fitted carpets
Strip room of all movable fittings
Cover fixed fittings with plastic bags

Structure and Services
Carry out structural repairs or alterations
Make alterations to services, e.g. relocating sockets (outlets)

Home Furnishings
Start making soft furnishings, e.g. curtains

Week-by-Week Schedule

for Decorating

a Living Room

Preparing a Master Plan

Once you have worked out whether or not any structural work is required, you can decide upon the decoration and furnishings. Again, rooms must be considered in order of priority: usually the priorities are the kitchen, bathroom(s), master bedroom, living room and hall, followed in due course by the other rooms. This order of priorities is what distinguishes a thought-out scheme from the all-too-usual patchwork process. As with most set plans, you can vary the order so long as you understand that doing so may well increase your costs and take longer. If you are planning to 'camp' in your house or apartment while the work is in progress, it will help to keep your spirits up if right away at least one room can be made comfortable.

To go back to the master plan, when the most important points have been decided (or mostly decided, because fresh thoughts will always be occurring) make another list for every room and include every single thing that you think you will need to install or replace or which could be improved or refurbished. The sample list supplied on page 13 might be useful as a guide; you can add or subtract as necessary. However obvious the items on the list might seem, so many things are all too easily overlooked in the grand scheme: a lot of minor items generally add up to a major problem – and a major expense. If you read the list you will probably start thinking of other things that ought to be done: note them all. Sensible decisions at the start will prevent much confusion and regret later on.

When it comes to deciding upon the actual decoration, plans should be dictated by the proportions and historical style of a house or apartment, its situation, condition and natural light. This is not to say that all buildings should necessarily be decorated according to their period, but rather that they should be treated with sympathy and that their natural ingredients should be used to best advantage. 'Natural ingredients' are not only doors, windows, view, and staircases, but also the different proportions of rooms, decorative flooring or mouldings (if there are any) and all the architectural details of a house (see pages 82–91).

Normally this sort of 'feeling' for a building can be achieved only after a number of relaxed visits to it while it is empty, or after you have 'camped' in a minimally decorated house for some time. After a period of time it should be possible to absorb the house's shapes, proportions, details and potential so that certain types and colours of furnishings can be visualized in their

Prepare the surfaces, e.g. strip off old wallpaper Put up lining paper if wall surfaces are rough	
Put up decorative mouldings	
	Lay carpets or sheet flooring Fix lighting, replace fittings Hang window treatments Put furniture in position
Install units, built-in cupboards, window seats	
Decoration Prime surfaces Apply undercoat	Paint ceilings and then walls If wallpapering, hang paper before painting woodwork Paint woodwork Treat floor, e.g. bleach floorboards

appropriate settings. Also, you should come to recognize those features to emphasize and those to diminish.

If you find it hard to settle on a starting point for a scheme, ruffle through relevant books and magazines looking for congenial arrangements. Investigate local shops, stores and showrooms (or catalogues, if you have a shortage of time) in search of wallpapers, carpets, rugs, hard flooring and fabrics, and collect or send off for samples of anything that accords with your impression of how your home should look. You may want to collect all these samples together in a file or stick them all up on a notice-board. Once you see them all together you should find yourself starting to have some definite ideas – if only on what to discard.

Get into the habit of carrying around a notebook in which you can jot down descriptions or make quick sketches of anything that appeals to you. A ceiling treatment, a particular way of covering a wall or of arranging a group of pictures, a certain juxtaposition of colour – all of these can spark off a train of thought. At the time this may lead nowhere, but you will find that later on many of these ideas will click into place alongside other ones, thereby contributing to your overall scheme. Remember that ideas hardly ever stay in your mind unless you have made some kind of a record of them in writing.

Decorating Schedule
Draw up a plan of the order of work before you begin, even if you are only tackling one room at a time. This will help you to coordinate the services of contractors.

Flexibility Crucial to your overall scheme is flexibility. A lack of flexibility inevitably leads to frustration. Pieces of furniture or light fittings that you have set your heart on may turn out to be too expensive, or they may have been discontinued. Fixed ideas may prove to be impracticable because of space or time or light or money. If you have lived in the city for years and then move to the country – or to another country, continent or state – your tried, tested and loved belongings may suddenly become unsuitable. All such difficulties may seem insuperable, but they can be overcome if you retain an open mind.

Never be bound by fixed 'rules'. Never think that it is absolutely imperative to have a certain item or a particular colour. Good interior decoration should ultimately be a background, an impression of personality, not an end in itself. It is therefore important to create an environment that is most comfortable for *you*, within the limits of practicability. It is never impossible to substitute what you can get for what you originally conceived – although of course it is important not to make a thoughtless substitution.

Part 2

Setting the Style

What is Style?

A sense of style is as intangible and amorphous a thing as having a good eye for colour, a fine sense of scale and proportion or a sensitive ear for music.

Then again, the word 'style' has so many connotations – quite apart from its alliance with that equally nebulous attribute, 'good taste'. When we talk about someone having style or taste we mean that they have a particular and sometimes memorable way of arranging things, of putting things together – whether they be clothes and accessories or furniture and possessions.

There are, of course, the so-called 'national' styles. These have been particularly well documented over the last couple of decades in numerous books with titles such as *English Style*, *English Country Style*, *American Country*, *American South West*, *French Style*, *French Country*, *Italian Style*, *Caribbean Style* and *Japanese Style*. Then there are 'period' styles, named for a particular age – Renaissance, Restoration, Régence, Directoire, Federal, Empire – or for a monarch or monarchs – Louis XIV, XV, XVI in France, or the Stuarts, William and Mary, Queen Anne, Georgian and Victorian in Britain. Then again there are general terms that conjure up in one's mind particular styles of furniture and decoration: the Baroque, with its elaborate wood carving; the Rococo, with its curves and shells (*rocaille*); the Neoclassic, with its simple classical forms; Art Nouveau, with its sinuous configurations; the Bauhaus, with its stark 'shock of the new'. Finally, there are styles named for particular furniture designers (Chippendale, Hepplewhite and Sheraton), loosely geographical terms (Country Style and Urban Style), and popular turns of phrase (Art Deco, International Style, Eclectic, Hi-Tech and Minimalism).

Finding a Style All in all, the question of what overall style you should choose – or of putting a name to some half-formed mental picture of a room or rooms – can become as intimidating as that of selecting colour schemes to put together for your home. It is easy to say 'Find the style which suits you best and with which you are most comfortable', but putting this into practice is a far more difficult task.

Again, just as in choosing colours, there are certain criteria to follow. As usual, learn to really *look*, take note of what pleases you, and try to analyse *why*. Think about why a particular room gives you pleasure. Look through

books and magazines. Look at room settings in stores and museums. Take more notice of theatre sets and the backgrounds in movies and television programmes. Think about what sort of architecture pleases you most. Old houses in general, or clean modern lines? Quirky, idiosyncratic designs or traditional?

Some people look hard for that indefinable thing, 'charm' – which, while they cannot adequately describe it, they can recognize as soon as they see: it may be something as simple as a good growth of wisteria around a porch, arched stone windows, a fireplace in most if not all rooms, or a general meandering higgledy-piggledy quality that immediately gives them a feeling of genuine pleasure.

In general, unless you are sure of your decorating prowess, if a building already has some distinctive style or 'feel' you should make a point of being sensitive to it. This does not mean that you should furnish it exactly to period: that could look stuffy and lifeless, however beautiful and however much money and knowledge you might have to carry such an exercise through to its best potential. Rather it is that you should try to be sympathetic to the synthesis of architectural coherence

2

1 Pleasing juxtapositioning in New England of a simple love seat, a complicated Austrian shade, a sophisticated 19th-century side table and an old rustic painted corner cupboard.

2 A decidedly eclectic mix in an old London studio: a kelim on a painted marble floor, crewel upholstery alongside faded brocade, an Indian cloth flung over a white sofa, gilded Queen Anne chairs with assorted over-scale pots, hand-blocked wallpaper sandwiched between a complicated painted ceiling, and a painted dado — not to mention the grandeur of the fireplace.

3 Hand-painted fabric and modern lines in a 19th-century room painted like a grey box.

4 A quietly luxurious all-marbled bathroom in a Parisian apartment.

3

4

Setting the Style
WHAT IS STYLE?

1 This thoroughly Middle Eastern interior comes as something of a surprise in a London home.
2 A turn-of-the-century Edwardian-style interior in the United States. This was designed for a 1980s US showhouse, and is complete with bamboo occasional furniture, papier-mâché and upholstery to match the chintz-lined walls.
3 Rose-on-white toile de Jouy, a white iron bedhead against brick walls, and white-painted boarding feature in this country-style New York bedroom.
4 The Eastern influences on the decor of this Western attic bedroom are all too clear.
5 A hi-tech/minimalist kitchen in familiar black-and-white styling.

and fineness of proportion that define the relevant period. In the case of a Georgian or Federal house – indeed, with any building you live in, whatever its architectural detail – a sense of style is really an attitude of mind, a sympathy with the overall 'feel' of the surroundings and a sensitivity both to what is fitting for those surroundings and to your family's needs. Clearly finance will affect your stylistic choices, as will the furnishings you already possess, whether they are from former homes, gifts or items you have inherited.

Obviously, there are certain commonsense factors to consider as well. For example, country houses look best when they are obviously geared to country living and the outdoor life. Floors, for instance, seem more fittingly rural when they are of wood, brick, stone or quarry tile, or covered with coir or rush matting, than if they have fitted carpets (except perhaps on stairs or in bathrooms and powder rooms). And, although a country look or 'feel' has a certain charm in a town house, a sophisticated urban look is far from appealing in the country.

Again, beach and summer houses do not look appropriate or suitably relaxed when they are too carefully furnished and decorated: they should be casual and slightly shabby, and full of familiar heterogenous objects. This is not, of course, to say that they cannot be pretty. But the whole idea of such houses is to make people feel relaxed, comfortable and carefree.

When you first walk into a new home there is usually a certain 'something' about each room that helps to set the style you will wish to employ. If, for example, a room is heavily beamed and low-ceilinged, you are likely to opt for a comfortable, warm-coloured eclectic ambience rather than a roomful of clean-lined modern furniture – although some people, quite sure of themselves and their tastes, might be tempted to do exactly the opposite to the obvious approach and make the furnishings stark and simple.

Another room might be well proportioned but dark. In such a case you would have the choice of exploiting the lack of light to make the room warm and cosy or resorting to artifice, making the place look much brighter through the use of light but warm colours (apricot, buttery yellow, pale terracotta, old rose, etc.) and plenty of artfully concealed lighting – at the top of windows

under a valance or pelmet (cornice), behind plants and large pieces of upholstery, or even, skilfully, at the top of sun blinds *outside* the windows so that the sun appears to be shining through.

You might have a room with a wall of windows and a marvellous view for you to exploit (use spare furniture and simple lines in order not to distract attention from the view outside) or, conversely, you might be confronted by a room that is boxy and characterless, in which case you can dress up the walls, try to make the windows more interesting, and add various touches of character of your own devising – from mouldings to a cleverly painted floor or exotic furnishings. The point is that, whatever the nature of a room, you should look for any clue that might help you determine the appropriate style of decoration. This clue might lie within the room itself but, if the room says nothing to you, it may be possible to find it among your own possessions.

Putting style into a home is, in fact, much like solving a puzzle in which you have to get the maximum number of words out of a collection of letters. Ultimately, it is all a question of juggling with possibilities.

4

5

INSPIRATION OF THE PAST

Up until the 18th century, style evolved in different countries, sometimes according to the dictates of fashion – for example, seating had to be redesigned to accommodate hoop skirts and crinolines – or as new woods, materials, skills, techniques and domestic articles were introduced. The general interest in Chinoiserie, for example, followed directly from the first appearance in Europe of oriental lacquered goods and silks, and small tables were invented for the new-fangled practices of tea-drinking and card-playing. There was, then, little nostalgic harking back to the past – at least, not deliberately – for the new was always the rage.

Once travel became more general, however, all this changed. The Grand Tour around Europe became *de rigueur* for the young men (and quite often women) of the aristocracy, and a direct result was the Neoclassical movement in Britain during the 1750s. Initially this movement was a product of Inigo Jones's discovery in the 17th century of the work of Palladio. The fashion for Palladianism dominated the 18th century in Britain, thanks largely to Lord Burlington and his protégé William Kent, and it fostered a general admiration for 'the noble simplicity and calm grandeur' of the ancient classical forms, especially the Greek. This was followed by studies of the Italian Renaissance and by the

*A very splendid Art Nouveau bedroom
in an American country house.*

Setting the Style
INSPIRATION OF THE PAST

extravaganzas of the Gothick revival, which spread around Europe and to North America. Late 18th- and 19th-century travellers to the Far East, India, the Middle East and Egypt, not to mention military expeditions and campaigns in those areas, were responsible for the emergence of the exotica of the Regency and for the introduction of ancient Greek and Egyptian influences.

Although the wholesale historical revivalism of the 19th century had more or less burned itself out by the 1900s – Art Nouveau, with its roots in the arts and crafts movement, owed little to other styles – decorative inspiration continued (and continues) to be provided by the styles of many different periods.

'Period styles come and go, and sometimes come again,' remarked Witold Rybczynski blithely in his beautifully written historical survey *Home*. His point would seem proved by such episodes as the rediscovery during the early 1900s of the Rococo, Neoclassical and

1 *A richly detailed Victorian restoration, with mahogany mouldings, Victoria plum walls, a modern carpet, and modern stencilling beneath the deep gilt border. All elements add to the feeling of warmth.*
2 *Painted faux marble bathroom with turn-of-the-century fittings and handsome 19th-century gilded mirror.*

3 Updated Regency in Manhattan: a magnificent round mahogany table, Thomas Hope-inspired chairs, a splendid 19th-century oriental rug, and terracotta scumbled and glazed walls.
4 Detail of an early 19th-century mantelpiece.
5 A rather Napoleon-III oriented bedroom in Paris, its green marbled dado matching the painted Empire bed, and its mahogany pedestal and handsome polished wood screen used in conjunction with a modern sculpted wool carpet.
6 This Parisian apartment revels in 1930s elegance.

5

6

Georgian delights of the 18th century – more often used all together. Another example is the resurgence of Regency ideas in the middle of the 20th century. The further revivals of Victorian, Edwardian, Art Nouveau, Art Deco and early modern styles and the sly allusions to classical motifs in today's Post-Modernism provide further support for Rybczynski's aphorism.

This harking back to the past is rarely a matter of slavish imitation of earlier interiors. Rather, it is the sympathetic use of traditional motifs and forms in conjunction with the best materials of the present to produce what can often be a highly memorable and pleasing result.

At the same time, it means nostalgia, a very salient part of decoration in the late 20th century: nostalgia for what are perceived to have been the 'good old days'; nostalgia, especially in the United States, for 'roots'. Although Modernism is now some 70 years old, the majority of people have been uncomfortable with its tenets, simply because it *is* uncomfortable. By contrast, the nebulous 'past', especially as glamorously recreated by designers such as Ralph Lauren, seems warm, cosy and leisurely, while at the same time distinguished and patrician. People today are therefore looking on the 'past' as a time to be envied – even though we all know it never really happened like that.

Rustic Charm

One of the particular fascinations of the past few decades has been with the country and 'below stairs' furnishing of the preceding generations. These can have harmonious charm – the old pine, yew and elm, cherry, American golden oak and simple English oak; the rustic painted or stained pieces of furniture (cupboards, wardrobes, dressers, dining chairs and side and dining tables); and the wall and floor tiles, rag rugs, bric-a-brac, stoneware, china, prints, engravings and needlework homilies. A fine list, yet nothing on it is at all grand.

The popularity of this type of decoration has been partly a result of the fact that prices were, and still are, comparatively cheap for such generally attractive objects. The main reason, however, has been that the furniture shapes are simple and spare enough, and the objects handsome and interesting enough, for them to be mixed comfortably with modern furnishings. They add a degree of warmth and idiosyncrasy to a room, yet are in no way aggressively antique.

1

1 *A comfortable Scandinavian rustic room, the whitewashed boarded ceiling contrasting with the dark boarding just beneath. The highly polished wood shelf running around the room just below the dark boarding is an interesting idea and provides a good display space for a miscellaneous collection. Below this again, the sombre green paint matched to the window blind is a good foil for the blond floor and furniture, the leather seating and the battered old rocking chair.*
2 *Battered painted furniture manages to look appealing against the barn siding wall in this US washroom. Note the geometric precision with which the old blue cotton rugs have been placed side by side. The feeling is good and solid – nicely time-worn. With this old background, even the towels hanging neatly on the wall begin to look like objets trouvés.*

2

3 Brilliant walls, a sculpted fireplace, rustic furniture, an icon and a crucifix adorn this Santa Fe style room.

4 An elaborately-painted 19th-century folk art hutch (dresser), complete with clock, works well in this Swedish country room with its deep green dado and dark wood boarding.

5 Rough plaster walls, deeply inset with a cobalt-painted window frame and a misty Swedish view beyond, make an interesting background for the rather more refined 19th-century furniture and polished blond floor. The contrast between rustic architecture and polished wood is very pleasing.

41

The 19th Century

In general, we tend to think of the 19th century in terms of the solidity and expansive opulence of High Victoriana. But style during the century was so much more diverse and fragmented than that. At the beginning of the century the exuberance of the Regency, with its exotic oriental and Indian influences, still survived. There were the Egyptian and Greek revivals exemplified by Thomas Hope; *Empire* in France; Empire in the United States; and the fanciful Gothick. In addition there was the anglicized Japanese of the aesthetic movement, the earnestness of William Morris and the arts and crafts movement and (in the United States) the Mission, and the sinuous shapes of Art Nouveau.

Today we appreciate 19th-century furniture, furnishings, art and accessories for much the same reasons as not so long ago we were rejecting them. Now we enjoy the solidity, slavish attention to detail, whimsy and sentimentality of so many of the objects and so much of the art: the fruit and classical figures under glass domes, the framed birds and fish and the bottled ships, the beautifully made brass scientific instruments, spectacle cases, pen boxes, lorgnettes and other collectables. Many of us love the bedsteads, the lamps, the samplers, the richness of the wallpapers, the silks and damasks and velvets, the floral charm of the Victorian chintzes. And there is a distinct harking after the palms and antimacassars, dados and wainscoting, arches, pillars, mouldings and balustrades of the Queen Anne revival and Victoriana in general.

1 *Lacy sheer curtains filter the light coming into this Swedish parlour filled with the elegant accoutrements of the 19th century.*
2 *Mahoganized skirting heating is carefully fitted into the harmonious whole of this restored Victorian room. Note the two pediments of window and closet.*
3 *Gentle late Victoriana at its bedroom best in a Louisiana house.*
4 *There is a distinct Victorian feel to this small room.*
5 *The old pine chest and velvet chair look comfortably 'old world' against the panelling and velvet.*

Art Nouveau and Art Deco

The Art Nouveau style was unusual in having little historical connection; it lasted less than a decade, from 1892 to 1900. It began in Brussels, and spread all over Europe and to the United States, being known by a variety of different names in different countries – *Jügendstil* in Germany, *Liberty* in Britain, *Style Moderne* in France, and so on. Art Nouveau rooms were full of extravagant, sinuous ornament based on forms drawn from nature: this extended throughout fabrics, wallpapers, furniture, rugs, carpets, lighting and ornamental objects to give an amazingly strong stylistic consistency.

Perhaps it was for this reason – that Art Nouveau was so complete in itself, so self-contained – that it had such a short life. Or perhaps it was too connected with the decadence of the Naughty Nineties. In its final form, the Vienna Secession style, it lost much of its floreate style: in the hands of the Austrian architect/designer Josef

1 A stunning recreation of an Art Nouveau dining room. Look at the structure of the chairs, the sofa under the turn-of-the-century painting, the wall sconces, the fire dogs, the spectacular fireplace and the oil lamp above it. The framework of the room (the fabric-lined walls, the green woodwork and the green-stained floor) has been carefully chosen to enhance the whole.

2 An equally stunning bathroom in the same house. Note the handsome bath and basin surrounds, the period lighting and bamboo closet.

3 Another detail of the extraordinary Art Nouveau collection in this spectacularly lavish American house. Everything is of the period.

4 Art Deco chair and cocktail stand show vivid juxtapositioning of shocking pink and shiny chrome.

Hoffman – as indeed in the hands of the Scotsman, Charles Rennie Mackintosh – it became somewhat more abstract and geometric, so that, along with Art Deco, it figured as a precursor of Modernism.

Art Deco was primarily concerned with sumptuous surface effects, superb ornamentation, and jazzed-up versions of old forms. Although named after the *Exposition des Arts Décoratifs* in Paris in 1925, it was sparked off by a radical movement in clothing towards sensual and flamboyant lines. Interior design to match this new exoticism followed swiftly. The style was not so much a denial of the past as the past reworked under the influence of new technology.

Art Deco also incorporated African influences (tropical woods for frames and inlays, and zebra and leopard skins) and echoes of the recent archaeological discoveries in Egypt.

5 *This Art Deco bathroom is in total contrast to the Art Nouveau bathroom.*
6 *London hallway in Art Deco: tawny marbled walls, typical stepped-top cabinet and the ubiquitous woven cane chair.*

4

5

6

MODERN MOVEMENTS

At the 1925 international *Exposition des Arts Décoratifs* there were two pavilions which were either scorned or almost unnoticed yet which would have an enormous influence on domestic design over the next several decades. These were the stark, geometric Russian Constructivist pavilion (people joked that it had been made from packing cases) and a little pavilion belonging to an art magazine called L'E*sprit Nouveau* ('New Spirit'), designed by the cousins Charles-Edouard and Pierre Jeanneret; the former was the editor of the magazine, and is better known by his nom de plume, Le Corbusier.

The L'E*sprit Nouveau* pavilion was roughly box-shaped, with a plain white exterior and an equally bare and Spartan interior. On exhibit were no ornamentation, no draperies, curtains or wallpaper, no mantelpiece or small tables on which to display photographs and family treasures, no comfortingly panelled study, no polished wood furniture, no rich materials of any kind ... absolutely no vestige, in fact, of familiar home-like things.

Instead, there was starkness. The walls were white, except for one which was painted plain brown. Industrial-type storage cabinets, painted yellow, were used as room dividers and the staircase was made out of steel

A modern interior with Bauhaus-inspired furniture and a marble floor.

Setting the Style
MODERN MOVEMENTS

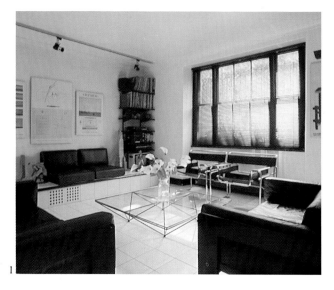

1

2

3

1 Another Bauhaus-inspired living room. This one is furnished with 20th-century classics such as the pair of Marcel Breuer 'Vasily' chairs (made originally in tubular steel and canvas in 1925, and used by the painter Vasily Kandinsky), the ubiquitous black leather and the track lighting.
2 The minimalist kitchen here, with its pristine whiteness, is given maximum interest by the Fornisetti plates which are cleverly displayed in a row above the kitchen cabinets.
3 A minimalist kitchen in shiny black and glass; another homage to Modernism and sleek technology.

pipes. The kitchen was tiny, and the bathroom – almost as large as the living room – had an entire wall made of glass bricks and was intended to double as an exercise room. As for the furniture, there were side tables of the kind usually found in restaurants, tables made of slabs of wood resting on tubular steel frames and some rather nebulous leather armchairs. The whole was meant to show the 'new spirit', the comprehensive rejection of decorative art, and was meant to shock.

However scornful the reaction to this building (one US critic said it exhibited the prosaic literalness of a cold-storage warehouse cube), its architect was actually trying to come to grips with modern living and the advent of the new technologies – to create with his 'machine for living' a style to mark the age. Undeterred by the hostile reaction of the critics, Le Corbusier went on to build a number of villas based on this same austerity. By the 1930s this 'new spirit' architecture was gaining ascendancy.

However, Le Corbusier's pavilion was certainly not the first building to demonstrate conspicuous austerity. As far back as 1908, the Viennese architect Adolf Loos had written a much abused essay called 'Ornament and Crime', in which he advocated the removal of all ornament from architecture and interiors – indeed, from everyday life as a whole. He argued that what had seemed appropriate in the past was no longer appropriate to an industrialized world. Loos had since 1904 been designing villas with plain white plastered walls that lacked any such decoration as cornices (crown moldings) or mouldings. What he despised, however, was not decoration but *ornamentation*, and his otherwise austere rooms were filled with beautiful surfaces. Although he was afterwards to change his mind about austerity, his *cri du coeur* for the elimination of ornament became the basis of a veritable crusade by the German, Dutch and French avant-garde.

The Bauhaus, founded in 1919 in Germany by Walter Gropius, was dedicated to reform. All vestiges of the past were to be removed, and luxury became as much of a crime as ornamentation. This extremism made its mark, for after 1920 there was a decided shift in popular taste: rooms became steadily less cluttered, a tendency which reached its apotheosis with the minimalism and hi-tech of the 1970s.

4

4 *This room is a microcosm of the modernist movement, combining as it does the austerity of the Bauhaus, the Modernism of the 1930s (the two brilliantly curved, white leather, tubular steel chairs and the standing chrome ashtray), and the hi-tech of the 1970s (the industrial carts or trolleys for television and stereo, and the wheeled base for the glass coffee table). Also there is the sleekness of the modern Italian designers as represented by the sharp metal Venetian blinds. In this setting, the tiniest bit of colour 'zings' — the large mauve and white flower arrangement sets off the whole scheme.*

If dance and clothes influenced the Art Deco style, economics, politics and World War II were the primary factors affecting the acceptance of the modernist style in the 1930s, 1940s and 1950s. With the Crash of 1929 and the Great Depression, Art Deco – which, with its exotic materials and faint air of decadence, had always been the province of the rich – ceased to be a domestic style, although it continued to feature in large buildings, restaurants, movie theatres and ships.

However, Le Corbusier's unglamorous 'cube' style was uniquely suited to post-Depression times, being more adaptable to slim budgets. There was also a political aspect to the style's sudden regaining of popularity during the 1930s: the new totalitarian states, such as Germany, Italy and Spain, were staunchly grandiose and monumental when it came to architecture, and so the new austerity came to represent a rebellion against totalitarianism.

Most of the modernist German architects and designers of the Bauhaus ended up in the United States, where men such as Gropius, Breuer and Mies van der Rohe were fêted and given many commissions. Thanks to this patronage, the new Modernism became regarded as chic, unfettered, an emblem of the 'free world', a refreshing change, and an altogether necessary break from traditions of the old world. The whole modern movement set new high standards for living. It not only influenced architecture and interior design but also created a general framework for daily living. It advocated a cleaner and more regulated environment and a way of life which would complement the new technological age. Le Corbusier attempted to redefine the home by calling it a 'machine for living'.

Rooms were pure white, uncluttered, glass-walled, and filled at first with the *de rigueur* modern classics of Le Corbusier, Breuer and Mies van der Rohe. Later the marvellous new shapes made possible by airplane-material technology, beautifully reinterpreted by Alvar Aalto, Arne Jacobsen, Charles Eames and Eero Saarinen, joined the works of Le Corbusier and the rest of his generation. Modern abstract and expressionist paintings were hung on the walls, and occasional furniture was made of glass and chrome, plexiglass, perspex or white moulded plastic. Often the only colour to be seen apart from in the paintings was in the leaves of large plants and the tan-and-beige of leather upholstery. Europe's Modernism was glamorized and made sleek and sophisticated. Renamed the International Style, it was for years a favourite of the enlightened rich, filtering down in due course to the enlightened middle classes.

Minimalism

Minimalism – the art of living with the least – uses Mies van der Rohe's dictum that 'less is more' as its creed. At its best, as in traditional Japanese interiors, it is a celebration of space, or of form in space, so that one can revel in the pure sculptural lines of a piece of furniture or architectural element.

Rooms are kept as sparse as possible, with pared-down furniture and no visible clutter. Often there are hi-tech elements: industrial grey carpeting, studded rubber flooring, crisp woven matting, slick tiles and gleaming lacquered or metallic finishes. In good minimalist rooms – as opposed to bad ones which can look merely bleak and uncomfortable – background colours are kept to a minimum, white being prevalent. The shapes of the furniture and all the objects, even the humblest of baskets or a single flower, combine to achieve a special and rewarding significance. In a minimalist environment storage is of course all-important, for the absence of the usual detritus of domestic living is essential to the style. For most of us, minimalism is a difficult style both to live with and to live up to – it is not an easy option. For the enviable and disciplined few, however, who can live without clutter, the visual rewards are great.

1

2

1 *Minimalism is not always just a case of black-and-white. In other words, a minimalist design need not be of such stark intensity that any coloured object or plant smites the viewer with all the subtlety of an alarm clock going off. Minimalism can just be very simple, very austere and, as in this instance, very pleasing with its clean-lined soft colours and lack of clutter.*
2 *Much the same feeling of fresh clean elegance is apparent in this small, basically white bedroom. The use of the mirror at the back of the bed is clever, as are the neatly striped and edged comforter and pillows. Colours serve to emphasize its freshness, while the room as a whole makes sensitive obeisance to the craggy green outside.*

3

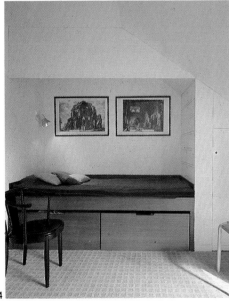

4

5

3 There is great charm in this spare room, all cream, bare wood and neutrality right down to the rooftops and houses outside the bare window wall. Indeed, so neutral is the room and so minimal the creature-comforts, the coarsely woven cane of the three empty baskets stands out — if not like a riveting work of art, at least with some considerable distinction.

4 A study-bedroom of quiet simplicity and concise planning. This time the lines are less crisp, less well defined, but the effect is still disciplined, with that peculiarly Scandinavian calm.

5 Red is used with deliberation in this ordered diner-kitchen to provide a contrast with the quiet beige stripes.

Post-Modernism

Post-Modernism is not so much just another manifestation of Neoclassicism – one of those styles which, like Gothic and Rococo, slips in and out of favour through the centuries – as a somewhat playful style based on allusion or reference to history and the classical order in a movement that is otherwise contemporary.

Pillars, pediments, arches and so on are incorporated on the outsides of buildings and in interiors in a rather dégagé manner – for example, free-standing pillars or pediments and other architectural elements are used as decoration rather than for support or delineation. Post-Modernism makes no attempt to recreate or revive a historical style, but rather it lightheartedly acknowledges the presence and influence of the past on contemporary spaces and elements of design.

The colours used are distinctive – both harmonious and strong. They are pale terracottas, sea greens, lilacs, washed pinks and sky blues – representing land, light, air and sky. In many ways they comprise much the same colour combination as those used in the Neoclassical and Adam rooms of the 18th century.

1

2

3

1 In this instance, the Post-Modernist influence is more in the colours: the apricots, blues, greens and lilacs. But it is also evident in the somewhat architectural look of the halogen lamp with its blue casing.

2 The Post-Modernist pillared fireplace-surround in this room has the same 'feel' as the 1960s style of the psychedelic colours on the spacey chairs.

3 Post-Modernism works well for this ingenious little bedroom with its interesting ceiling, oeil de boeuf window, wall lights cleverly integrated with the ceiling, closet, drawer and the bookshelf space, not to mention the ladder up to the bed. It is extremely well thought out, even down to the idiosyncratic frieze, with its odd photographs of leaders through the ages.

4

4 This kitchen door, with its elliptical window and applied decoration, opens onto a Shoji screen window and geometrically painted units – a good strategy for improving a mediocre little space.

Freestyle

One thing the mixture of historical and creative revivals with the modern movement during the last part of this century has done is to create a sense of release, of freedom and experimentation in decoration. This is true especially among the young, the impecunious, the avant-garde and the unconventional.

According to various surveys, the majority of us tend to nostalgia as we grow older, more settled and more solvent, decorating more like our grandparents (or how we would have *liked* our grandparents to have decorated!). But for the more uninhibited minority anything can go, from wonderful (but expensive) experimental furniture by sculptors, painters, architects, craftsmen and designers, through brightly coloured contemporary pieces like the Italian Memphis work and its copies, to ingenious made-up pieces and revitalized junk. All or any of these can be set against a variety of backgrounds and can be rearranged at will.

1 This French dining room has not one but two different kinds of painted finishes.
2 In another French dining-kitchen there is a play on black-and-white checks.
3 The stepped-up 1960s wall and frivolous blues make sense in a narrow space.
4 There is deliberate repetition in this somewhat hi-tech room.

AN ECLECTIC TASTE

When all is said and done, most people – including most professional designers – are happiest or at least more at ease with a rather eclectic look. It is, after all, only natural: you like a bit of this, a little of that, and maybe a touch of something else. One can draw an analogy with cooking: the most interesting dishes are an amalgam of different influences, the alchemy of the various flavours producing a delicious synthesis.

It is precisely this sort of mixing that makes decorating so exciting and varied, and which gives you such scope for your imagination. After all, purist decoration of whatever period by definition has to be fairly predictable. There are only so many early 18th-century styles – or, for that matter, available pieces. The same can be said of any other period. However different the backgrounds, the walls or the window and floor treatments, there cannot be any 'shock of the new' or even 'shock of the different', because, despite any overall beauty of the design or of your collection, the purist approach restricts you to ideas that have been realized a million times before in every combination imaginable.

Eclecticism, on the other hand (and if well done), is a real art. You mix periods and nationalities of furniture,

Aquamarine blue, used on walls, tablecloth and cushions to make a soothing framework for the furnishings in this living room.

56

Setting the Style
AN ECLECTIC TASTE

1 *This mixture of modern upholstery with Victorian needlework cushions, 17th-century Dutch paintings and an early 18th-century bureau bookcase with ancient painted blue doors (echoed in the seats of the painted terracotta chairs) is well framed by the lively yellow walls built up with coat after coat of subtly coloured glazes.*

2 *At the other end of the same room, two watercolours of Petworth House by Teddy Millington-Drake are juxtaposed with coloured stripes of Italian silk. While the enormous windows allow plentiful daylight into the room, a traditional table light draws attention to the carefully composed corner of this living room.*

paintings, sculptures, materials, objects and lighting to create, from all the disparate components, a whole that is completely harmonious. And it is an art of endless permutations. You can mix furnishings of different periods, linking them together with the best of modern background materials: beautiful cottons and wools, matting and tiles and wood. You can use 20th-century furniture in conjunction with classical Roman sculpture, 18th-century gouaches, Expressionist paintings and 19th-century oriental rugs. Other combinations are modern Italian, fifties, and classic Scandinavian furniture with a fine collection of photographs and folk art; abstraction and early oak; or Japanese lacquer, together with matting and Regency.

What you need to be successful when decorating eclectically (and make no mistake: if you are unsuccessful the results can be disastrous) are a sense of form, scale and colour, courage, most definitely a sense of humour and a willingness to experiment. One of the great things about the eclectic style is that it need not be at all costly, for any sensitive eye will be gratified by a judicious choice of colours and thoughtful juxtapositioning of even the most inexpensive of items.

3 The matting underscores the garden theme in this room: the real flowers and greenery are matched by the painted ones — some are even appliquéd on the throw.

4 Here, different shades of cream in the walls, curtains, upholstery, lacquered coffee table and lampshade provide the common denominator. However, the potted plants are an important ingredient in this scheme, adding dashes of green to the basically monochromatic effect of this living and dining area.

5 In this room, on the other hand, the grouping of glass tables, chair and light against the wall has much the same kind of graphic quality as the contemporary framed poster.

3

4

5

Living Rooms

In living rooms almost anything can be used – but there is one proviso: key or anchor pieces, such as sofas and armchairs, should be as comfortable as possible. However idiosyncratic or curious the general assemblage of furniture, paintings and objects, much of the interest and vivacity will be lost if it is impossible to feel physically comfortable in the room.

However different from each other the elements of a room might be, there should be some sort of common denominator – some theme – to unite them all. This is most usually colour – used as a harmonious background on the floor, the walls, or at windows and on some upholstery. For instance, you might have a large old rug whose colours you could lift and repeat here and there in the room – in an armchair and a sofa, on an occasional chair, in some throw pillows or cushions, in the window treatments, the mounts or matts of prints, and so on. Or it might be that you paint the walls in a warm colour or a dark one, such as dark green, blue or red; any of these will act like the lining in a jewel box to

show off your possessions, however disparate those possessions might be.

Another excellent background for a disparate assembly of furnishings is all-over white: white walls, white window treatments (shutters, perhaps) and a white floor (maybe tiles or bleached or painted floorboards). This approach generally makes everything look sculptural and three-dimensional. The use of coir or rush matting has a similar unifying effect, making a mixture of old and new, conventional and bizarre, seem cohesive and right.

3

1 The uniting factors in this room, with its cheerful red-checked fabric and painted armoire, are the country feeling and the cushions which repeat the terracotta colouring of the panelling.

2 Greeny-grey and greeny-white are the prevailing colours in a room predominantly furnished with different weaves of cane.

3 The extraordinary row of windows topped by equally extraordinary objects can hardly help but distract from the furnishings. However, the mixture is nicely contained within a pale colour scheme.

4 Almost any number of things can be placed with impunity in an off-white room.

Dining Rooms

Interestingly, although rooms devoted exclusively to dining were a fairly late invention, the modern dining room is often the most traditional room in the house, with 'Baronial', late-18th-century, Regency or Victorian table, chairs and sideboard. Yet an eclectically furnished dining room can make for much more interesting eating – as long as it is remembered that the main purpose of a dining room is, of course, to provide a comfortable place in which to enjoy food, drink and conversation, and that any decoration should enhance the meal rather than distract from it. This means that background lighting should be soft and flattering, with specific lighting directed onto serving areas. Chairs, whatever their period, should be comfortable, and walls and floor and window treatments should act as a framework.

1 *A Victorian cast-iron fireplace with original stove and grate was stripped, sandblasted and boot-blacked to make a handsome feature in this basement dining-kitchen area of a 19th-century London terraced house. The room is made cheerful and interesting by the use of well-worn bentwood chairs, a 1930s advertisement, synthetic marble tiles, and modern units made to look an indeterminate age with just one coat of eggshell paint.*
2 *In this kitchen-dining room a polished pine table with Edwardian chairs sits comfortably under a modern Italian light fitting. The pillared 19th-century chest-of-drawers makes a good contrast with the painting.*
3 *The dining corner of this French kitchen has dark panelled wainscoting, flowered cotton curtains and tablecloth, striped wallpaper and 19th-century cane-backed chairs, all contrasting with the spareness of the green painted kitchen units.*

3

4 In a St Tropez apartment, modern bentwood chairs, a pine refectory table and an adjustable Tizio lamp are mixed with an old pine side table, an old ginger jar and a painting of a window.

5 A painted rustic hutch (dresser) and brick walls in a New York brownstone are in sharp contrast to the mid-18th-century Irish table, the 19th-century elm chairs and the collection of silver. Paisley curtains and shades look good against the distressed blue-and-terracotta walls.

4

5

Bedrooms

Since bedrooms are generally the most personal of rooms and are not usually on show to outsiders, they tend to evolve in somewhat haphazard ways. Thus, they are often the most eclectic room in the home. Very often memorabilia, photographs and small collections of 'this and that' jostling for room with books, mineral water, handcreams, make-up, hand mirrors, prints, small paintings, pillows and cushions, can all too easily – albeit charmingly – smother the actual furnishings. And this is nice for, with the best will in the world, it is less difficult to create a beautifully designed room than to keep it that way.

In fact, a precisely and carefully decorated bedroom, however beautiful, can look soulless and uninviting if it does not have its fair share of the detritus of personal life, which is almost by definition eclectic in nature. Be careful, though, not to accumulate too many bits and pieces on dressing tables and bedside tables. They could end up looking like a jumble of possessions and may distract from a well-planned decorative scheme. A judicious clearout once in a while helps to keep your bedroom clutter under control.

4 An elegant four-poster with sunburst roof. The lively colouring, repeated in the velvet sofa and armchair, is balanced by the oversize lace-edged pillows, the glazed walls in subtle grades of apricot, the Victorian needlework chair and cushions and the handsome overmantel mirror with its pale blue and gilt.

5 Coir matting, an old kelim and palest yellow walls make a framework for mixtures of different blue-and-white designs on bed, cushions, pillows, tablecloth and window treatment. The blues are then repeated in the lamp and the Bristol blue goblets on the mantelpiece. These are balanced by the strong dark lines of the oval mirror, the old cane-sided chair and the little sewing table.

1 A little vignette of disparate objects on a lace-covered bedside table. The books, the gilded skullcap on a plaster head, the tarnished gilt palm, silver mirrors and odds and ends, the old manicure set – all look good against the smooth greeny-blue paint.

2 A charming stepped-up sleeping recess lined with bookshelves and supported by drawers has been formed between two closets in this bedroom. The subtly painted woodwork matches the ceiling, and the stencilled border has much the same feeling as the border on the flowery black rug.

3 Framed cards surrounding a green marbled mirror look neat in this checked and striped room, with its old polished floor and nice old oak furniture.

Studies and Other Areas

The time-honoured image of a study – somewhat battered leather armchairs and footstools, a well worn sofa, a flickering fire, a club fender, a capacious desk and shelves crammed with books – stems directly from the average ambience of the library in a typical 18th-century English country house. However, as that century drew to a close, domestic libraries changed: they turned more and more into general family living rooms, and men were forced into smaller versions of their grander libraries – their studies. Today, most studies tend to be somewhat eclectic, if only because, like the grander libraries of the past, they too tend to be family rooms, or casual smaller living rooms containing a desk and bookshelves. Generally speaking, they are comfortable, cluttered, warm and informal, and more often than not they have a sofa that can be converted into a bed for occasional guests. The bookshelves may have a pediment or a Gothic curve, or be modern wall fitments with an integral working surface. The chairs may be of the capacious wing variety, or Charles Eames-style loungers. The rug or rugs could be oriental or calfskin or needlework. Whatever its varied ingredients, if a study is to be successful it must always seem warm and inviting.

1

2

3

4

5

1 A beautiful arched fanlight over glass doors sets the scene for an equally splendid graphic room with its collection of architectural drawings and bronze objects.

2 A handsomely complicated 17th-century writing table, old leather chair, oriental rug and collection of bronzes are strikingly contrasted in this study with the Tizio lamp, the modern paintings and the hi-tech stereo and projection equipment.

3 Subtle blue-green upholstered walls with matching dragged skirting boards (baseboards) are paired here with a modern carpet, rose-and-green chintz and a collection of 19th-century furniture in mahogany, bamboo and various painted finishes.

4 The very different whites and off-whites in this room (the cotton of the chair, the tweed upholstery and the petals of the orchid) are the common denominator binding together disparate furnishings.

5 This hall, made to seem extremely palatial, was in fact created out of a Manhattan apartment gallery. The exotic burled wood is actually painted faux bois, with glazed terracotta panels to match the border of the freshly installed marble floor. The handsome 18th-century mirror and Empire side table, however, are genuine, as are the Chinese pots. Note the dramatic effect of the uplights behind the torchères and the framing projectors set in the ceiling.

COUNTRY
STYLE

The term 'country style' embraces a vast diversity of styles, in that every nation's country style is different in character and easily distinguishable. Nevertheless, whatever their dissimilarities, all of these styles have something in common: they are comfortable, comforting, warm and relaxed. Moreover, they are interestingly different from any other style in that, whatever their nationality, they are equally adaptable to a cramped town apartment, a suburban villa, a rambling house or a small cottage. Endearingly, too, decorating in country style does not require too much money, for the essence of true rurality is simplicity. Here, of course, we are not talking about 'smart country', which is an entirely different kettle of fish: it requires either the passage of many years or the expenditure of a good deal of money to implement. Country style proper has an atmosphere of freshness and prettiness that is redolent more of nature than of sophistication.

English Country is, as the writer and critic John Richardson once put it, principally noted for 'its simultaneous look of relaxed elegance and benign neglect'. Unforced English country is cluttered with slightly bedraggled loose covers of chintz, and typically has worn oriental or

Country kitchens are much the same throughout the western hemisphere: this one is in fact English.

Setting the Style
COUNTRY STYLE

1

needlework rugs on old wood, matting, brick or pamments (large old terracotta tiles). Other typical elements are battered white plaster walls and old pine furniture, great baskets of logs and flowers or leaves and nice old paisley throw spreads. Open fires blaze, dogs stretch luxuriously in front of the hearth, and, at least in summer, French windows open out onto lavender-fringed brick terraces. Grander country houses have delicious Colefax and Fowler prints, swags and festoon blinds, mellow polished mahogany and walls decorated with pictures of horses, dogs and other subjects related to field sports and country life.

French Country vignettes are divided between Provençale and provincial. The former are full of charming little cotton prints, often bordered with rich dark backgrounds (e.g., deep red or intense yellow, green, terracotta or blue). There are old, sun-baked, terracotta-tiled or stone floors, sometimes with straw mats. The furniture is typically old and made of chestnut with cane seats, and has those slightly curved legs so particular to France and Italy. Cupboards and dressers are primitive in style. Provençale interiors look as if they have grown up in the sun and seem set in the knowledge that the sun will always shine – well, almost always.

Rightly or wrongly, one's immediate decorative images of the other parts of France – Normandy, Brittany, Burgundy, the Dordogne and the Pyrenees – are of small red or blue checks, faded *toile de Jouy* on walls and windows and bed alike, lovely old elm or chestnut refectory tables with those practical *tirettes* (extensions that pull out to accommodate yet more children for Sunday lunch), flagstones and terracotta tiles, ceilings with low beams, pewter everywhere and window boxes bustling with bright geraniums.

American Country is all about primitive furniture in faded burnt-out reds or dusty blues, simple bare board, and the lovely spare lines of Shaker furniture. Checks and small all-over print cottons abound in various guises. Other features are stencilled borders and painted floor cloths, rocking chairs and floorboards, rag rugs and four-poster beds with spanking white linen and crisp embroidery. Then again there are the samplers showing tracts and homilies, the wide stone fireplaces with leaping flames. The pervading smell in winter is of woodsmoke and mulled cider, cloves and cinnamon. Summer is typified by old cane and chintz, and rocking chairs on porches for those long still evenings.

American South West is distinct from the general American country style. It features stone and adobe, rough-hewn, solidly-built rustic furniture, faded patched textiles, Navajo rugs, carelessly thrown blankets, Indian sculpture and ceramics, straw matting on terracotta tiling, and great terracotta pots.

Mediterranean Country styles – from Italy, Greece, Turkey, North Africa, Spain, and so on – are something else again. There are cool stone walls and floors, deep window recesses in pink or blue or lemon wash, simple wood and cane chairs, old chests, sun filtering through latticed window screens or elderly shutters, crisp white cotton or linen, and baskets of herbs and flowers, aubergines, peppers and zucchini.

Scandinavian Country style is typified by distressed painted wood, elaborate ceramic and iron wood-burning stoves, bare wood floors, a pervading blue and white, and a clean crispness.

All of these are, of course, nothing more than quick sketches, a kind of shorthand list of ingredients. But you can mix these ingredients in a vast number of recipes to get the kind of look (or looks) you want.

1 Simple wooden shelves over a modern unit and a roller towel holder acting as a mantelshelf on the chimney breast. Both features are contemporary, but do not look out of place in a country kitchen.

2 Grey-painted stairs and woodwork give a pleasant feel to a casual hall with rural pine pieces.

3 A good old English back hall with orderly rows of hats and boots and a chair that has definitely seen better days upstairs.

4 A simple four-poster with an old chest at its foot. The result – a nicely relaxed country bedroom.

5 Painted floorboards are the outstanding feature of this beautiful country bathroom.

Living Rooms

There are two particular points to bear in mind about country living rooms. One is that, however beautiful they might look and whatever their particular country style, unless they are 'loungeable-in' they simply will not work. A country living room must have deep, squashy sensibly covered seating, well placed stools, good light for reading, soft lights for atmosphere, and comfortable pillows or cushions and soft rugs for lazing about on. Other essentials are a capacious fireplace, deep window sills for abundant flower arrangements and windows that open out onto sweet-smelling terraces or gardens – or at least onto the landscape outside.

The second point to remember is that it is more important for country rooms to be easy on the eye than it is for them to be impeccably coordinated. Country rooms are more for relaxing in than to be impressed by, more for peaceful contemplation than aesthetic confrontation. Certainly they should not in any way be 'demanding' rooms.

1 *Dark beams and decoy birds in a room packed with geraniums.*
2 *A Christmas tree, faded-rose fabric and bleached beams in the brick-floored living room of a converted country barn.*

3 *More beams and an interesting rounded corner fireplace in a room which, despite its cathedral-type ceiling, remains cosy.*
4 *An interesting horizontally beamed North American room, with a lovely old faded rug, painted mantel and wing chairs upholstered in pale damask. The crewel-covered camel-back sofa and airy whites add freshness.*

1

1 The painted light-brown checks
on the floor, exaggerating the
checks of the curtains, are matched
by greeny-grey wainscoting and
mouldings in this quietly decorated
dining room.

2 An unusual painted dresser
and a collection of Victorian jugs
provide the decoration in this simple
glass-roofed dining area.
Whitewashed brick and coir
matting add to the relaxed feeling of
casual rurality.

3 The massive family table in this
room is balanced by an equally
massive dresser packed with china.
A collection of old and new family
photographs goes surprisingly well
with the 19th-century country
chairs and the old rise-and-fall
pendant lamp.

2

3

Dining Rooms

The same feeling of peaceful relaxation and informality should certainly be the chief characteristic of a country dining room. If you are generally a gregarious person or family, it is useful if your table is expandable to cope with guests, or if you have another table nearby that you can bring into service. Likewise, you want to have plenty of spare chairs. Although it can be difficult to achieve, it is well worth trying to design your dining room so that during the summer it is cool and redolent of the outdoors, while during the winter it is warm and snug.

Apart from practical points such as these, there are no real decorational rules to follow. Certainly it is appealing to have country accoutrements – old dressers, sideboards, plates, and collections of antique curios; these latter can be particularly effective if the items have a common theme of eating and/or drinking.

The idea of modern furniture in a country dining room seems like a contradiction in terms, probably because when we think of a country style we are thinking of some imaginary timeless idyll. If, nevertheless, you do wish to incorporate into a scheme items of contemporary furniture, it is felicitous to pair them with more-rustic objects, old or new.

4

5

4 This dining area off a cottage kitchen is furnished with unstudied charm. The tiny space – big enough for four at a squeeze – is crammed full of baskets, plants and hanging shelves for china and other bits and pieces. The interior merges very naturally with the garden outside. It could hardly be called a decorated room, but it definitely seems none the worse for that.

5 A collection of old corkscrews mounted on pine panelling above the jumble of tennis racquets, and mahogany doors panelled with etched glass – these are only a few of the disparate ingredients in this welcoming kitchen-dining room. Differently coloured woods add to the casual charm, as do the extra-tall chairs matching the high table.

Kitchens

The very mention of the words 'country kitchen' is apt to bring to mind comforting thoughts of delicious cooking smells mixed with equally comforting visions of worn chopping blocks, bunches of herbs, garlic and onions, shelves massed with stoneware, crocks, utensils, spices, and esoteric oils and vinegars. *De rigueur* in such a traditional country kitchen would be an old wood table at which one could sit quietly slicing away. The reality of a modern country kitchen is that, instead of the welcoming table, there is likely to be an efficient island in the middle of the room. Nevertheless, all the units should be capacious and made of wood rather than any sort of plastic laminate; the presence of plastics instantly destroys any romantic visions of rurality.

Another practical ingredient for a modern country kitchen is good storage space which might include: glass-fronted cupboards to use for attractive displays; old pine dressers; capacious wooden plate racks; and, perhaps, if you are lucky enough to have the space, a walk-in larder.

1

2

1 *An awe-inspiring wire-mesh grid, massed with pots and pans, almost covers the ceiling of this old kitchen. Beautifully made cabinets have what amounts to a frieze of old bottles running along the top shelf. The old apothecary chest in the middle of the room has a practical marble top. The antique fireplace is inset with a stove top. The ovens are set into another brick wall which has the further function of providing hanging space for saucepan lids.*

2 *Beautiful cabinets, pottery and a nice old table and chairs in this room are softened by the hanging plants and bunches of herbs strung from the ceiling.*

3 *White glass-fronted units in this room look good against the wooden countertops, floor and old country chairs; the window treatment provides further enhancement.*

4

4 An old fireplace in a kitchen otherwise full of traditional furniture and equipment has been updated with stencilled designs and immaculate white tiles. It now holds the stove as well as providing convenient display space.

5 A very 1980s country kitchen, using all the old traditional ingredients yet in an entirely modern way.

6 This pleasing city room, with its ragged ceiling and walls and its dazzling white tiles, has all the 'feel' of the country.

7 Old cane chairs, a collection of jugs, bunches of herbs and rustic cupboards and shelves turn this kitchen into something much more than just a room for cooking.

3

5

6

7

Bedrooms

The general feeling you should aim to achieve when decorating a country or country-style bedroom is one of gentleness. Country-style bedrooms can be overwhelmingly romantic, chastely fresh, demure, simple and folksy, just plain simple or packed with rustic collectables. Whatever their style, though, they do not try to overtly impress – except, possibly, with a sense of complete ease and comfort.

Victorian and Edwardian iron or brass bedsteads, still fairly easy to pick up in antique shops (or junk stores if you are prepared to paint and rehabilitate them), are very useful for country bedrooms. So are sleigh beds and some old wooden beds. Reproductions of these can fit in almost equally well. Old stripped or painted dressers and chests of drawers look good, as do needlework rugs, rag rugs and old patchwork quilts.

If you have sleep problems, or if you dislike the too-early morning, you should use either layers of curtains and blinds or draperies and shades lined with blackout material to mute the bright country dawn and the chorus of waking birds.

3

1 Old white-painted boarding and a battered brick wall gives this city bedroom a decidedly rustic character. The mood is compounded by the high Edwardian iron-and-brass bed with its plump feather mattress, pristine white linens and rose and white Roman blind.

2 A quite different 'feel' in another room with a boarded ceiling. The graphic quilt, tartan blanket, crisp walls and pine furniture and floor all make for a much more masculine atmosphere.

3 A child's room with a decidedly turn-of-the-century air. Cotton-lined walls are adorned with plates and samplers, as are the windows, while the floor is covered with old cotton rugs.

4 The blue frill on the pull-up curtain adds a delicate touch to an already pretty room.

2

4

Part 3
The Elements of Design

Architectural Character
Light
Colour
Furnishings
Pattern and Texture
Displays

ARCHITECTURAL CHARACTER

A room's style is generally dictated by its size, proportion and detailing – or lack of these. Clearly, it would be incongruous to furnish a small, low-ceilinged and dark room with massive soaring furniture, or a large high room with delicate spindly pieces. And, although panelled rooms, or rooms with elaborate mouldings, *can* be furnished with entirely contemporary furnishings to interesting and idiosyncratic effect, the treatment needs a sure eye and a good deal of confidence. For most of us it is usually more effective, and certainly a great deal safer, to be sensitive to the general 'feel' of a space, and to design and furnish accordingly.

This does not mean that a poorly proportioned space cannot be altered in any way that seems feasible. Ceilings in cavernous spaces can be lowered at moderate expense, and this might also allow a more flexible lighting plan with a system of downlights, wallwashers and pinpoint spots. (Such light strategies can, of course, also change the look of a space at night quite significantly.) Any existing mouldings should be restored or replaced. If there are none why not think of putting some in? This may be expensive, but the overall effect should be well worth the cost.

Ceilings that seem too low can often be made to seem less oppressive by visual means. For example, you can paint them a much lighter colour than the walls, or you could have them in a slightly darker shade but put in a 30cm/12in stripe around the ceiling's perimeter so that the central space seemed to be raised. Vertically striped wallpaper or fabric will make rooms seem taller, as will uplights judiciously placed in corners so as to splash light onto the ceiling.

Sometimes the simple expedient of blocking up a door and putting in a new one in a different part of the room can make a huge difference to the seeming proportions of a room; additionally, the resiting of a door can make a room a great deal more comfortable and elegant. Also, if there is more than one door in a room and they are of different heights, they can be equalized to make the space seem more harmonious. A room can be made to look considerably more gracious and effectively longer if you replace the built-in shelves and cabinets at one end with a handsome free-standing piece of furniture – for example, a bureau-bookcase with, say, mirrors or paintings on either side and perhaps an accompanying pair of chairs. Alternatively, a small

1 Imaginative use of colour and arrangement, coupled with an eye for balance, helps this awkward space. White paint expands the apparent size while the paintings and photographs between the beams, the objects along the ledge, and the dressing table at the end of the bed make maximum use of the available area.

2 Here the lofty shelf helps to lower the ceiling. The arches and the clean lines and colours make the most of natural light and the view of the river beyond.

3 This very low attic space is helped by white paint, the oeil de boeuf window (which adds a sense of perspective), the low line of the couch, and the darker colours of the rug which visually 'drop' the floor. **2**

characterless room can be made infinitely more appealing if you line it with bookshelves, maybe leaving alcoves for sofas.

Mirrored alcoves either side of a chimney breast can add inches to the apparent length and height of a room, quite apart from improving its light. You can get a similar effect by mirroring between a pair of windows.

Lengthening windows – or installing French doors in their stead if a room leads onto a terrace, deck, balcony or garden – invariably has a miraculous effect on the appearance of a room, provided, of course, that such windows do not look incongruous from the outside or spoil a carefully designed facade. In the same way, an additional window or two – assuming once again that they suit the exterior and you have the relevant permission – will vastly improve the sense of light and air in the room.

A final way to disguise poor proportions is to use a wood floor that is either much lighter or much darker; such a tactic makes an immediate statement. If the floorboards are in bad condition they may have to be replaced with new boards and parquet; or they could be bleached, stained or varnished.

4 *An incredibly difficult space has been cleverly disguised using mirror along one wall to double the apparent size, a painted geometric floor and ragged walls to give depth, a large painting to add grandeur, and an interesting mix of furniture and objects.*

5 *Here the walls have been made to look further apart by painting them a darker shade between the pillars, creating the illusion that they are deeply recessed.*

6 *The space in this very high loft area has been effectively 'tamed' through the use of different levels, platforms and stripes.*

Period Details

All through history, interior architectural detailing – ceiling decorations, mouldings, pillars, columns, arches, chair rails, dados, wainscoting, panelling, door-cases, pediments and so on – has been considered an essential part of a room by those who could afford it. Although the Bauhaus movement in the 1920s resulted in a paring-down of such elements to rely on form and structure for decoration, rather than on embellishments, the more eclectic of the general public have never given up exploring antique shops, country sales, auction rooms, junk shops and demolition yards for decorative elements to incorporate in their homes.

The Post-Modernist movement of the 1970s and 1980s has, of course, put ornament, or an approximation of it, back into the mainstream. Now there is, too, a brisk trade in well detailed fibreglass, plaster and wood columns, mouldings, balustrading, niches, corbels and panelling as people attempt to add character and atmosphere to the plain rooms of new apartment buildings and housing developments. In the same vein, just as it was fashionable in the middle years of the century to rip out or cover up and fill in old beams, mouldings and all too often (alas) old fireplaces, in the course of 'modernizing' old houses it is now equally *de rigueur* to renovate and revive, to try to uncover, open up, and generally restore or replace all the former details.

It is interesting how even the simplest cornice (crown molding) can add elegance to a space and, of course, if a ceiling is sufficiently high, the more elaborate the cornice, the grander the room appears.

If, as in so many rooms built in mid-century and later, the ceiling is not high, it is still possible to add simple slim beading or, as an alternative, one of the many paper borders available; these now include well drawn architectural cornices and dados, as well as the more usual floral and geometric designs. Fabric wallcovering can always be finished off using polished, stained or painted wood beading, decorative braid, or even lengths of picture frame in gilt, silver or polished wood. Stencilled borders (available in kits or made yourself) look decorative on plain painted walls (see page 191).

A good approximation of a dado or chair rail can be effected by simply applying lengths of 4–5cm/1½in–2in moulding to a wall at waist height and either painting or papering the space below in a way that contrasts with

the general wall colour or finish. Painted panelling can be simulated by lengths of moulding applied in rectangles or squares (see page 167). Lengths of moulding in various designs can generally be bought from good hardware or decorating stores.

A final sense of attention to detail will certainly be imparted by the room's hardware: the door handles, fingerplates, window catches, light switches and dimmers. All of these fixtures look handsome in brass, but light switches and sockets (outlets) can alternatively be effectively painted in with the walls to achieve a simple touch of character and style.

4 Simple turned banisters and a dado rail with Lincrusta beneath it are classic turn-of-the-century details in many halls.
5 The addition of an old stained-glass door adds character.
6 Mirrored panels, a graceful fanlight and a gilt strip along the bottom of the moulding give distinction to a small Italian hallway. The new details give it light, space and elegance.
7 The marbled applied pilaster contrasts well with the blue-grey paint and adds character.

1 The applied ceiling mouldings in this room add visual interest.
2 Panelling adds warmth to a small country hallway.
3 Original stained-glass panelled door makes a bold decorative statement as well as defining the space of the hallway.

Fireplaces

A working fireplace – long sacrificed in favour of the assumed higher efficiency of central heating – is once again considered to be one of the best aesthetic assets a room can have. However efficient the heating system, however beautiful the contents of a room, nothing as comforting as flickering flames and sweet-smelling smouldering wood ·or coal has yet been invented – although gas-fired imitations set into a pretty mantel are reasonable runners-up.

Even if a fireplace is not functional, the mantelpiece still provides a natural focal point for a room, and in any case, with some expense and determination, it might well be possible to open up a chimney again or to divert a flue or create a new one. Consider matters carefully before you remove a fireplace or mantelpiece unless it is really hideous. If a building is at all old, the fireplace and its surround may well be original and will almost certainly suit the proportion and 'feel' of the room in a way that no replacement could – unless, perhaps, it is a superior model of the same period and style taken out of another building.

If you are trying to make a room much grander than it already is, you could install a grander fireplace. Some-times, too, the original will have been removed already, in which case the choice is either to find another of the period or suited to the style of the room, whether an original or a good reproduction, or to introduce some other classic fireplace. Old French marble fireplaces, or copies of them, seem to fit in with almost any style of furnishing, and are often used when upgrading a room. You might prefer an old English pine mantel to a marble one, or *vice versa*.

It may be difficult or undesirable to remove an existing fireplace that is undistinguished rather than unattractive. In this case it can always be 'marbleized', *'faux bois'd'* or given some other painted finish – or just painted the same colour as the walls. If the mantel is not bad but the slips (the stone, marble or tiles framing the actual fire-hole) are awful they can (at worst) be replaced – an expensive, messy job. Alternatively, they can be painted; boarded over and then *faux*-finished; tiled over, if they do not stand too proud on top of the old tiles; or even mirrored on top of the old tiles in a room that could benefit from a bit more sparkle.

If a mantelpiece is unattractive and the room has no special architectural characteristics, a comparatively

1 This French fireplace is treated like a painting with a gilt frame around it. The fender and hearth are made out of heatproof glass.
2 Another modern fireplace, this time in Germany. The hood is integrated with the walls, and a continuation of the hearth has been made into seating. Note the space beneath for storing logs.
3 Traditional New England fireplace, untraditionally painted yellow with a painted checkerboard floor for contrast.
4 English between-the-wars mantelpiece and overmantel with a small cast-iron grate filled with dried flowers.

1

2

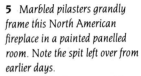

easy solution is to remove the offending mantel, and either install a basket grate in the hole or plan to burn logs directly on the hearth or on fire dogs. Alternatively, once the old mantelpiece has been removed and the recess tidied up, it can be framed.

One technique worth thinking about is – assuming it is feasible – to take down the walls either side of a chimney breast, leaving a central grate between two rooms. The grate can be either knocked right through, so that one fire is shared by the two ends of the enlarged space, or rebuilt so that there is a separate fire on each side; on the whole, the latter is the most satisfactory solution if you want to minimize excess smoke. The exposed chimney breast will usually form a striking shape in the room. There is no reason why the hearth should not be raised a couple of feet above the floor to give extra warmth, and perhaps extended along a wall to form a long brick base that can hold books and magazines as well as providing more seating.

If there is no fireplace at all in an otherwise ideal country house, do not despair. Wood-burning stoves can be added to outside walls provided flues are carefully engineered and the wall is insulated and fireproofed.

5 Marbled pilasters grandly frame this North American fireplace in a painted panelled room. Note the spit left over from earlier days.
6 A simple pine surround for a French fireplace makes all the difference.
7 Wild flowers and Victorian cast iron, surrounded by unpretentious marble, and a set of variegated 1920s tiles.
8 An unusual and sophisticated Swedish fireplace inset into a wall of careful panelling.
9 French mantelpiece in an Edwardian house.

Doors

Doors, whether internal or external, can make an immediate difference to the feeling and 'stature' of a home. Luckily, it is not very difficult to change them. You can choose from a large range of standard and custom-made designs which can be painted, left natural, stained and/or sealed to suit a particular scheme. There is also a growing choice of insulated French doors and both single and double interior doors with glass panes which, substituted for the solid variety, can totally change the feeling of light and airiness in a room.

You can find old doors in demolition yards, at antique dealers specializing in architectural elements, or at demolition sales. These latter are especially useful if you are carrying out a renovation or conversion where the ceilings are high enough and enough walls are down that you can dictate your own terms as regards door openings. A handsome pair of double doors or a collection of pediments and beautiful door-cases might well dictate the entire style of your conversion.

Existing doors can, of course, be embellished. Mouldings can be superimposed on flat surfaces to give the impression of panelling (see page 167). Conversely, unattractive mouldings can be stripped off and better

1 This double-sided mirror-panelled door between a study-bedroom and a bathroom is indistinguishable from the mirror-panelled wall when closed.
2 Glass-panelled internal doors in a French apartment. These are often found in 1920s buildings in the United States as well as in European apartment blocks.
3 Handsome etched glass-panelled doors from France, used here to great effect in a US home.
4 Floor-to-ceiling folding doors make a neat space-saver in a very small kitchen area.
5 A softly draped doorway leading to a tiny dining room.
6 The same draped doorway as in 5, but from the other side, showing the reverse lining.

7

5

6

7 *Graceful panelled double doors in a French room lead to a draped sofa bed with pillows hung from a wooden pole.*
8 *Extremely ornate archway leading to an Edwardian-inspired ante-room in a US show house.*
9 *Heavy cotton drapes frame panelled glass French doors.*

8

ones put in their place. Doors can be veneered, stripped or wood-grained (see page 188), or they can have their mouldings picked out in subtle gradations of colour. Undistinguished flush doors can be painted or papered in with the walls – or painted, for example, pastel colours in an otherwise all-white room. Door-cases can be painted in a colour that contrasts with that of the door itself, or left white to frame pine or mahogany panels. In an old house, it is always worth scraping away at a painted door to see what type of wood lies underneath. You may find a series of beautiful old pine doors in a particularly felicitous mellow tone lurking under a shabby coat of white paint.

Good hardware, although often quite shockingly expensive, might well give pleasure long after the shock of the price has worn off. Such hardware can make an enormous difference to the feeling of quality in a home. It is well worth making a careful choice. Alternatively, you might consider sending off old hardware to be cleaned. On modern flush doors, coloured or matt chrome hardware can add a cheering note.

9

1

2

Windows

A window is a lot more than a source of light and air, a base for good window treatments, and a view. Quite apart from how you treat the window – your decision to leave it alone to stand on its own merits, or to put up curtains, shades or shutters – do not forget the decorative potential of the window itself. There is no reason why a pedestrian frame should not be imaginatively treated, as long as it fits in with the general design of the room; after all, window frames are part of the background. Extra trims of wood can be added to make frames seem more substantial. Frames and surrounds can be stained to match the floor, or they can be painted in a contrasting colour and left to stand on their own. A window with an especially pleasing view can be treated like a painting in a frame. Short windows can be made to appear long and graceful by giving them a floor-to-ceiling frame, perhaps with a window seat stretched across, and softening the sides with long, caught-back curtains, or drapes.

Windows, too, can make excellent frames for glass or perspex (plexiglass) shelves which can be used to display glassware or plants. Windowsills are also useful for displaying all kinds of objects, such as china and flower arrangements.

Do not forget that windows are just as visible from the outside as from the inside. Do not decide to alter their structure in any way until you have made sure that the outside view of the building will not be adversely affected and that your new window will not clash with the old ones. In addition, you must remember to obtain permission from any local authorities.

Another important point to be considered is how problematical the windows are. How do they open – inward or outward? How are they set in the wall? Are the windows all the same size and regularly spaced, or of different sizes, asymmetrically spaced? All these points should be thought about *before* you plan any kind of window treatment. How should pivot, French, arched, corner, clerestory and dormer windows be treated, quite apart from those awkward varieties with odd-shaped or sloping tops?

But, just as elegant doors can give an entirely different look to a room, so can more appropriate windows. And remember that well fitting, well insulated windows make a lot of difference to your general comfort.

1 *A large skylight gives pleasant lighting to this Connecticut hallway.*
2 *The window behind the basin of this bathroom shows a pretty view of farm buildings. Its sill provides space for a pair of orchids.*
3 *Wooden shelves stretched across the window of a North American room hold an attractive collection of glass and bibelots, enhanced by the greenery outside.*
4 *A simple treatment for an attractive arched window. The sill makes a good display area.*

4

5

7

5 <u>Plants are the sole window dressing for this bay window</u>.
6 White Austrian shades against a dense background of greenery, cane furniture and matting.
7 A rod for hanging jugs makes a good-looking display area out of a very simple little window.
8 This large round window in a Scandinavian house is spectacular by day and hidden by an extension of the wall covering at night.
9 Draped sheer cotton looks good in this Italian room.

6

8

9

Stage II (see page 112) *Stage III (see page 128)* *Stage IV (see page 144)*

Kitchen: Stage I

Room Schemes

In order to show how a room can be built up logically, practically and comfortably – to show a true 'before and after' sequence – this book illustrates the shells of four main spaces: a kitchen, a living room, a bedroom and a one-room studio apartment. These illustrations demonstrate the natural progression of lighting, decorating, furnishing and adding accessories, in that order. The thinking behind the various transitions becomes clear if you read the sections – on lighting, colour, furniture and fittings, and pattern and texture – which immediately precede each set of illustrations.

By examining the progression of the four different rooms carefully you can analyze exactly how a room can be made to work to fit your particular needs. You can also work backwards – gradually stripping away each layer, as it were – until you are left with an empty shell of a room. If, too, you happen to prefer a less-cluttered look, you can ignore the final stage altogether.

Stage II (*see page* 113)

Stage III (*see page* 129)

Stage IV (*see page* 145)

KITCHEN

The aim here was to build on an extension to a home to make a good-sized kitchen/dining room. The owners desired an efficient and spacious working kitchen, yet at the same time they wanted both rooms to be warm and casual. The most difficult thing to be sorted out was the lighting in the dining area. Since the new space was going to be so much longer, everyone was afraid that

the dining part would be too dark. The architect overcame this problem by stepping down the ceiling in the kitchen extension and adding a row of windows at the junction. However, to avoid too much of a break and to assist the warm 'feel' his clients wanted, he decided to tongue-and-groove both ceilings with pine boarding (see page 205) and to repeat this wood on the skirting boards (baseboards).

LIVING ROOM

This living room in a 1920s apartment block, although spacious, was at the back of the building and thus had very little daylight and a dreary view of rear brick walls. On the other hand, it had nice natural details: a polished hardwood floor, a well proportioned fireplace, high ceilings and good cornices (crown moldings), cased-in radiators under the window and

to the side of the fireplace (with potential, respectively, for a window-seat and extra shelf space) and shutters. It also had a graceful arched doorway with internal windows on either side so that what little natural light there was could filter through to the entrance hall beyond. The main tasks, then, were to get more light and warmth into the room and to take maximum advantage of the good points.

Living Room: Stage I

Room Schemes

Stage II (see page 114)

Stage III (see page 130)

Stage IV (see page 146)

Bedroom: Stage I

Stage II (*see page* 115)

Stage III (*see page* 131)

Stage IV (*see page* 147)

Studio Apartment: Stage I

BEDROOM

During the 1940s and 1950s, in the first flush of enthusiasm for Modernism, many people tore out old architectural details from period buildings. Now, with the new spirit for preservation and restoration, people are seeking to put back the detail – or at least to restore the same sort of feeling. This was the case with this bedroom, which happily still retained its fireplace and handsome window frames and doorcase, although it had, unfortunately, lost its old floorboards and all its former mouldings; also, the room had been made much darker than it needed to be. The decorative aim was to give the room back as much of its former distinction as possible and to make it lighter, yet all this had to be done within the constraints of a fairly restrictive budget.

STUDIO APARTMENT

The main virtues of this studio apartment were, first, that the rent was low and, second, that the unusual dais leading to the kitchen and bathroom areas gave added flexibility and some rationalization to the limited space. The main problems were that, apart from the bathroom fixtures, the apartment was alarmingly empty and that the young owner had a tiny budget and very few possessions (a few family cast-offs, such as a 1930s chest of drawers and an old pair of curtains, as well as generous presents including a stereo system, television, Tizio desk lamp and halogen floor lamp). Nevertheless, this studio-apartment dweller was resourceful and ambitious for his comfort. Also, he had good design sense and, best of all, a willing carpenter friend.

LIGHT

Good light and good lighting – the one natural and the other manmade – are as essential to the success of a room as they are to sight, and yet, curiously, they are often the least planned, the least thought-about, of all decorating ingredients. How often do people fail even to think about the light factor in their rooms, or about how they should control, filter, or enhance light, until long after the decoration is underway?

Natural Light   Many people tend to think of artificial light as the counterfeit of daylight, regarding the two as totally separate issues. In fact, an effective lighting system that will provide comfortable light at all times requires you to strike a balance between the two, the one discreetly boosting the other when necessary. To do this successfully, you must understand the limitations of daylight – as well as its qualities. Daylight has, of course, all the advantages of variety: variety in intensity, in the form of almost hourly changes as well as seasonal ones; and variety apparent in colour, from intense blue to overcast grey, from the clear light of early morning to the pale lavenderish dusk of evening.

During each of these phases the interior of a building will look subtly different. That is why small windows should be left as uncluttered as possible to make the best of what light there is; why large windows should have screens, shades, blinds or sheers that can filter any superabundance; and why it is useful to see a room in as many lights as possible before deciding on a colour scheme and furnishings.

However, you should remember that daylight does not actually have great qualities of penetration, although the low angle of the sun in winter gives deeper penetration at certain times of the day than in the summer. In most average rooms, about 1 per cent of the available daylight outside will reach the parts of the space furthest from the windows, as opposed to as much as 10 per cent near the windows. In rooms with windows at both ends, the level of light from outside will fall off towards the middle. For large periods of the year, demanding visual tasks like reading, writing, drawing, painting and sewing can be done in solely natural light only if you are close to a window, and many rooms in buildings with a narrow frontage surrounded by other buildings will have poor lighting at most times of the day, whatever the season. This means that a good many rooms will always need the boost of artificial lighting for some purposes, and that many dark central areas in deep buildings – kitchens, bathrooms, as well as halls and passageways – will need constant artificial light.

4

6

7

5

This can raise quite a problem. During the day the eye becomes so adapted to the high level of natural light that, in order to remain equally comfortable in darker inner areas, it requires an equally high level of electric light – i.e., a higher level than is usual at night, when the eye will have adapted to the lower overall levels of artificial light. This means that *ideally* you should have either separate lighting systems in perpetually dark rooms – one for day, one for night – or some form of dimmer integrated into the existing system so that the level of lighting can be controlled.

8

1 Gauzy white cotton crêpe gently filters and whitens the sunlight pouring through the large windows of this cool-floored country room.
2 Skylights can help make the best use of natural light in the middle of the day when the sun is at its height.
3 The light entering through the thin glass of this utility room's door is caught and magnified by mirror-backed shelves.
4 For bathrooms, where privacy has to be considered, shutters which open at the top keep prying eyes out and allow sunshine in.
5 Do not be tempted to think of artificial light as just the poor substitute for natural light. Any daytime lighting scheme must constitute a partnership between the two, in which artificial light is allowed to boost natural light.
6 The large square halfway up the stairs lets in a great deal of light.
7 Installing glazed doors is an inexpensive way of allowing more natural light to enter your home.
8 Three unusually framed and mullioned windows flood this US bathroom with sunlight.

Lighting a Room

Room lighting can be divided into three distinct types:
- general or background lighting
- task or local lighting
- accent or decorative lighting

Ideally, every room should have a combination – to a greater or lesser degree, depending upon function – of two if not all three of these types. Ideally, too, each form of lighting should meld into the others to form a sometimes dramatic but always harmonious whole.

In order to achieve this kind of lighting harmony it might help to remember that artificial light is, after all, a *substitute* for daylight, which is never static but always shifting and flowing. Think, too, of the three types of light as representing different moods of daylight – the shaft of sun that lights up a particular corner or area; the way a sunbeam highlights a piece of glass or silver or the top of an old polished table – and about how you can use artificial lighting to create similar effects.

1

Living Rooms   The best effect is achieved if all three types of light are used. Background lighting is more subtle coming from well placed wall lights used on their own or in conjunction with uplights set on the floor and concealed behind plants or furniture or in decorative pots; this set-up will give a soft wash of light as opposed to the bland light that comes from a central ceiling fixture. Another alternative for general lighting is to use a selection of strips of one kind or another so as to bathe the walls with light. These arrangements will, in fact, soften the hard confines of a wall and make a room seem more spacious.

Task (local) lighting is provided by table lamps and floor lamps placed judiciously beside sofas and armchairs for comfortable reading, or by angled wall lamps set just above seating areas if there is not very much floor space. Desk lamps are desirable for writing.

Accent (decorative) lighting comes from eyeballs or spots of various types inset into the ceiling – if at all possible – or in some way angled to highlight paintings, objects, tabletops and so on. Accent lighting can also come from the pools of light cast by table lamps.

One important point to remember if you have the chance to rewire a room for your own convenience is that all of these light fixtures can be controlled and subtly modulated by separate switches and/or dimmer switches set by the door. If you are using uplights positioned on the floor, do remember to ask your electrician to have them switched from the door, for this will save a great deal of irritating stooping and crawling around on the floor to switch them on and off. Alternatively, if the rewiring involved is too difficult, ask your electrician to install kick switches by any floor lamps so that you can control them with your foot.

Dining Rooms and Dining Areas   These look best and certainly more romantic by candlelight, but make sure that candles are either above or below eye level, not flickering directly in the diners' eyes. A combination of candlelight with a discreet downlight or two in the ceiling, controlled by dimmer switches, is better still. Pendant rise-and-fall lights with an opaque shade cast a pleasant light, but again they should have a dimmer switch and be so placed as to avoid uncomfortable dazzle. The serving area should be lit separately, perhaps by a well angled spot or downlight or by concealed overhead lighting in the form of an incandescent strip set behind a cover or pelmet (cornice).

Halls, Corridors and Staircases   Far too many halls and staircases have hopelessly inadequate lighting.

2

3

1 A small lamp accents a tiny sculpture whereas a larger, angled lamp provides illumination for typing and writing.

2 A halogen uplight gives a general punch of light in this hallway whereas the recessed spot washes the wall.

3 The pair of table lamps in this bedroom provide both accent and reading light.

4 A chandelier gives general light whereas a series of table lamps provides both accent and decorative light in this living room.

5 A brass lantern supplies general light. Storm lamps illuminate the mirror, the Chinese ginger jars and the botanical prints.

4

5

6

7

6 The wall lights give background light, the table lamps are for reading, and the fire provides a subtle accent.

7 Spots give both general and accent light.

The Elements of Design
LIGHT

They should be well lit at all times, with light on the floor to show any changes in levels and surfaces and light on the walls to show switches and door handles. When starting a lighting plan from scratch, the ideal is to have a night circuit of low-level lights in those areas, controlled by a dimmer switch so that you can turn them down to the right level at bedtime. Alternatively, you could have a separate circuit of miniaturized lights that could, if desired, be left on the full 24 hours, because this system, although somewhat expensive to install, uses very little electricity and is therefore cheap to run. Both systems have the added advantage of acting as an effective deterrent to burglars and prowlers.

Do not forget to try to light hall closets from the inside, so you do not have to grope frustratedly in the dark for coats. Staircases should be lit to emphasize the distinction between treads and risers. The best way to achieve this is to have a good strong light above the stairs and a softer one below. If lights are on a dimmer switch, they can be turned down to an acceptable level and left on all night with very little waste of power. (You may find, though, that you have to replace bulbs more frequently). This is particularly useful in households where there are small children or elderly relatives. Any paintings and mounted objects – sculpture and so on – can be lit using different varieties of spots, preferably attached to a dimmer.

1 In this beamed dining room, ceiling spots give general light, lamps and candles providing decorative accents.
2 Track lighting gives general illumination and a rise-and-fall lamp lights the table in this spare-lined dining-kitchen.

3 Spots give overall light and the candles and strip light accent. The floor lamp is for reading.
4 Another mixture of general light from the mantelpiece spot and the candles on the wall mirrors.
5 At night goose-neck lamps light the table in this dining room.

3

4

5

6

7

6 *Judiciously placed ceiling spots give good, even background light in this tidy kitchen. The pendant lights over the stove top give supplementary light when cooking.*
7 *These bedside lamps serve as general and task lights. The mirror doubles the illumination.*

Bedroom Lighting   This should be almost as flexible as that in the living room: soft enough to be relaxing and peaceful; bright enough to see to dress and perhaps make-up by; and well placed enough for comfortable reading in bed. Bedside lamps should be high enough to shine directly onto a book. A light above a mirror used for making-up is less helpful than lights placed at either side. Lights positioned to shine outward are much better than lights set to shine onto the mirror itself. The same applies to full-length mirrors: the light should be directed onto the viewer rather than onto the glass.

Children's Rooms   In rooms for small children all sockets (outlets) should be childproofed and lighting fixtures should be kept well out of reach. Wall lights are useful here, for they give a softer general light than central ceiling fixtures. Dimmer switches are useful for children who are afraid of the dark; alternatives are very low-wattage skirting (baseboard) fixtures. Older children will want good light for homework, hobbies and reading in bed, so provide adequate lighting on desks and work tables and above beds, and make sure these fixtures are well positioned.

Bathrooms   Small bathrooms may well need no more than a single ceiling light or a couple of downlights (one set over the bath, with a waterproof bulb). Lights should be fixed either side of any mirror used for both making-up and shaving, or just above if used only for shaving. Unfortunately, all too many bathrooms have wiring for light only above the mirror and often people find it just too much hassle to get the situation changed.

Kitchens   All kitchens should have good general light plus booster light for any precise activity – e.g., reading cookbooks, chopping, assembling ingredients and washing dishes. Well placed general diffusing lights fixed flush to the ceiling, inset spots or a mixture of downlights and angled spots make good background light, supported by strip lights concealed under high-level wall cabinets to shine down on the work surface. Any fluorescent lights should be of the warm white variety, because they make food look more appetizing than do most other fluorescents. Also, try to light the inside of storage cupboards or closets.

Directional Lighting

Task or Local Lighting This is a most important part of any room, providing the right level of illumination for a wide range of activities from reading and writing to cooking, eating, sewing, painting, making-up, shaving and playing cards, as well as creating warm, soft pools of light in the room.

In general living areas task lighting is usually provided by table, desk or floor lamps; in bedrooms it is given by bedside lamps, dressing-table lamps and perhaps 'theatrical' white bulbs set at either side of a mirror. In kitchens and laundry rooms, items such as fluorescent strips or a diffusing ceiling fixture give the sort of bright, even light that is required; this can be locally stepped up by spots angled from the ceiling. In bathrooms, you can obtain task lighting by installing the same sort of 'theatrical' strips suggested for dressing-table lights, as well as appropriately placed downlights.

Often people are beguiled by the shape and look of a table or floor lamp but fail to think very much about what the lamp actually achieves in the way of light output. Lamps should, of course, be as functional as they are good-looking; they should provide both generous light for tasks and reading and add a comfortable feeling to a room.

Other moot questions are the height of lamps and how they should be placed. A good guideline to follow for table lamps is that the total height from the floor to the lower edge of the shade (including table height) should equal eye height from the floor – i.e. 100–110cm/ 40–43in, if you are seated on an easy chair. For reading choose three-way or regular soft white bulbs with a maximum of 150W; this might sound a high wattage, but it is a sensible intensity for close work. Three-way bulbs, if available, are preferable because they can be turned on low when not needed for reading or writing. Alternatively, a table top dimmer can be fitted so that you can vary the level.

The base height of floor lamps should be 100–125cm/ 40–49in to the lower edge of the shade with 150W–200W soft white bulbs, or 50W/150W/200W three-way bulbs – or best of all, a halogen bulb with a dimmer switch. For reading, the lamp should be placed behind your shoulder. This obviously cannot be done if a chair or sofa is against a wall; here you can use something like a swing-arm lamp with a dimmer attachment.

1 In this sleek kitchen strip lights concealed beneath the cupboards give good light for cooking, food preparation and washing up.
2 A flexible angled lamp gives excellent work light as well as providing elegant accent in this Swedish study.
3 A brass floor lamp giving reading light.
4 An interesting double-angled halogen light shines into the bowl.

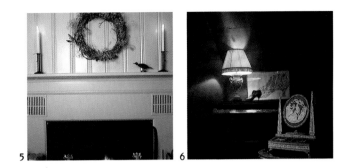

4

5 *Candles and firelight provide warming accents.*
6 *The table lamp on this desk gives dramatic but mellow accent light to a little study area.*
7 *Angled spots wash the walls with light and illuminate all the art in this fabric-lined Parisian apartment. Candles on the dining table provide the more mellow accent light. The unified effect is quite dramatic.*

7

The base height of a bedside lamp should be in line with your shoulder when you are in a semi-reclining position, and the lower edge of the shade should be at your eye level. Extended arm wall lamps are particularly good for bedtime reading and are useful too for saving space on overcrowded bedside tables. Bulbs should again be of the three-way variety if possible: if not, the lights should have a dimmer switch so that one partner need not be unduly disturbed if the other has to switch on the light in the middle of the night.

Accent Lighting Accent lighting creates focal points, emphasizes paintings, plants, flower arrangements and ornaments, and can be used to add interesting drama to a room. The sort of fixtures to employ for this sort of highlighting are the various types of spots, wallwashers, pinhole or framing projectors, uplights, and those strips of tiny lights (like Christmas-tree lights) that can also be used below shelves, in bookcases and so on to delineate angles and give sparkle. Not to be forgotten are candles.

For a wall of pictures, prints, wall hangings or other art use recessed wallwashers, or, if this is difficult, surface-mounted strips, which can be bought in any length with any number of sockets to which to attach lights; alternatively, use track lighting with individual housings that are adjustable for spacing and targeting, so that you can illuminate individual paintings or objects as well as wash the whole wall with light.

The ideal for lighting individual paintings and objects is a pinhole or framing projector; note, though, that they are expensive. When their lenses and shutters are adjusted accurately they will focus exactly on the item to be highlighted, with no overspill. They should be recessed into the ceiling 90–110cm/36–43in from the wall. Alternatives are surface-mounted fixtures similar to those specified for track lighting on page 160; these can be used either in conjunction with track or mounted individually on a ceiling or beam.

If you want to highlight a painting over a mantel, for example, but cannot use recessed lighting or surface-mounted lights, you can utilize uplighting provided by very small portable spot fittings, or by halogen lights concealed in a vase or small canister on the mantelpiece. Alternatively, you can use a high-density lamp aimed from below in order to avoid unwanted reflection in picture glass. Should you use a conventional picture light mounted on the picture so as to illuminate from above, it ought to have a rotating reflector and be adjustable to adapt to an extra-thick picture frame.

For plants, floor sculpture and hangings near to floor level use standard uplights or small adjustable floor uplights concealed behind the plants, in corners or just by the object to be lit. These will either bounce light up, or 'graze' the given object with light.

COLOUR

Colour is both the most immediately noticeable and the most malleable element in decorating. Different combinations of colour can make the same room and the same furnishings seem warm or cool, restful or stimulating, harmonious ·or jarring, welcoming or impersonal. In other words, colour is of the utmost importance – and for that reason it is the source of considerable worry to many people.

Inspiration Some rare indivîduals can carry a colour around in their heads and match it absolutely. They look at a room and know instantly what will or should suit it, and how a single colour will look in this or that colour combination. The majority of us, however, have to work at developing our sense of colour. The easiest and most efficacious way is to get into the habit of *looking hard* at any combination of colours that pleases and appeals to you, and deliberately to analyse the build-up of the colours within that image.

Most visual artists develop the habit of patiently observing colour – of noting all the different shades and nuances that exist in an object or a scene. The Impressionists in particular developed the practice of describing everything they saw in terms of the most detailed breakdown of tones and shades. It is an interesting experiment to take a single item – a rug or a painting, a piece of china or a particular fabric – and to write down the various colours and tones of colours you see in it; not just those that predominate but also all the ancillaries that together make up the whole image. Once you have got used to looking at and analysing colour, you can draw inspiration from almost everything that visually pleases you – particularly, of course, from the natural world.

Think of country or forest or sea or sky colours, or of the build-up of tones in a Mediterranean village or your own garden. Most rural scenes contain innumerable shades of green harmoniously blended with bright flashes of colour from flowers, blossoms, berries or crops. Similarly, looking at an old-fashioned rose garden can tell you how to make successful blends of pinks, yellows, peaches, greens and terracottas, creating a subtle and pleasing scheme of equal tones against a background of the green of trees or the rose-terracotta of an old brick wall.

Another way to build up ideas for a scheme is to observe your own and other people's emotional responses. People often have extraordinarily violent reactions to different colours for no logical reason. 'I loathe green,' they say, or 'I just can't tolerate anything pink.' It is difficult to see how people can possibly object when these colours are used well and with the right balance of contrasts but, whatever the logic of these responses, you can use them positively. Take your favourite colour and think about it in depth. Think, for example, of yellow, and remember everything floral and yellow from the palest creamy yellow of honeysuckle or freesia to the thick

1 Warm red walls enhance this Victorian bathroom.
2 Scarlet walls make a dramatic foil for antiques.
3 Sunshine yellow drenches a living room in light.
4 A palette of light tones promotes a sense of airiness.
5 Adding a sense of depth to a predominantly white room, loose covers on the sofa are palest blue.
6 The rich malachite green of the festoon is echoed in the wall colour.
7 A dresser painted cobalt blue makes a perfect background.
8 A combination of different blues gives a look of serenity.
9 Deep blue walls in the dining room of Charleston House.

creamy velvet of rose petals, through narcissi to daffodils and marigolds. Think of other colours in the same kind of depth and it should be easy to translate all these subtleties and variations of tone into interesting monochromatic colour schemes, especially when the colours are translated into textures to make up a room: wood and wool, cottons and velvet and tweed, paint and paper; all of these and many more can be used to give differing depths and surfaces.

If you are not sure what style of decoration you want to use and are still uncertain about the colours that you find comfortable to live with, there is a useful trick. Buy

The Elements of Design
COLOUR

as many decorating books and magazines as you can. Mark the pages showing pictures of rooms that particularly appeal to you, put the books and magazines aside for a few days, and then look at all your favoured photographs at once. You will notice almost certainly that there is a common style and balance of colours between them.

Matching Colours to Style Although certain colours and colour combinations are definitely connected with particular periods (dark plums, reds and greens for late-19th-century style; stripes and apricot for the Regency period; perhaps orange, green and cream for the 1930s) and indeed are sometimes called after a period, style or culture – as in, say, 'Pompeiian red' and 'Adam green' – there is no need to feel you are rigorously bound by such traditional conventions.

A comforting example can be found in the recolouring of the William Morris designs by Liberty: these look good today, yet they do not in any way sacrifice William Morris's original style. Or again think of the extraordinarily pretty chintzes revamped from old designs by Colefax & Fowler, Scalamandré, Sandersons and others. It is all a question of balance and proportion.

As far as rooms are concerned, the degree of your success will depend on the way you *personally* manipulate style and 'feeling' to your own best comfort.

1 *Aggressive colour is subdued by the delicate furniture to create a strong design statement in this 1950s kitchen.*
2 *Yellow walls provide a good background for antiques.*
3 *The classic kitchen colours, blue and white, give a look of freshness to this contemporary design. Pale grey tiles provide a softening link between the two colours.*
4 *This streamlined kitchen displays a colour combination evocative of the 1930s: buttermilk counters and units banded in bright chrome and duck-egg blue, set off with bright red.*

8

6

9

5 The shiny black and white of this slick modern kitchen is counterpointed by the dramatic injection of lipstick-red details.

6 The restrained elegance of the soft cream colour scheme suits the curved shapes and warm tones of the 1940s-style furniture.

7 Crisp white with dark wood is the perfect combination for suggesting a cool African interior.

8 Pink candy-stripe wallpaper makes a feature of the unusual angles and corners in an attic bedroom.

9 An authentic 'retro' look is achieved by the use of classic Art Deco colours.

10

7

11

10 There are echoes of Tissot in this languid Victorian-style garden room, with its moss-green festoon blinds and painted furniture.

11 A classical treatment for a Georgian dining room: powder blue walls set off with cream woodwork.

Putting Schemes Together

Thinking up colour combinations for a particular style of room is one thing. Achieving the right balance is another. Preparing schemes for an entire home is the most intricate exercise of all.

There are several types of permutation you can use to achieve an interesting balance. One way is to keep most of the room in shades and variations of a single colour but to have a number of items in a harmonious secondary colour, while using objects of quite different colours for the purposes of accent. For example, you could use a warm but pale cream for walls, window shades and carpet, mix it with rose for the upholstery and curtains and add, as accent colours, white (chairs and frames), green (plants and a stencilled design on the walls) and burnt umber (a dried flower bouquet).

Another effective permutation is to keep walls, curtains, floor and furniture all in one colour, perhaps white, the interest being provided by the varying textures. Alternatively, to the same basically white room you could add green-and-white cushions or pillows as well as groups of plants.

Again, you could use a soft blue for walls, a slightly darker shade for dados or wainscoting, paint woodwork a crisp white, and have touches of pale lilac. Another variation on the same theme would be to have the colours as above but with the addition of chairs or even the carpet in olive green.

Planning the colour scheme for a whole house or apartment depends very much on its overall size. If a home or apartment is very large you can afford to have, if you wish, quite different schemes in every room, as long as you remember to pay attention to the meeting points of floor and wall finishes, and to make sure that differing colours, textures and patterns work well together between corridors and the rooms that they adjoin. If the space is small, however, then it is sensible to create a harmonious whole – to think up an overall palette of colours that can be used in differing proportions and combinations in the various rooms. For example, suppose you were particularly happy with apricot, dark blue, burnt umber and green. In one room you could have apricot walls combined with white shutters, a dark polished wood floor, a golden Afghan floor rug, and upholstery in dark blue, cream and plain white, accented with green plants and old needlework cushions or pillows in shades of yellow and apricot and with blue paisley fabric at the windows and on chair seats. Another room could have apricot and off-white wallpaper used with plain deep blue upholstery, and a third room could be basically off-white with an apricot-and-blue border or stencilling, polished floorboards with a blue-and-apricot dhurrie rug, off-white shades with a double border of apricot-and-dark-blue grosgrain, and a mixture of blue, off-white and apricot upholstery, or blue or apricot bedspreads.

Each room would seem entirely different, but each would meld with the others to create an overall impression of harmony.

Manipulating Space and Colour It can be seen from the above that in a small apartment or house the space can be made to seem much larger if more or less the same colours are used throughout, but in different juxtapositions – especially if they are rooted to the same general floor covering (or perhaps a polished wooden floor). Strong or warm colours like red and burnt orange will make walls appear to close in and the space seem smaller. Cool colours will appear to stretch space, to push the walls out, particularly if the floor, walls and ceiling all relate to each other. A long corridor will seem less so if the end wall is painted or covered in a warm colour, just as a small space will seem larger if all the

1 The Empire look, in rich cream and purple.
2 A sugar-pink kitchen, carefully coordinated (right down to the teapot), is set off with a jolt of green.
3 Subtle, muted shades of pale terracotta, pale leaf green and light blue blend beautifully.
4 Plastered walls washed in light green create an atmosphere of contemplation.
5 A 1950s 'retro' look, with a splash of paintbox colours.
6 The graphic lines of the modern furniture are softened by light spilling through translucent curtains.

surfaces are painted the same white colour and the walls are washed with light.

A high ceiling will seem less so if it is painted a darker colour than the walls. Another way of making a high ceiling look lower is to add a false wainscot at waist level around all the walls, painting it a darker shade than the walls above. A low ceiling will seem higher if it is painted a lighter shade than the walls, and higher still if you fix moulding around the perimeter of the ceiling and paint it a darker colour than the ceiling.

Colour, of course, has an immediate effect on the 'feel' of a room. Rooms painted in deep warm colours such as rust red seem warm and comfortable; such a scheme would be appropriate, for a home in a northern city, with long winter months. The same room painted white or pale yellow would seem light and airy in a hot climate, especially if it was filled with white wicker furniture.

A rather dark, rich room can be brightened by using accents of more intense colour and lightened by painting the woodwork white. A light, somewhat bland room can be given much more interest and character if you stain the floorboards a deep, very dark brown and add large plants in oversized baskets or terracotta pots. Large pieces of furniture will look smaller if their covering is the same colour as that of the walls; a smaller piece of furniture covered in an accent colour can then be used to balance the effect.

Mixing Colours

When you are on the verge of finalizing a colour scheme it helps to take samples of all the ingredients you plan to use in a room (flooring, curtains, window shades, wallcovering, paint, tablecloths, bedspreads, valances or ruffles, trims, tie-backs and so on) and put them on a table, if possible in the room itself. Then you should give them, as it were, a good squint with narrowed eyes. This is what Emily Malino, the US designer, suggested in her excellent book, *Super Living Rooms*. I have often followed her advice, for it works very well. By squinting at all those assembled colours and textures you can see which really works with the others, and in what proportion; what stands out too harshly; and what patterns and textures contribute to the most harmonious whole.

That, of course, is to assume you have already selected your colours. Sometimes you may have in mind a colour for walls or a piece of furniture that you cannot find in any paint shop – and, indeed, cannot yourself precisely visualize. The best thing to do in such a situation is to browse through magazines (including the advertisements) and look at samples of coloured wrappings, bits of dress fabric and so on. As soon as you see the colour you desire – and if you do this you almost inevitably will – you have something to show what it is

that you want. Take your 'sample' along to a paint shop to get the colour mixed, or show it to a painter, who might, if he or she is good, be able to achieve exactly the same subtle effect by tinting a glaze and overpainting a wall, by painting on different layers and rubbing the paint off until the desired effect is achieved, or by some other means.

Then again, you might find exactly the right colour for a curtain in a dress-fabric department. The fabric will be of a narrower width, and you may have more trouble working with repeats, yardage and seams, but it could all be well worth it to get the exact shade you want. Do not forget about antique textiles – and, indeed, old fabrics in general. Dyes vary over the generations, not to mention the centuries, and it is often possible to find beautiful old draperies and tablecloths in thrift stores as well as antique shops.

Finally, do not neglect chance or happy accidents, or think that once a room is done to your satisfaction it is finished. You might suddenly see a new (or old) fabric that seems to go perfectly with, if not match, an old rug. All you have to do is cover a cushion or pillow with the fabric, or use it to make an overcloth for a table, and again the room has a new dimension.

1

2

3

4

5

1, 2 *Here two connecting rooms with different schemes are given unity by the repetition of colours. In the blue dining room, red needlepoint seat cushions and a red lacquered lamp-base tie into the glimpse of red wall through the doorway. In the scarlet living room, blue-and-white china on the mantelpiece and a blue covered footstool link to the dining-room colour scheme.*

3 *A Mondrian-style painted table-base acts as a colour code for the decorative scheme.*

6

7

How Many Colours Can You Put Together? This is a point that often worries people. Major areas (walls, floors, window treatments) should generally be restricted to three colours at most, but there is no real limit to the number of accent colours that can be used with pillows, mouldings, accessories, flowers and so on. For example, in a room with glazed yellow walls, the carpet could have a yellow-cream ground with odd touches of various blues and rosy terracotta. The curtains could be yellow-and-white stripes with the undercurtains in creamy white. One sofa and an armchair could be cream, another sofa yellow, and a second armchair could pick up the blue in the carpet. Two other occasional chairs could have frames painted in soft terracotta and faded blue-green seats – again to pick up the carpet's colour. A final colour could be provided by the greens of plants.

The main point is that you do not have to stick to matching colours exactly. After all, in nature colours are never perfectly matched.

4 *A strict two-colour scheme can give coherence to an area such as a kitchen where there are many different types of surface.*

5 *The consistency of the red, black and white scheme is carried right through.*

6 *The turquoise background of the patterned fabric on the chair, stool and screen is used to draw together different areas of the room.*

7 *A black-and-white background is a sympathetic frame for pretty floral chintz, plants and ferns.*

111

Room Schemes

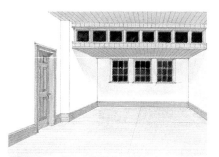

Stage I (*see page* 92)

Stage III (*see page* 128)

Stage IV (*see page* 144)

Kitchen: Stage II

Stage I (*see page* 93)

Stage III (*see page* 129)

Stage IV (*see page* 145)

Living Room: Stage II

KITCHEN

The next step was to install the lighting and tiles. To make a deliberate distinction in atmosphere between the kitchen and the dining area, a chandelier was put in above where the dining table would go. Recessed ceiling lights were set in the kitchen (see page 158), there being ample recess between boards and roof. Sockets (outlets) were installed above the counters to allow both for further lights and for appliances. Large Mexican tiles were chosen for the floor in both the kitchen and the dining area to provide continuity; smaller quarry tiles were set into the wall above the sink and the counters (see page 200). The walls were all painted in white eggshell, and the ceiling boards were lightened with a white stain to raise the apparent height. This also helped the overall lightness.

LIVING ROOM

The first thing to be done was to boost the natural daylight while avoiding having to have artificial lamps switched on all through the day. The best way was to use a system that had enough flexibility to give bright light by day and interestingly subtle light by night (see page 150–161). To this end, 'warm white' fluorescent strips were slipped behind the wood pelmets (cornices) above the window to simulate sunlight filtering down through the shutters. Uplights were placed in the corners, a picture light was installed over the fireplace, downlights were recessed in the internal windows, and a halogen floor lamp was installed on the premise that it really looked like sculpture. Walls were ragged (see page 184), in warm apricot and the woodwork was painted white to add to the lightening effect.

113

Room Schemes

Stage I (*see page* 94)

Stage III (*see page* 130)

Stage IV (*see page* 146)

Bedroom: Stage II

Stage I (*see page* 95)

Stage III (*see page* 131)

Stage IV (*see page* 147)

Studio Apartment: *Stage* II

BEDROOM

Although restoring or adding mouldings can be reasonably inexpensive, in this case the cost still went over the budget. It was therefore decided to use a small floral wallpaper with a coordinating border, and to paint all the woodwork white (see page 181), so that lightness was restored as well as character. However, before the decoration was done, heating panels were installed along the skirting (baseboards), as well as wall sconces to enhance the period feel. The less than distinguished 1940s floor was improved by first sanding it down (see page 169) and then staining it in a darker, richer colour; finally the floor was given a couple of coats of polyurethane and a waxing. This at least made it a better-looking background for the collection of cotton rugs.

STUDIO APARTMENT

Clearly the first priority was getting the framework right, followed by obtaining good kitchen equipment. There was no money to add new electric sockets (outlets), but ceiling fixtures were found on sale in a lighting store and a job lot of old spotlights in the local charity store. Although the original intention had been to paint everything white, the scheme was changed to yellow walls with grey woodwork once the major decision had been made to splash out on close-fitting grey industrial carpeting (laid everywhere except in the kitchen), the aim being to give a substantial improvement to the overall appearance of space and comfort (see page 224). Black and white vinyl kitchen tiles were found in a nearby store; they were stuck down with adhesive.

FURNISHINGS

It is quite possible, if you have the money and the time, to plan the furnishings of a room from scratch and, within a few weeks or months, have the room exactly as you originally envisaged it. The result, however, may have all the impersonality of a hotel room or a store advertisement. It may be comfortable, workable and well designed – even lush – but it will have nothing of your own particular character and individuality.

If you have considerable experience of decorating, either because you are a professional or because you have moved frequently, you can get round this problem, but on the whole the most interesting, idiosyncratic and memorable rooms *evolve*. People change their minds. It may be that they have to change them through lack of funds or simply because they cannot find what they originally conceived. Alternatively, though, some different arrangement or juxtaposition might suddenly present itself through a chance happening – perhaps someone gives you a good piece of furniture or a painting, the inclusion of which will affect the design of your room. For whatever reason, half the fun of decorating is living through the gradual changes – the interesting evolution – of a room.

This is by no means to say that you cannot or should not plan the furnishing of a room from the beginning, or have any idea for its eventual style based on your particular needs and preferences as well as the overall 'feeling' you wish to create. It is important to get the framework – the bare bones – right from the start, and to go about the arrangement of a room in such a way that at every stage it *looks* finished, even if it has yet to reach the ideal you envisage for it in the long term. Doing this is not difficult if you make a practice of always buying compromise 'fill-in' furniture, with an eye to recycling it to other rooms as and when you can afford what you really want. For example, inexpensive canvas, cane or wicker chairs can be used in the living room in the meantime and then later they can be moved to a bedroom or a porch.

It has to be repeated emphatically that you should be prepared to change your mind if necessary – to add here and subtract there. Above all you must be flexible, because your tastes and ideas may change, as may your financial status (or lack of it). Happily, even if money is at a premium, imagination need not be.

1 A warm, neutral colour scheme and the natural textures of the coir and the slatted wooden blinds together make an appropriate setting for a collection of wooden furniture.

2 The country pine table and chairs are the focal point in this dining room, blending with the floral festoon and modern print.

3 Living rooms often need to accommodate different activities. Here the right angle made by the pair of long sofas echoes the angled laminate worktop.

4

3

5

6

4 A traditional living-room arrangement: a pair of facing sofas on either side of the fireplace, flanked by occasional tables.

5 In this spare Swedish bedroom, an iron bed, Victorian dining chair and modern leather recliner are set around the perimeter of the space, as if they were objects on display.

6 A truly eclectic mix: canvas director chairs ranged around an antique table, and a simple wooden stool used as a plant stand.

117

Choosing Furniture

It helps when planning furniture for various rooms to think in terms of 'rooted' and 'peripheral' or 'floating' pieces. Sofas, beds, pianos, bookcases, dining tables and storage walls are definitely rooted pieces, as are armchairs and any sort of storage. In the peripheral or floating category come occasional chairs and side and coffee tables; these contribute to the overall effect of contrast – solidity and lightness, permanence and fluidity. Clearly, you will have to buy first the large, comfortable root items. Once these are installed you can adjust your ideas about the floaters, perhaps even improvising them – for example, you could make your own coffee table using a sheet of thick glass set on a cube-shaped base.

Make lists of (a) what you already have that can be used 'as is', (b) what needs to be re-covered, revarnished, relacquered, repainted, stripped and waxed or otherwise titivated, and (c) what needs to be bought; list (c) should also include notes as to when you are likely to be able to afford the various items.

Since, if you are planning ahead for any length of time, you will need to keep colour in mind, it is probably best to start with a neutral palette, arranging your contrasts by means of textural differences and subtle gradations: you can always add the colours as you go along. Remember that dark walls will always make a room look more 'furnished' and richer than in fact it is. Dark greens, Pompeiian or Victorian reds, terracottas, deep blues and chestnutty browns are all extremely helpful colours to use if your budget is restricted.

When you purchase a piece of upholstered furniture – a sofa, armchair or chaise – opt for the very highest quality you can afford: you really do 'get what you pay for' when buying such pieces. A good combination for chair and sofa seats is a foam core surrounded by down; this gives you both softness and firmness.

However beguiled you might be by light colours – the luxurious look of creams and whites, soft rose and blue – do not even think of buying such fabrics if you have children or pets or do a lot of entertaining. While there have been quite radical improvements in fabric treatments, it is best not to test providence too hard. Reupholstering is expensive, so if you act on your preference for light colours you may have to forfeit or put off other elements of your ideal room.

3

4

5

1 There is an interesting juxtaposition here between the soft simplicity of the love seat and the crisp geometric lines of the large side table.

2 Black cane chairs and sofa look elegant in this simply decorated living room.

3 The pale wood table, chairs and stools look clean-lined against the brick floor and darkish units.

4 The cantilevered chairs of tubular steel and rough canvas, and the wicker armchair go well texturally with the somewhat off-beat table and the units.

5 This sofa is very much anchored by the storage units which are placed on either side of it.

6 Good advantage is taken of the deep window recess in this airy North American work room. The specially created window seat works well with the seating arrangement grouped around the desk.

6

The Elements of Design
FURNISHINGS

Arrangement

Most rooms in a home arrange themselves, in the sense that there are only so many places that you can put the bed, storage units, the dining table or whatever. Living rooms, however, are a different kettle of fish: it is the living room that almost invariably exercises our imagination and flexibility the most. In the first place, this is the room that is most on view to other people; in the second place, a living room always requires at least one focal point and this is always difficult in one of our modern box-like apartment rooms without any fireplace or particular view.

Obviously the shape of the room – long and narrow, square or irregular – will dictate arrangement as much as the various activities that will go on in the room: general relaxation, conversation, reading, music-making, watching television, and so on. Also, you must allow for easy movement to and from the door and around pieces of furniture. About 90cm/3ft is the optimum space to allow for a passageway. There should be about 45cm/18in between a coffee table and a sofa or chair, and about 75–90cm/30–36in should be allowed at the back

2

3

1 A relaxed seating group in a smallish room is supplemented by patterned floor pillows. The room is made to appear considerably larger by the use of white for the walls and the floor.
2 A comfortable right-angled seating unit makes the maximum use of this quite small but pleasant attic space.
3 Comfortable armchairs and an upholstered stool nicely angled for conversation in a book-lined study.
4 In this US living room the white-covered day bed with its comfortable squashy cushions sits perfectly under the window without crowding the main seating group.
5 A well arranged area in an old house in New York State. It combines a bar, wine storage, general storage and stereo, not to mention the collection of sticks.

4

6 The abstract rug defines the seating area and the rise-and-fall lamps give height to this room.
7 Black-and-white gives a graphic quality to a French dining area.
8 Airy open bamboo furniture keeps a small room looking light, uncluttered and fresh.

of dining chairs around a table, whether that table is in the living room or in a separate dining room.

A good plan is to think of seating first, the other furniture afterwards. The optimally comfortable arrangement for good conversation and general relaxation is a large sofa and a small sofa or love seat at right angles, faced by two comfortable armchairs and supplemented, if there is room, by occasional chairs and ottomans. This provides the classic conversation group. Occasional chairs can then be pulled up to the main seating group or used to form small groups of their own, by the side of a small round table, for example. A small, narrow room might take only one sofa and a couple of armchairs, or a pair of sofas opposite each other with a couple of occasional chairs. In other small rooms there will be space only for an L-shaped arrangement – modular seating, say, flanking a large coffee table. Again, a small room can be milked of every inch of space if you build bookshelves or storage units all around it leaving two recesses on right-angled walls to take a pair of small sofas. Other ways of getting in extra seating without taking up too much actual floor space include the use of benches around the fireplace and window seats.

The Elements of Design
FURNISHINGS

A foolproof way of tackling any sort of room arrangement is to make a scale plan of the room (see page 18) and to cut the shapes of your items of furniture out of thin coloured cardboard. These you can move around until you think you have found the best solution. Obviously, every seat should have good light as well as some sort of small table nearby on which to put books, drinks, sewing and so on. Again, depending on the room's size and shape and your spending power, you may need bookshelves or some form of wall storage for things like your stereo, VCR tapes, records, drinks and games, as well as side tables, a coffee table and perhaps some sort of round table with a cloth on it to add softness as well as an extra display surface.

It is important to remember that a room is made interesting as much by the differences in scale of the various pieces as by the pieces themselves. This is not so much a matter of aesthetics as of variations in the sizes – especially the heights – of the various items, for a good sense of balance in a space is as visually necessary as a contrast in texture and colour. A room will look boring, however beautiful the furniture, if everything is much the same height. The usual problem is that everything is around or below waist-level. This can be remedied by adding a tall secretary desk, if you can afford one, or a tall bookcase or storage wall, or a screen, or, of course, tall plants and lamps (especially the sculptural halogen variety). Even the most modern and minimal of rooms will benefit from the addition of some larger taller piece.

Another way of obtaining the same effect is simply to position a large picture – or a block of smaller prints or paintings – over a side table, sofa or chest. Paradoxically, in a low-ceilinged room tall objects will actually deceive the eye in such a way that the ceiling appears higher, just as tall objects placed at the end of a corridor or hallway will give the space good perspective.

Making a Focal Point If you have no fireplace and no other particular focal point around which to arrange the room, do not despair: it is quite possible to create a focal point if you are prepared to use a little ingenuity. If, for example, there is no particular view and the windows themselves are undistinguished, you can still convert

1 *The curved pine-lined cooking island with its multicoloured tile top makes a good focal point in this spacious kitchen-dining room.*
2 *Kitchen window sills provide extra storage space in this attractive Swedish kitchen, whose odd shape required the design to be meticulously planned.*

1

2   4   5

6

3

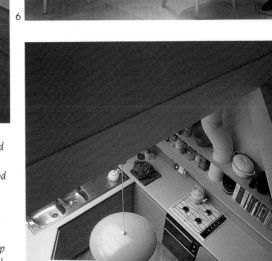

7

3 This crisply tiled German kitchen fits into the narrow space available. An added attraction is the slatted upper shelf massed with plants echoing the garden.

4 A well designed unit combining a black-glassed double oven and marbled counter with ample shelf and drawer storage to hold a multitude of kitchen accessories.

5 Eclectic storage is well arranged here, with the books and stereo equipment stashed on natural wood shelving next door to the kitchen.

6 Space for everything, and everything in its proper place, in a Swedish storage wall.

7 This geometric kitchen has crisp sharp lines, a good work space and good storage.

them into an attractive feature by framing them with a lambrequin (a valance that goes over three sides of the window) made of painted or covered wood or of stiffened fabric (lined, perhaps, with buckram). Alternatively you can frame a window from floor to ceiling using 3cm × 15cm/1¼in × 6in planks of wood cut to order by your local supplier, applying the thin edge to the walls so as to give added length. If you do this you can even add a window seat by stretching a shelf across the two sides at sill level (or whatever is the best seat-height) and putting on it a piece of foam slip covered to match or contrast with the window treatment. Windows can also be edged by full-length folding screens or by shutters, which might be louvred, painted, lacquered or covered with fabric.

Other focal points around the perimeter of a room can give it added character: a generous wall of books or storage set neatly with stereo components or a collection of memorabilia; or a dresser or hutch, commode or console (old or modern) with a mirror over it.

In a bedroom, the natural focal point of the room will be the bed itself, particularly if it is a brass antique. To emphasise an unspectacular bed, you could position it diagonally in the room or create a dramatic drapery headboard (see pages 206–207) using fabric which matches or coordinates with your other soft furnishings. To attract attention away from a bed, decorate the window with an elaborate treatment.

1 A clever arrangement for a child's room. Bed, storage, and the work and play areas are all encompassed by the gaily painted tubular steel units.

2 Cottage-style curtains and rose walls in a room that is really all bed – albeit a handsome Edwardian example.

3 The window of this ordered London study-bedroom is framed

5 An angled bed can make the
most of the space in a smallish
bedroom.

6 Bathroom and bedroom cleverly
divided by a bedhead wall.

7 Grey-and-white walls, a white-
painted floor and white-draped
furniture make a tranquil
bedroom. The only flashes of colour
are in the patterned bedhead and
the objects.

8 Walk-in hanging storage off a
London bedroom, thoughtfully
arranged to take both partners'
clothing and personal possessions.
A little dressing-table unit has been
skilfully tucked in at one end.

9 Grey tiles in the open bathroom
area off this bedroom match the
bedspread and the Austrian shade.
Clothes are kept behind the space-
and-light-enhancing mirrored
doors.

with bookshelves. The panelled
screen behind the slightly angled
writing table contrives to make the
work area both definite and elegant,
and disguises the slightly awkward
corner.

4 An intelligently thought-out
sleeping and storage area in a
corridor-like space at one end of a
child's room. The rest is left free and
unencumbered for playing.

The Right Balance

It is very difficult to be a purist about furniture unless you have enough money to buy only the most ravishing pieces. Even then, with the best taste and intentions in the world, the result can look sadly disappointing and museum-like – perhaps even downright cold. That sense of *balance*, always important in decoration, applies as much to the 'feeling' of a room as do physical proportions. It is so much more interesting to mix a bit of flamboyance with simplicity, humour with very serious pieces, and flippancy with solidity.

In an otherwise modern room, at least one or two old things, even if they are only accessories (a painting, some old prints or an antique shawl or rug), will make all the difference to the room's warmth – and will, indeed, show off the spare clean lines of good 20th-century furniture all the better. And 19th-century furniture – especially japanned and turned bamboo, chesterfields and bentwood rocking chairs – goes well with today's contemporary furniture, with its light woods, lacquered cubes, glass and natural textures.

Of course, mixing requires a certain amount of nerve. Many people have a fixed idea in their heads about what goes with what, and tend to be overly careful. Moreover,

1 *Deep-seated old cane chairs in a comfortable room are mixed with Kentia palms and other plants to create a conservatory atmosphere.*
2 *Coir matting makes a good uniting background for this Gallic living room with its old chaise, country pine, 19th-century furniture and modern sofas.*
3 *Late 19th- and early 20th-century chaises in a quite different French room.*

4 *Spare lines and a lack of clutter in a Japanese-inspired bedroom.*
5 *An asymmetrically arranged day bed, floor pillows and a 19th-century chair are balanced by the screen, the urn on its pyramidal plinth, and the mirrored fireplace wall in this New York City apartment. Louvred blinds shield the radiators as well as the windows. The checks echo the colours of the rug.*
6 *Amazing pink upholstery in an Art Deco room, its exuberance tempered by the basically grey framework of the room.*

to experiment in mixing several styles demands a sureness of taste and a degree of experience.

A unifying background certainly helps in such experiments. Coir matting, for example, is a perhaps unexpected unifier of different styles, and is much better than wall-to-wall carpeting or a varnished wood floor with rugs. Another good way of unifying a room is to have an all-white background: white walls, floor and windows and window treatments.

Balance and Harmony The balance of furnishings and accessories is an important consideration. A large sofa, for example, should be balanced by a sofa-table, desk or work table. A large plant in one corner can be balanced by, say, an étagère or a bank of bookshelves in another. Balance the mass of an armoire or a bureau bookcase with a large painting or group of paintings on the wall opposite – but be careful not to hang a large painting over a piece of smaller furniture: the whole set-up will look hopelessly top-heavy. Similarly, too small a painting or print on a large wall will look just as unfortunate and lost.

The same points about balance apply to colour. Repeat the same colour here and there in a home. The colour of a pillow or cushion at one end of the room can be echoed in a painting or the mount or mat of a print at the opposite end. The tones of a rug can be repeated in upholstery, and flowers can be used to reflect the colour of a throw. All of these may seem quite small details, but they are all the sort of touches that give an agreeable sense of harmony to a home, and harmony, after all, is what most decoration is all about.

5

6

Room Schemes

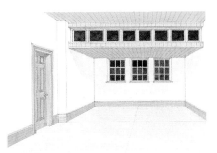

Stage I (*see page* 92)

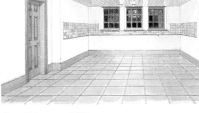

Stage II (*see page* 112)

Stage IV (*see page* 144)

Kitchen: Stage III

Stage I (*see page* 93)

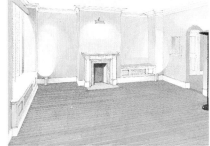

Stage II (*see page* 113)

Stage IV (*see page* 145)

Living Room: Stage III

KITCHEN

Once the shell was all sorted out, the kitchen units were installed and the lights were fixed under the run of cupboards to illuminate the counters and the stove. A butchers' chopping block was bought and placed in the centre of the kitchen area. A long pine refectory table was found for the dining room; the oriental rug on which it stood served as yet another distinction in 'feel' between the two areas. Old pine country chairs were brought in for seating. Further to enhance the difference in 'feel' between the two rooms, the owners added a capacious old pine settle along the door wall. This had the added advantage of making the dining wall look half panelled, while at the same time balancing the solidity and bulk of the kitchen units which might have looked too modern on their own.

LIVING ROOM

Once the appearance of lightness had been enhanced and two reading lamps had been added, the next step was to emphasize this new 'feel' using furnishings that, clearly, had to be as fresh-and light-looking as possible. We associate white wicker with sun, just as we associate window-seats with light and a view. So a Victorian chaise was bought, its cushions covered in warm light rose, matched by the checked cotton of the seat cushions above the radiator casing. A Portuguese rag rug in rose, apricot and cream was chosen to balance the rose and apricot. The rocking chair was cushioned in blue, a colour repeated in an armchair, stool and a tablecloth. The glass coffee table and side tables take up little visual space. The sofa was covered in cream fabric.

129

Room Schemes

Stage I (*see page* 94)

Stage II (*see page* 114)

Stage IV (*see page* 146)

Bedroom: Stage III

Stage I (*see page* 95)

Stage II (*see page* 115)

Stage IV (*see page* 147)

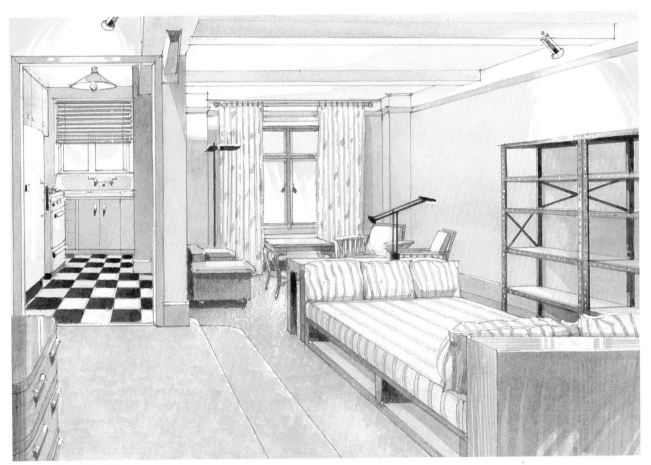
Studio Apartment: Stage III

BEDROOM

To preserve both the period look and the feeling of light engendered by the pale paper and woodwork, the windows were framed with the sort of ruffled treatment common in Colonial houses; roller blinds (shades) in the same fabric were concealed underneath for night-time use. The patterned cotton tablecloth matches the walls and has an overcloth to repeat both valance (bedfrill) and chair. Good balance was achieved through the solidity of the mahogany military chest, the bedside table, and the stools, counteracting the elegance of the slim-lined four-poster bed (which again preserves the room's new lightness). Tall skinny bedside lamps repeat the vertical lines of the bedposts, further contrast being supplied by the horizontal stripes of the rugs and the large rounded basket by the fireplace.

STUDIO APARTMENT

Kitchen units and equipment took up a sizeable portion of the rest of the budget. The main window treatment was taken care of by hand-me-down curtains hung from an unpainted wood pole and rings. A matchstick blind was sprayed coral for the kitchen window at negligible cost. But how should the room be furnished? The occupant already owned the old chest, which was positioned on the dais between kitchen and bathroom, but what about the rest? The young owner decided to kill several birds with one stone by getting his carpenter friend to make up a wide bed unit, which could also double as a sofa; at one end would be a table, and beneath the bed there would be storage space. Industrial shelving was fitted and the remainder of the furniture was second-hand.

PATTERN AND TEXTURE

As we have seen, the effects of colours are radically changed by differences in texture and pattern, so that a nearly or totally monochromatic room can be as lively and memorable through its subtleties of texture as a room with vividly contrasting colours. The thicker or stronger the texture, the softer or more diminished a colour seems. Flat, smooth glossy surfaces project a much brighter image than soft ones: a painted surface in a particular colour will be very much 'sharper' than the same colour in carpet or felt or velvet.

The Effects of Soft and Hard Surfaces   Just as rooms need balance in colour to keep them harmonious and comfortable, so they also need a good balance of textures – matt with gloss, soft with hard. Gaining the knowledge of what contrasting textures go best together is really a matter of experience. You must experiment and develop your taste and a good eye for such things.
· To get into the habit of thinking in textural terms, it helps to make lists of all kinds of different surfaces and materials and to conjure them up in your mind's eye, appropriately distributing them around walls, floors, ceilings, windows and furniture. Such a list might be rather like the one shown overleaf.

There are, of course, certain conventions, and there is no doubt that some textures contrast with each other better than others. For example, brick walls or floors look better with quite strong textures such as linen, hessian (burlap) and cotton than with velvet or silk – although there is no reason why, if you like it, you should not contrast brick and silk.

Comfort is, of course, very much connected in one's mind with softness (even though firmness is often better for the spine), so the softer-looking the covering on a sofa or armchair, the more comfortable and inviting it will seem. Inside the sofa, as we have seen, you can combine both firmness and softness by having a foam core enveloped in down, but if you cover this filling in silk velvet, linen velvet, glove suede or buffalo hide it will look as deeply luxurious as it is harshly expensive. A less

1 *Handmade blue-and-white Mexican tiles on the chimney breast, blue-and-white Dutch ceramics and the charming antique quilts blend pattern and texture beautifully.*
2 *Contrasting marble tiles give a sharp definition to this bathroom. The naturally mottled and flecked surfaces provide a sense of depth.*

3 Wood is inherently textural.
Slatted wooden blinds, polished
floorboards and wooden bath
panelling combine with lush plants
to promote a tropical atmosphere.
4 A restrained colour scheme is
enlivened by the use of contrasting
textures: coir matting, leather
upholstery, glass-topped tables, old
beams and a lacquered cabinet.
5 The rhythmic pattern of free
strokes makes a textural finish.
6 Unpainted plaster has a
softness and subtlety that can be
very attractive. New plaster can
simply be sealed with matt varnish
or rubbed with layers of wax; here
layers of paint were stripped to
leave a mellow surface displaying
traces of old distemper.

2

4

3

5

6

133

The Elements of Design
PATTERN AND TEXTURE

expensive cotton, linen or chintz covering, while not so luxurious-looking, can be made to *seem* softer if you juxtapose it with, say, a wood or tiled floor of some kind and use scatter-rugs rather than a carpet.

Sofas, armchairs and beds can be made to look more deeply inviting if you heap them with throw pillows or cushions, and more interesting by varying the textures of these cushions. For example, a linen sofa could be piled with cushions made of old velvet, *gros* and *petit point* and silk. A bed covered in a simple quilted cotton will look luxurious if it is piled with white lace and broderie-anglaise pillows. A harder chair – say, a tight-covered or buttoned occasional chair – can have a shawl or throw tossed across its back or an arm.

MATERIALS OF DIFFERENT TEXTURES

Hard	Soft
floorboards	plain cotton
barn siding	chintz
brick	linen
flagstone	satin
marble	silk
slate	ottoman
parquet	corduroy
travertine	velvet
plaster	silk velvet
vinyl	linen velvet
glass	tweed
perspex or plexiglass	wool
brass	cashmere
steel	leather
chrome	felt
lacquer	quilting
ceramic tiles	velvet Wilton carpet
terracotta tiles	shag
cork	low-pile textured carpet
cane	kelims
wicker	dhurrie rugs
mahogany	silk orientals
oak	oriental rug
pine	coir matting
walnut	sisal
teak	hessian (burlap)

The contrast of softness and hardness can also be exhibited on floors. Whether you put a rug on a wood floor, a sheepskin on brick or old tiles, or an oriental on coir matting, you are making use of their differing textures. And think of the feeling of comfort you experience when you see large, soft fluffy towels against the tiles of a bathroom, or the sybaritic effect of a soft warm carpet contrasted with bathroom fixtures.

This same juxtaposition of hard and soft can be carried through by the use of contrasting accessories and possessions. You can offset a piece of sculpture with an interesting plant, or you can line a china or glass display cabinet with velvet – or at least paint a background so that the cabinet looks soft and deep.

5

6

1 A living-room corner rich in detail includes a damask cushion, quilted sofa upholstery, inlaid table and needlepoint rug.

2 Striped cotton ticking curtains and soft furnishings make a simple but effective textural contrast with the rough-hewn stone walls.

3 Old and new: the smooth white walls and wooden mantel make a foil for the mellow old bricks, antique carved clock, spinning wheel and old metal toy train.

4 The sense of warmth and enclosure provided by knotty pine panelling is emphasized by the pretty floral cotton of the bedcover and at the window.

5 A light summery mood is created through the use of cane and basketwork, together with plain white calico upholstery and white cord carpeting.

6 A comfortable country blend of traditional trellis and chintz patterns is set off by plain coir matting and enlivened by the bright-red cane table.

Pattern as a Feature

1 *This room, entirely lined in flowered chintz with chairs to match, has considerable pattern underfoot as well. Note the interesting window treatment.*
2 *A brilliantly coloured quilt flung over some corner seating immediately draws the eye, but the massed Picture Post covers challenge for attention.*
3 *Walls, floors and windows share one pattern and the chairs another in this French room: roses are almost everywhere.*

In many modern buildings, rooms tend to be somewhat featureless: they have no fireplace, no strong architectural elements like mouldings, and not much in the way of a view unless you actually stand on tiptoe to peer out of the window. Yet even the most uninspiring box-like room can be enormously cheered by the clever use of pattern. Obviously you can use beautiful additions – for example, paintings and wallhangings – but an interestingly designed or a subtly coloured needlework carpet or an exquisite rug will immediately distract the eye from any architectural mediocrity, as will a well-chosen patterned wallcovering or a stunning upholstery fabric.

Patterned paper, or stencilled border running around a room just below the ceiling and perhaps down corners and above skirting boards (baseboards), makes an excellent and colourful substitute for mouldings and a cornice (crown molding). And dull rooms can be made to look mysterious and beautiful if you resort to comparatively inexpensive 'disguisers'; for example, you could first paint the walls a strong colour and then shirr them with cheesecloth or a light cotton (see page 206). You can achieve this effect by stretching a generous amount of fabric between two sets of rods, one fixed just below the ceiling and one just above the skirting boards.

When you have no natural focal point in a room you can create one by hanging a good rug on a wall, or even by framing a beautiful piece of fabric or an old paisley shawl and hanging it up. It does not really matter if your windows have no view and are less than graceful, because you can dress them up with attractively patterned fabrics – particularly, you can contrast framing or dress curtains or draperies with inner curtains or with roller, Roman, festoon or ballroom shades or blinds, and add yet more contrast using edges or fringes, trims and tie-backs. A trick you can use with dull windows is to frame them from just below the ceiling, cornice or moulding to the floor using fabric-covered two-by-fours or pieces of plywood. The windows can then have either contrast curtains or a shade within the frame.

Another way of creating an interesting focal point in a monochromatic room is to have a single piece of seating – a large armchair or a sofa – upholstered in an interesting pattern. Or you could set two contrasting tablecloths – one over and one under – on a round table, with perhaps a fringe trailing to the floor.

4

6

5

7

8

4 The interestingly combed painted floor – with its large diamonds of natural wood and arresting malachite-green border – makes the statement here.
5 Mondrian-like tile design makes effective use of the limited space in this dramatic bathroom.

6 Only the carpet, the underside of the canopy and the door frame escape the ubiquitous pattern.
7 In this North American bedroom, the dhurrie rug – although stronger in colour – picks up the design of the fabric.
8 Rose chintz offset by linen.

137

Combining and Coordinating

A very great deal of the pattern in a room is effected by objects and possessions, furnishings, plants, lights and light itself, with its play of shadows, as well as by the varying textures of so-called 'plain' fabrics, carpets and matting and their juxtaposition with each other. There is pattern in the way paintings are hung on the walls. There is pattern in shelved books, with their diverse jacket designs and the gradations and contrasts of their colours – there is even pattern in the arrangement of the shelves. There is pattern in vases of flowers, in the jagged edges of leaves set against a wall or window, and in the way an uplight can shine through the foliage at night to cast shadows on the walls and ceiling. There is pattern in the arrangement of furniture, and in the display of accessories and collections.

If you think about the way all these things form a pattern in their own right, you can see how you should not worry too much about mixing patterns in fabrics. With all the other things that are going on, one fabric more or less will hardly make a difference so long as the scale, tone, proportion and colour are right. Nevertheless, many people remain very nervous about mixing patterns. To counter this lack of confidence, fabric and wallpaper manufacturers often get together to produce coordinating prints and plains, using perhaps a large floral design together with a small, more open pattern having similar but scaled-down elements; these in turn can be combined with a geometric pattern or basket weave or some similar all-over design in matching colours. In this way one design can be used for curtains, another for shades, and yet others for different pieces of upholstery, combined perhaps with some plains. One of the designs can also be used for wallpaper, or at least for a border. This sort of coordination has proved very popular. Manufacturers have also expended a good deal of effort to find other complementary designs in their ranges. Their catalogues are usually filled with photographs of room settings to show you how well different designs can look together.

However, suppose you have the requisite confidence and want to be a little more idiosyncratic in juxtaposing designs, to do your own mixing and matching. What is the best way to go about it?

As we have seen, scale, tone and proportion are of prime importance, and to this list you might add

1 Collier Campbell updated designs in a superb combination.
2 Grey-blue and roses combined in different permutations of colour and texture.
3 The same colours used to good effect in a quite different way.
4 Wall, sofa, cushions and rug merge into each other, but all retain their own intensely floral identities.
5 A host of different designs given an overall harmony by the common denominator of colour.

4

5

similarity as well as overall suitability. Always bring home as large a sample as you can get so that you can see what the design will look like *in situ*, with your sort of light and in the context of your other possessions. Unless you possess a very good sense of scale, larger patterns that you thought eye-catching in the store may look fairly dire once you have brought the materials home and set them up in your own private setting. Likewise, the colours may clash if the room is otherwise gentle. Conversely, very small, detailed patterns can often blur so that they give the impression of a single colour when actually used for curtains. On the other hand, small-scale repeats in upholstery or soft furnishings of a larger pattern on the walls, curtains or shades can give an interesting sense of perspective. It is worth experimenting to see what looks good.

You can often use together materials of the same pattern but in two different colour schemes, or you might opt for the same pattern reversed or in negative – for example, a predominance of terracotta on cream for some items and a predominance of cream on terracotta for others.

Patterns that are fairly but not exactly similar – that is, patterns from the same 'family', like a large rose print with a smaller rosebud print, a floral abstract or a single colour on white like a *toile de Jouy* – will look good together. To the combination suggested here you could alternatively add a damask in one of the deeper colours, or a stripe, check or small geometric in the same

colouring as the leaves of one of the flowers. Very often, as we have noted, an old fabric or textile thrown across a sofa, chair or table will add an interesting dimension.

The best thing is always to experiment. Get together all the samples of fabric that you like and look at them simultaneously – and look at them, too, in conjunction with your chosen rugs and/or carpets. It should quickly become obvious as to which fabrics enhance each other and which detract from each other.

Another good way to learn about mixing patterns is to look at a collection of Indian fabrics and dhurrie rugs. The various designs look effortlessly harmonious, their patterns all being of much the same size and in good proportion with each other. Once you have studied the way their colours repeat and intermingle with one another, and the way in which colours are balanced yet subtly contrasted, the whole business of mixing and matching will seem less of a matter of trepidation.

It is reassuring, too, to recall that people have throughout history mixed patterns and textures with, if not abandon, then at least a sense of richness. Look at the intricacies of oriental rugs, the extraordinary linen-fold panelling, rich plasterwork and tapestries used together in the 16th and 17th centuries; the complicated but beautiful ceilings and floors of Robert Adam, with the various damasks, silks, embroideries and plaster-work of the 18th and 19th centuries; the pattern-on-pattern of the Victorian age; the sinuous complications of Art Nouveau; and the jazzy mixtures of the 1920s.

DISPLAYS

Furniture and furnishings make a room comfortable and, with luck, good to look at. The pictures, objects and accessories are the elements that give the room personality – although it is important to remember that, if you are to achieve a truly personal room, the objects themselves must be personal, liked for their own sake, thought about deeply, lovingly chosen and put together with care and enthusiasm. Buying objects because they are fashionable or because they were displayed in the store alongside the furniture is not at all the same thing. Just as you buy paintings for their own sake and validity or for their subject matter, rather than because their colours suit those you have chosen for your room, you should select objects because you *like* them. Mind you, serendipity can creep in here as anywhere else: happy accidents, after all, have a lot to contribute to the character of a home.

There are two quite separate schools of thought concerning the possession and display of artworks and objects. One school opts for simplicity, the other for

3

4

1 *A collection of pictures always adds interest to a hallway. Here an entire alphabet of characters is hung close together, reading as a single composition.*
2 *A tabletop of disparate objects leads the eye up to a collection of framed prints, creating a corner full of delight and surprise.*
3 *Even homely objects can be worthy of display. A collection of carpet beaters makes an unusual frieze, baskets look suitably rustic on top of a wooden dresser, and a fine clock is the centrepiece for a collection of delicate coloured prints.*
4 *Architectural fragments, portrait busts, paintings and engravings are arranged in splendid profusion.*

1

2

clutter. The difference is between offering up one or two exquisite, interesting and/or rare objects and presenting a magpie collection of objects and possessions which can generally be termed 'memorabilia'. The difficulty with the former proposition is that the few objects must either be really beautiful or extraordinarily well displayed; the trouble with the latter is that the clutter must be organized in an interesting way or else it looks like nothing more than, well, clutter. This means you have to assemble the items carefully and thoughtfully according to their colour, shape, texture or theme. Thematic collections of small objects – for example, glasses or butterflies, birds' eggs or stones – should always be grouped together rather than scattered all over the house. To take another example, old coloured glass is often shown to particular advantage against other pieces of glass, so group such items on window sills or on glass shelves stretched across a window. Larger objects, however disparate, can be contrasted with each other, but their arrangement looks best if they have something in common with each other (e.g., colour); as ever, balance is all-important. If arrangements are grouped on low tables that are used also as adjuncts to chairs and for the casual dumping of books

5

7

8

6

9

5 *The shape of the brimming pitcher of wine in the painting has suggested an abundant arrangement of richly coloured ceramics and lacquerware.*
6 *In among the colanders, sieves, graters and ladles, holly and mistletoe add a festive touch.*
7 *The polished gleam of copper pans makes an inviting and practical kitchen display.*
8 *Beautiful objects have drama and importance when displayed singly. This modern ceramic piece, standing in a sculptural alcove, has all the calm tranquillity of a Grecian urn.*
9 *A riot of painted plates and teacups has a dolls-house cheerfulness.*

and drinks, leave appropriate space so that the composition will not be ruined.

If arrangements are on a glass shelf, try lighting them with an uplight from below: this gives extra sparkle. If they are on a solid shelf, try lighting them from above with a downlight or spot, or with a small strip of lights (see page 154). It is important to realize that collections of objects can be as idiosyncratic as you want them to be. In fact, assemblages of quite ordinary things – like old spectacle cases, watches, keys, snuffboxes, toast-racks or whatever – can often be much more interesting and decorative than much grander objects.

Hanging Pictures Although some people who own serious art collections see a wall as a means to an end – a convenient space for display – most of us want to use that space to its most decorative advantage, and therefore need to find some unifying factor to bring together our disparate collection of prints and paintings, posters and objects. A miscellaneous series of prints, for example, can be given a unity it would otherwise lack if each is mounted with the same distinctive colour – say buff, deep red or dark green – and framed in the same way. Again, you can group similarly sized and shaped

frames together – ovals with ovals, small squares with small squares. One of the easiest ways to get good groupings without making an awful mess of the walls while experimenting is to lay out on the floor all the pictures you want to hang. After you are satisfied with the arrangement you can measure out the spaces for the hooks on the wall itself, using pencil or chalk that can be rubbed away easily.

In general, you should be careful not to hang things too high or too far apart. Do not fix anything so low over a sofa that people will knock their heads on it – although, when your seating is at a very low level, there is no reason why paintings cannot be hung much lower than usual. Vertical arrangements will make walls seem higher; horizontal ones will make them seem longer.

Posters are best slipped into special holders so that they do not tear or curl up at the corners. They can be balanced by size, subject or colour, depending upon which seems most appropriate to the room.

Wall hangings can be made from just about any piece of decorative fabric, from fragments of old robes to pieces of abstract modern cotton. Hang very heavy fabrics or rugs on slim curtain rods suspended from hooks, or stretch them like canvases over a frame.

Plants

1

2

There is almost no gap in any room which cannot be filled and improved by a plant. There is no piece of furniture that cannot be balanced and somehow freshened by a spread of leaves, and there are no hard lines and formality that cannot be softened and lightened by foliage. If books furnish a room, the same can be said of plants. Tall plants, small plants, flowering plants and exotic indoor trees add a quite different dimension to any space – a liveliness and freshness that are gratifyingly cheap in relation to the year-round pleasure the plants give.

On the whole, small and medium-sized plants look best massed together or at least grouped in twos and threes. You can get a good effect by grouping different sizes of plants of the same species together, or by putting a shorter, bushier plant at the foot of a taller, skinnier one. A bushy indoor tree set in front of an uncurtained window can make it look full-dressed, and you can get the same effect by hanging plants from a traverse rod from just above a window. Two standard plants set in front of a pair of windows can strike quite a grand and harmonious note.

In the summer, hanging plants strung from the ceiling of a porch give the whole area a cool greenness just when it is most needed. Windows crossed with shelves in either glass or wood and massed with a mixture of upright and trailing plants can look very attractive indeed. This is a particularly good solution for windows that are otherwise difficult to curtain or dress.

Tall plants and indoor trees make subtle room dividers, and planters can be set on casters or wheels for easy movement. One especially effective set-up I have seen was a green balustrade of plants at the edge of a dining platform in a living room; another living-room set-up employed a group of Kentia palms to form a gentle division between the dining and sitting areas, so that the room was for all the world like an exotic Edwardian conservatory.

Conservatories, in fact, are currently enjoying a well deserved revival. They are marvellous adjuncts to a room, especially if they are stocked with scented jasmine and stephanotis, lilies and gardenias, and give off that heady, warm damp smell of well watered foliage. If you do not own one and have neither the space nor the

3

5

1 A sunny arrangement of coneflowers and foliage, highlighted by the warm glow of a pair of table lamps, makes a natural focal point in a country living room.
2 Classical white pedestals of varying heights and cachepots are an elegant way of displaying decorative house plants such as aspidistras and weeping figs.
3 Trailing plants either side of this stark white stairwell, complement the rational 'feel' of this home and add colour.

4

6

money to add one, you can always at least simulate the impression of one by setting the panelling at one end of a room with mirror glass and massing plants in front of it so that their reflections have the effect of doubling the number of plants there. Extra appeal can be added by hanging plants from the ceiling: these, too, can be dramatized by placing uplights beneath them, or you can put uplights behind planters to shine up through the leaves and create interesting shadow effects.

There is a choice of planters to suit any room: stone and terracotta, chrome and brushed steel, comforting baskets and graceful wooden Versailles boxes. Even when rooms are dark and receive little natural light there is no need to be deprived of greenery, for using the new and sophisticated bulbs that simulate natural light it is quite possible to give foliage all the light it needs.

7

4 Palms set either side of a wood-framed mirror appear to add depth to a modern bathroom.
5 A tall yucca acts as a room divider and also helps to integrate kitchen and living space.
6 A single spindly cactus, set in a Moorish-style alcove, makes an amusing statement.
7 An arrangement of ginger jars and glass vases on an ornate mahogany table are framed by overhanging palms, jasmine and fuchsias.

Room Schemes

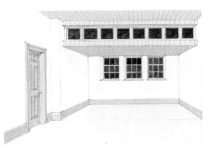

Stage I (*see page* 92)

Stage II (*see page* 112)

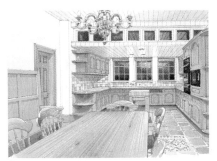

Stage III (*see page* 128)

Kitchen: Stage IV

Stage I (*see page* 93)

Stage II (*see page* 113)

Stage III (*see page* 129)

Living Room: *Stage* IV

KITCHEN

In a way, dressing up the two parts of the room was easy once the main ingredients had been put into place. The wooden ceiling made it a simple task to screw in hooks to hold bunches of dried flowers and herbs. The kitchen shelves just begged for a variety of good-looking canisters and casseroles, always particularly important when the room is going to be used for eating (albeit at a distance) as well as for cooking. The row of old prints, hung vertically, was something of a stroke of genius, since the vertical lines exaggerated the height of the dining area. Moreover, the prints made the area seem very much more of a *room*, and the frames went beautifully with the golden tones of the pine. To these were added other, larger prints and paintings, as well as cushions.

LIVING ROOM

Now that the room looked altogether lighter and warmer, the final exercise was to add liveliness and freshness, using texture and pattern, art, accessories and plants. Rose, apricot and blue cushions were added to the seating as were a few others covered in painted linen in the same colours, which are repeated in a different design in the overcloth on the round table. Further textural interest is introduced through rush log baskets, the iron grate filled with logs, and the old cloisonné urns on the mantelpiece and internal window sills. Paintings were hung above the mantelpiece and on other walls. The room is kept full of flowers and plants to add conservatory-like freshness. By keeping the white shutter semiclosed the dreary outlook is gently disguised.

Room Schemes

Stage I (*see page* 94)   Stage II (*see page* 114)   Stage III (*see page* 130)

Bedroom: Stage IV

Stage I (see page 95)

Stage II (see page 115)

Stage III (see page 131)

Studio Apartment: Stage IV

BEDROOM

To add more softness to the room a pile of snow-white lace-trimmed pillows was added to the bed with, behind them, much the same kind of fabric treatment as used on the windows, although on a larger scale. The general effect of this backdrop was almost to create the illusion that there was a third, bigger, window. The bedcover introduces more of the warm rose colour of the bricks surrounding the fireplace, a hue repeated again in the heap of pillows on the chair as well as in the flowers (in their blue vase) by the bed. Notice how every flash of colour, however soft, stands out against the calm, neutral background. Other odds and ends – the dressing mirror, candles, boxes, photographs, paintings and the jokey firedogs in the grate – add a warmth of their own.

STUDIO APARTMENT

The apartment was now reasonably furnished and ordered. Four transparent Plia chairs had been purchased for use at the desk/dining table; these could be hung on a large hook (not in the picture) next to the chest of drawers when not in use. At the sink area in the kitchen a cheap adjustable desk lamp was clamped to the side of a storage unit. To liven up the colouring, the owner found a 1930s geometric rug as well as some vivid cotton in the same colouring which he had made up into a tight cover and extra pillow covers for the sofa-bed. Books, records, tapes, television and stereo equipment fill the shelving units, prints are hung on the walls, odds and ends are placed on various surfaces, and the space is generally freshened by plants.

147

Part 4

Successful
Decorating

Lighting
Preparation
All About Paint
Paint Effects
Wallcoverings
Floors
Window Treatments

In some countries it is illegal to install or to alter electrical systems
without a professional qualification. Always check regulations before
you attempt electrical work.

LIGHTING

Domestic lighting fulfils a number of functions in the interior. In practical terms, it is a supplement or substitute for natural daylight activities, enabling ordinary tasks to be performed safely; it can provide additional brightness in a work area or dark corner, as well as an even level of background illumination. However, just as important is lighting's ability to generate mood and atmosphere. Subtle interplays of light and shade soften and enhance the decoration of a room. Directional light picks out architectural detail, displays, objects and pictures. And the design of the light fitting can in itself be a source of style and interest.

TYPES OF LIGHTING
Broadly speaking, all domestic lights have two components: the light source itself (bulb or lamp) and the light fitting. When choosing lighting for your home, you should consider not only the style of the fitting but also the quality and distribution of the light that it produces. Depending on the fitting, light can be distributed
● evenly in all directions
● principally in one direction with some diffusion
● in a concentrated beam

Background Lighting
Background lighting essentially acts as a replacement for daylight; typically it is supplied by a ceiling-mounted fitting or a pendant. Alternatives include wall lights, uplights and table lamps, all of which can produce something more interesting than a single bright light overhead, whose effect can be dull and uninspiring.

Task Lighting
Areas such as kitchen counters, workbenches and desks – anywhere that specific tasks are to be performed – need an extra level of light. Task lighting should be positioned so that shadows do not fall across the work surface: directional lights which can be angled to suit needs – such as downlights, angled desk lamps and spotlights – are often a good choice.

Another form of task lighting is utility lighting. Practical rather than aesthetic, utility lighting is the type used to illuminate dark and potentially dangerous areas, such as stairways and exterior paths.

Accent Lighting
By picking out decorative displays, accent lighting creates a sense of drama. Strongly directional spotlights are particularly effective: they can be angled to highlight a collection of

Bulbs and Lamps
1 *General purpose tungsten bulb*
2 *Tungsten striplight*
3 *Parabolic aluminized reflector lamp*
4 *Halogen display bulb*
5 *Halogen reflector (cool beam)*
6 *Halogen reflector bulb*
7 *Globe bulb*
8 *Candle-shaped bulb*
9 *Fluorescent long-life bulb*
10 *Reflector bulb*
11 *Fluorescent striplight*
12 *Circular fluorescent tube*
13 *Crown-silvered bulb*
14 *U-lamp*

objects, a set of bookshelves or a group of pictures. Other types of accent lighting include traditional bracket picture lights, concealed lights in display cases and floor-standing uplights.

TYPES OF LIGHT SOURCE
The three main types used in the home are tungsten, tungsten halogen and fluorescent. The differences between them concern the efficiency of their use of energy, their average lifetime and, most important in aesthetic terms, the quality of colour they lend to whatever they illuminate.

Tungsten
The commonest domestic light source is the tungsten filament bulb. This consists of a filament which glows

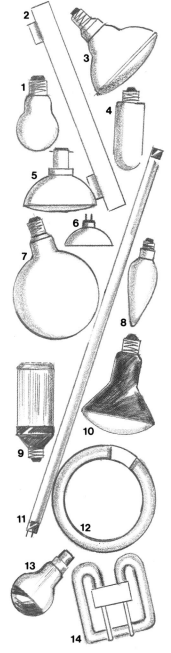

Types of lighting: *background lighting provided by uplights (**1**); task lighting (**2, 4**); accent lighting on a stairway (**3**).*

QUALITY OF LIGHT		
LAMP	**COLOUR APPEARANCE**	**COLOUR RENDERING**
Tungsten	Warm	Orange and reds bright, blues dull
Tungsten Halogen	White, crisp	Orange and reds bright, blues less dull
Metal Halide	Cool, white	Slight colour distortion, reds fairly dull
Fluorescent	Warm or cool	Variable
Neon	Range of colours	Variable

The distribution of light
This varies according to the design of the light fitting. Highly directional light is provided by downlights, spotlights and some types of uplights. Table lamps, on the other hand, diffuse light in more than one direction.

inside a pearl or clear glass bulb that is filled with an inert gas (e.g., argon) in low concentration. Compared to daylight, tungsten is a warm light, yellowish in tone, and is well suited to interior use. It does not alter colour relationships significantly and provides a good tonal contrast. Tinted tungsten bulbs are available in a range of pastel and primary colours.

However, tungsten lights are somewhat less practical than other light sources. The bulbs do not last very long, they generate a fair amount of heat, and they do not make efficient use of electricity. But they are inexpensive and can function with dimmers.

Tungsten Halogen
Tungsten halogen has a cool, crisp appearance, whiter and brighter than ordinary tungsten. The lamp is filled with one of the halogens (a family of chemical elements), and this reacts with vapours from the tungsten filament.

Like tungsten, tungsten halogen is effective at colour rendering and at revealing contrasts, but it also has a vital, sparkling quality which makes it particularly suitable for use in uplights, spotlights and accent lighting. There are two main types, mains-voltage and low-voltage; the latter can be used with a transformer. Both can be dimmed.

Fluorescent
Unlike tungsten or tungsten halogen, fluorescent light has a significant effect on both colour and tone. However, there are modern fluorescent lights available that simulate daylight, and special covers can be used to make the light more sympathetic.

151

Ceiling Lights

An overhead fixture – either a pendant or one or more ceiling-mounted lights – is one of the commonest ways of providing general lighting. Used on its own, however, overhead lighting can distinctly lack subtlety, be rather obtrusive and have a deadening effect. Wherever possible, supplement it with other types of lighting, and fit a dimmer switch so that the level of light can be adjusted according to need.

Alternatively, consider downlights or spotlights as substitutes.

Pendant Lights
Pendant fittings vary widely in design, price and the quality of light they produce. Glass and ceramic globes and paper lanterns diffuse light evenly in all directions, whereas shades, whether of paper, metal or fabric, tend to direct light downwards, an effect which is emphasized if the pendant is suspended on a long flex (cord). There are also rise-and-fall pendants, where the fitting can be pulled lower – for example, over a dining table – to provide more concentrated light. If the source is visible, you can use a crown-silvered bulb to minimize glare.

Chandeliers are highly effective types of pendant because they support several smaller sources of light, but they are often expensive.

Ceiling-mounted Lights
Generally rather plain and utilitarian, some ceiling lights are mounted on the ceiling rather than suspended from it. The bulb is shaded, often with a glass or plastic globe, half-globe or cylinder, which creates an even light diffused in all directions.

Downlights
Downlights are ceiling lights that are either recessed (fully or partially) or surface-mounted. Functional and unobtrusive, they direct the light downwards. Depending on the type of fitting, they can produce either a narrow concentrated beam or a wider flood of light. Eyeball downlights on swivels can be angled to direct light at a wall or other surface.

Downlights are a useful and attractive way of lighting work areas such as a kitchen counter. They can be used also to provide subtle background lighting,

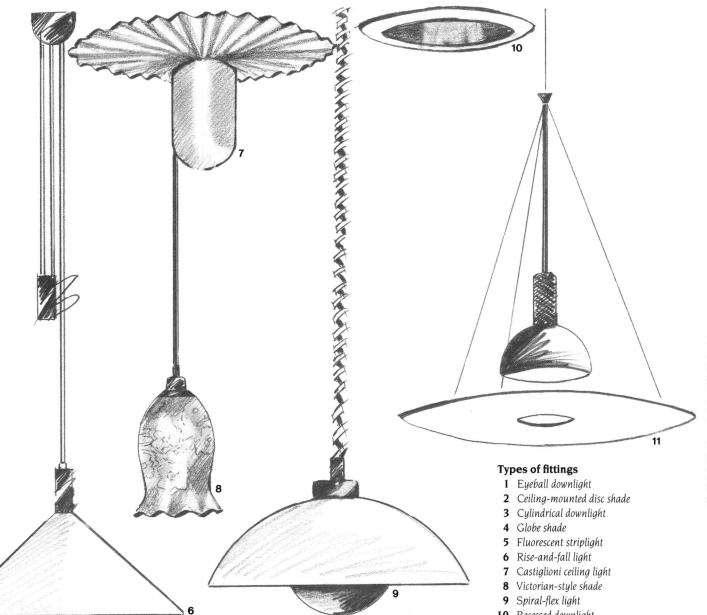

Types of fittings

1 Eyeball downlight
2 Ceiling-mounted disc shade
3 Cylindrical downlight
4 Globe shade
5 Fluorescent striplight
6 Rise-and-fall light
7 Castiglioni ceiling light
8 Victorian-style shade
9 Spiral-flex light
10 Recessed downlight
11 Castiglioni 'Frisbi' light

especially when controlled with a dimmer switch.

Other Types of Ceiling Light
Spotlights can be ceiling-mounted or on a track and used either as background lighting or to accent particular areas.

Ceiling-mounted fluorescent striplighting is suitable only for utility areas. To cut down glare, shade the tube with a diffuser.

2

1 A modern pendant fitting suspended over a dining table and counterbalanced by ball weights looks like kinetic art. Light is directed at the centre of the table, creating a soft, welcoming glow without glare.

2 Ceiling-mounted lighting need not be strictly utilitarian in appearance. This stylish, graphic-looking ceiling light, fixed over a dining table, echoes the designs of Charles Rennie Mackintosh.

Spotlights and Wall Lights

Spotlights

Spotlights are one of the most flexible forms of light fitting: they can be used not only as accent and task lights but also to provide a general level of illumination. Although generally mounted on the ceiling, spotlights can alternatively be fixed to a wall; they can be used either individually or in series on a track. Also available are spotlights fixed to a stand, clusters of spots on a ceiling fitting, and spotlights with clips or clamps so that they can be attached to a shelf and moved at will.

There is a wide range of sizes and designs. Spots can give you anything from a broad pool of light to a fine concentrated beam. Many are shaded with deep metal or plastic cowls so that the bulbs themselves are hidden; if this is not the case, it is a good idea to use a crown-silvered bulb to cut down glare. Combining a crown-silvered bulb with a parabolic reflector will create a narrow beam of light.

The great advantage of spotlights is that it is easy to position and adjust them, allowing you to angle light in different directions. This effect is best exploited by grouping more than one spotlight in each location – a track mounted on the wall or ceiling is an easy way of achieving this.

Wall Lights

Unlike spotlights and downlights – which, although relatively inconspicuous, are contemporary in style – wall lights come in a range of designs, from traditional to very modern.

Traditional types of wall light include shaded small bulbs which project out from the wall on decorative metal brackets, simulating the look of old-time gaslighting or candle-lit sconces.

Modern types of wall light include curved black-metal halogen uplights, and uplights in ceramic or plaster which can be decorated to blend in with the wall. The distribution of light varies with the fitting, but as a basic rule wall lights provide a sympathetic background light. Wall lights are usually fitted in pairs.

More utilitarian wall-mounted designs include bulkhead fittings – designed for exterior use but with a hi-tech appeal for interiors – and plain globes or half-globes similar to ceiling lights. One of the best ways of lighting a bathroom mirror is to frame it with unshaded lightbulbs, as in a theatrical dressing room. This type of light illuminates the face without creating shadows.

● Never buy a light without turning it on first to see what it does.

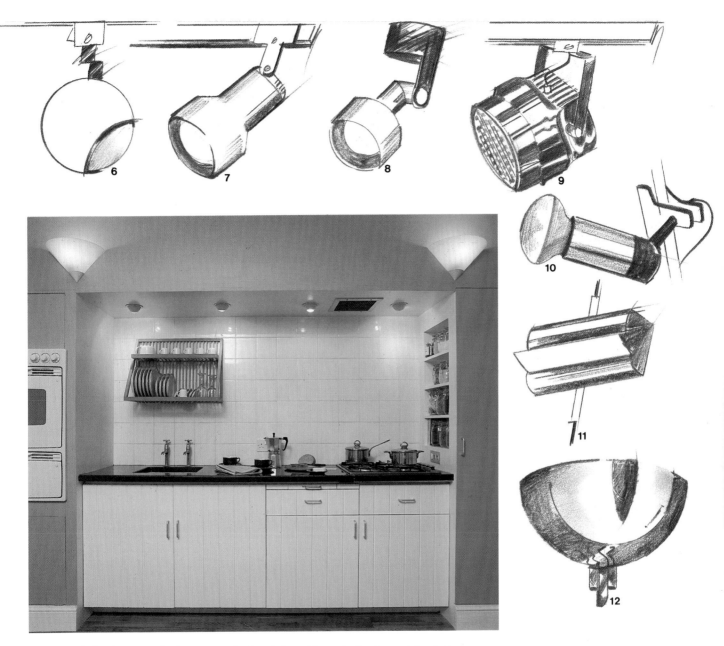

Eyeball spotlights illuminate a kitchen counter; the alcove is framed by a pair of wall-mounted uplights.

SWITCHES

As well as the ubiquitous white plastic variety, a range of more decorative light switches is available, from traditional brass or wood to modern black metal or chrome. You can exploit this diversity to coordinate the style of the details with the rest of the interior.

Dimmer Controls

Whatever the style of lighting or light fitting, the effectiveness of the result can be greatly increased if you are able to vary the light level. Dimmer switches are easy to fit and they are particularly useful in a multi-purpose room – such as a kitchen-diner where light may need to be quite bright in one area but softer in another.

Types of fittings

1 Halogen uplight
2 Wall-mounted desk halogen
3 Double wall bracket
4 Angular wall light
5 Brass picture light
6 Globe spot
7 Track-mounted spot
8 Jointed halogen floodlight
9 Multi-directional spot
10 Spotlight with clamp fitting
11 Adjustable wall shade
12 Chrome hemisphere uplight

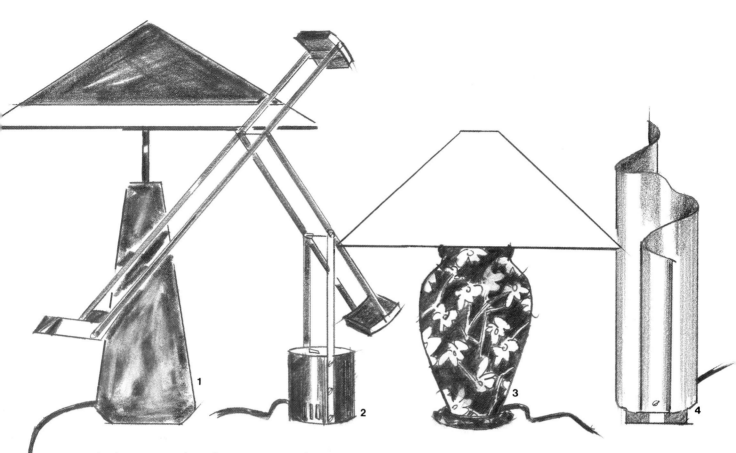

Table and Floor Lights

Lights which can stand on the floor or on a table are a popular choice both for task lighting and for general or background illumination. Decorative as well as practical, they come in a wide range of colours, designs and sizes to suit every type of decorative scheme.

Table Lamps

In many ways the mainstay of domestic lighting, the typical table lamp has a heavy base (often ceramic) which holds the bulb and carries a shade that may be paper- or fabric-covered, made of shell, etc. Even within these specifi-cations, however, there is tremendous variety. The base may be in different colours, patterned or textured, or in different shapes and/or materials. The shade can taper or have straight sides, and can be opaque or translucent. Also, table lamps are available not only in a plethora of traditional designs but also in many modern versions.

Table lamps provide a soft, diffused light at low level. Several of them placed around a room will create pools of light and shadow, an effect that can be very atmospheric. At least some of the light is directed upwards towards the ceiling (quite how much depends on the shade), so table lamps are also a good way of increasing general light levels.

Desk Lamps

The purpose of a desk lamp is to provide a bright, directed source of light for a specific area. The classic design is the anglepoise, a metal light with a deep cowl shade and an angled stand which can be adjusted to many different positions. Other types include modern cantilevered lights, lights which clamp or screw onto a worktop, brass or chrome lights on flexible arms, and traditional-style desk lamps (such as Victorian brass lights with opaque green glass shades).

Floor Lamps

Free-standing floor lamps help to raise the general level of illumination as well as provide local task lighting for reading or other activities.

Except in period rooms, the floor-standing standard lamp can look rather old-fashioned; the modern equivalent is the floor-standing uplight, often fitted with a tungsten halogen lamp to give a clear crisp light. Other modern designs include angled floor lights and spotlights mounted on a portable stand.

Floor lights need not be particularly tall. Uplights in the form of cylinders or flutes or translucent omni-directional lights placed at a low level can be an effective way to light a collection of in-door plants or just to provide an additional lighting accent.

Types of fittings

1. Modern table light
2. 'Tizio' task light
3. Traditional base and shade
4. Sculpted table light
5. Anglepoise
6. Standard halogen uplight
7. Portable uplight
8. Chrome uplight
9. Curved desk lamp

Halogen uplights have a classically elegant appearance which suits many styles. Intriguing table lamps provide a soft accent light.

FLEXES (Cords)

The accessories of lighting fixtures do not *have* to be plain and functional. Coiled, twisted, striped or spotted flexes can add visual flair to your lighting scheme. There are many available in bright primary colours to give you a cheerful hi-tech look – especially if they are coordinated with coloured switches and sockets (outlets).

1

1 In an elegant kitchen, brass-rimmed downlights provide a general level of illumination and coordinate with the brass light switches.

2 Downlights add dramatic accent to a display of sculpture. The fall of light brings out the warm tones of the coir matting.

3 The downlights fitted in the bathroom area of this bedroom are a means of dividing two quite distinct areas; they give the bathroom a more intimate and self-contained 'feel'.

2

3

Fitting a Downlight

Downlights are not difficult to fit, assuming there is a power source nearby – there is no need to remove floorboards and to work from above, nor do you have to remove an entire section of ceiling. Downlights can be surface-mounted; however, fully or partially recessed types are more effective and less obtrusive.

The first task is to ensure that there is enough space above the ceiling to take the fitting. If there is too little for a fully recessed light, choose a partially recessed one instead. The particular design will be specified in the manufacturers' catalogues and/or on the packaging. Downlights can be fitted with plastered ceilings, plaster-board or wood panelling. Before you start, plan where the lights will go. If you need to illuminate a worktop, ensure that the fittings are placed close enough together to create overlapping pools of light. They must be positioned directly above the work surface. Otherwise you will find yourself shadowing the work because you are standing between it and the light source.

SAFETY It is vital to switch off power at the mains or fuse box before you begin. Do not switch it on again until you are sure that the light is correctly connected. Always follow manufacturers' instructions when connecting the light flex (cord) to mains wiring, and always use a terminal block. In the United States and Australia, check local regulations before you attempt electrical work.

Materials and Equipment
● downlight(s) and bulb(s)
● template or pattern constructed to diameter of the fitting
● pencil
● padsaw (keyhole saw)
● screwdriver, if necessary
● filler

METHOD
1 Ensure that there is enough space above the ceiling (i.e., between the ceiling and the floor above) to fit the downlight. Required depths are usually listed in manufacturers' catalogues.
2 Switch power off at the mains or fuse box. Draw the template to mark the size of the opening.
3 Cut out the opening with a padsaw. Keep the edges tidy; smooth irregularities with filler.
4 Connect light to mains supply, as instructed, using a terminal block. Fit the downlight into place. If it has clips for fitting, swing both up and push the two longer arms into the hole.
5 Snap the fitting into place and clip on the trim, or fix according to the instructions.
6 Once you are sure that the light is properly connected, add the recommended lamp or bulb and restore power.

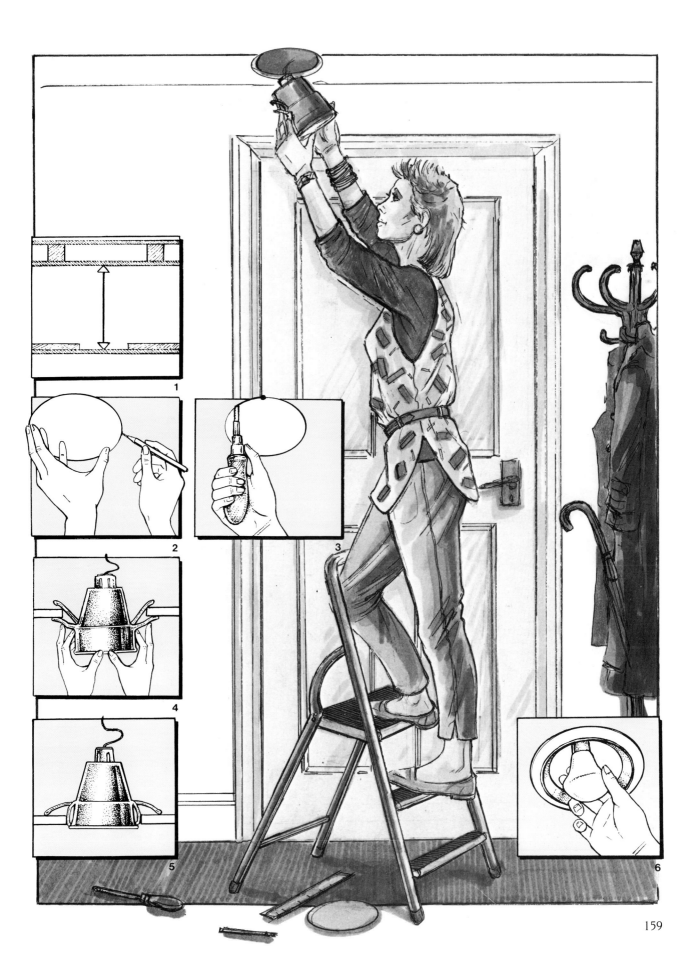

159

Tracks and Wiring

Putting Up Track

A spotlight track is electrified along its entire length so that a series of lights can be fitted. The tracks come complete with mounting clips and are in plastic or metal. There are basic lengths to which extensions can be fitted; some types can be turned around corners by use of flexible connectors.

1

2

Covering Electrical Wires

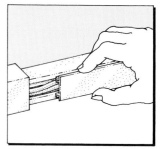

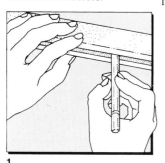

1

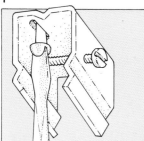

2

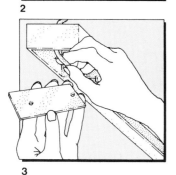

3

1 Decide where you want the track. It must be screwed to a solid surface, such as a ceiling joist. Remember to locate the live end of the track near to the power point. Turn off at the mains or fuse box and mark the position of the track through holes in it. Drill holes at these points.
2 Screw the mounting clips in position.
3 Remove the terminal box's cover plate and feed the cable through it.
4 Clip the track into the mounting clips and secure it by tightening screws. If a different system is used, see the manufacturers' instructions. Connect the cable to the terminals and replace the cover.
5 Slide the spotlights onto the track and lock into position. Restore power.

● In the United States and Australia, you must check local regulations before you attempt electrical work.

1,2 Originally designed for industrial and commercial use, track lighting is a versatile fitting that works well in either traditional or modern interior settings. Its main advantage is that any number of spotlights can be fitted easily to a single track, and directed at different areas.

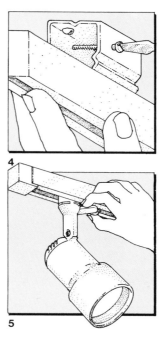

4

5

Cover and protect wires in situations where you want to extend your electrical circuit but cannot run the new wiring under the floor or do not want to conceal it behind plastered or finished walls. Covering is available in plastic, metal or wood sections, running at floor-level as a mock skirting board (baseboard) or at ceiling-height as a cornice (crown molding). Plastic types have a clip-on cover.

First plan the route of the circuit around the room. Drill and fix the main body of the covering by screwing through the base or, if the surface is suitable, using contact adhesive. Snap the fittings – couplers, bends and T-pieces – into position. Fit the lid by sliding one end under the cover of the first fitting. Cut 5mm/¼in past the first fitting, spring under the next fitting and snap the lid into position along the main body. Repeat the process between every fitting.

Making a Lamp Base

With a little ingenuity, you can improvise your own table lamps from a variety of containers, provided that whatever you choose is sturdy enough to support a bulb-holder and shade. Old bottles, narrow-necked jugs, interesting vases – all can make attractive bases. All you need to buy is the bulb-holder, flex (cord) and plug;

perhaps also a cork stopper if the neck of the container is too wide.

If you want to thread the flex down through the base, you will have to make a hole in the bottom of it. However, if the base is a treasured vase or a particularly brittle container that you do not want to drill, there is no reason why you cannot leave the flex coming out at the side. In which case, you may want to use a more decorative type of flex for the lamp – for example, striped or coloured (see page 157).

1 If the bottle or jar is light, weight it down with pebbles or sand.
2 Wedge the bulb-holder into the neck of the container. If the neck is too wide, take a cork disc and, using a craft knife, cut a hole in it in which the bulb-holder can sit.
3 Insert the bulb-holder into the cork and wedge the assemblage into the bottle. To drill a hole in the base, use a spear-point drill bit in a power drill set at a slow speed. Lubricate the drilling area with turpentine or white spirit contained by a sealed ring of putty.

SAFETY When drilling glass, ceramics or other brittle materials, *always* wear protective goggles or special safety glasses.

3 A *marble-based lamp is the centrepiece of this conversation area.*

SAFETY
Living with Electricity
● Have your electrical wiring system checked every 5 years, or at once if you are buying an older property
● Any system more than 25 years old should be replaced
● Do not overload a socket (outlet) with plugs
● Replace damaged flexes
● Replace plugs that are broken or cracked
● Ensure trailing flexes are kept out of the way
● Store electric blankets flat and in a dry cupboard
● Keep electrical appliances away from the bathroom

Working with Electricity
● *Always* switch off power at the mains supply before carrying out any repairs or replacements
● *Always* disconnect an electrical appliance before working on it
● Use a circuit tester to check that you have shut off power to the area of your home you are working on
● Use a circuit breaker plug on household tools, such as drills and sanders
● If you are not sure how to do the job, call in an electrician

PREPARATION

Preparation is one stage of decorating where the rewards are not immediately evident. Although making a good surface can be time-consuming, laborious and messy, proper preparation is essential if you want a successful result.

Almost all decorating finishes require a surface that is clean, even and dry. The first step is to analyze the condition of the surface and assess how much work has to be done to bring it up to standard. In some cases, all that may be needed is to wash and degrease the area and then allow it to dry thoroughly. More often, though, there will be small holes or cracks to fill, existing finishes to be stripped, and some minor repair work. Occasionally, you will discover that what seemed to be a minor fault is in fact the outward manifestation of a major one requiring remedial action before you can continue to decorate.

Major Problems
Symptoms of major problems can include:
● patches of discoloured or mouldy plaster
● wide cracks in walls which continue to widen
● cracking, warped or crumbling woodwork
● excessive moisture

Whenever you suspect an underlying defect it is crucial that you treat the cause, not just the symptoms: simply ignoring the problem could, at worst, lead to the overall weakening of the entire fabric of your home.

Structural decay, as shown up by poor surfaces, has several causes, including dampness, structural instability, infestations of woodworm or beetle and fungal growths such as dry rot. One cause may lead to another: for example, dampness can create the conditions for dry rot to flourish. If you suspect any of these defects, call in an expert to treat the condition – or, if you are extremely lucky, to allay your suspicions (see page 25).

Walls and Ceilings
Preparation can be dusty and messy, so you should protect furnishings and fittings as carefully as you would if you were already starting to decorate. Clear the room of furniture as far as possible. Remove lampshades, take down curtains and cover floors with dustsheets. Before you start to work, assemble all the tools and equipment you will need.

Painted walls and ceilings that are in good condition may just need to be cleaned before you begin decorating. First brush or vacuum off loose dirt and dust. Then, using a solution of warm water and detergent or sugar soap, wash all the surfaces with a clean rag or sponge.

Small cracks and holes can be filled with any number of fillers: some are ready-mixed, others come in powder form and must be mixed with water. Choose the filler that suits the surface and degree of damage.

Foam Fillers

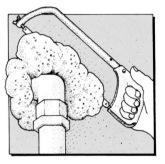

Foam fillers expand and can be used for awkward gaps.

Filling Cracks

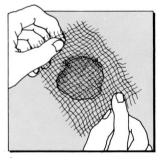

1

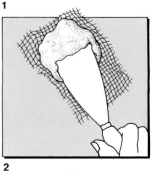

2

1 Rake out loose material and undercut edges.
2 Moisten surface. Press filler into crack. Level off proud of surface and sand.

Filling Holes

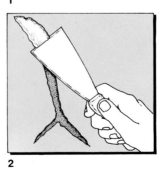

1

2

1 Prepare as for cracks, cutting round edge for a firm line. Cover with mesh tape, which will act as a backing.
2 Apply thin film of filler.

Filling Gaps

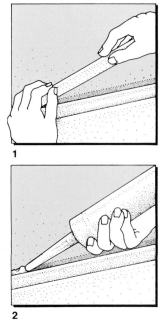

1

2

1 Gaps, such as those between skirting boards (baseboards) and floors can be filled using a bunched tissue or newspaper or a strip of expanded polystyrene.
2 Apply sealant to fill and seal the gap. Smooth with wetted fingertips.

Fitting a Ceiling Rose
(Medallion)
To fix a polystyrene ceiling rose, apply adhesive to its back and simply press it into place. If you are using it in conjunction with a light, you can feed the cord down through a hole drilled in the middle. Fill any gaps around the edges.

Architectural Details
Cleaning decorative plasterwork is extremely time-consuming, but it may be the only way to restore its original beauty.

Test a small area by sponging with water. If the paint comes off, soak the plasterwork for 30 minutes and then scrape off the paint using small knives and brushes, working gently into cracks and crevices. If the paint is not soluble in water, try a chemical solvent or a hot-air stripper.

Where architectural detail is lacking, you can buy ready-made cornices (crown moldings), ceiling roses (medallions) and mouldings in fibrous plaster or polystyrene.

SAFETY Do not paint polystyrene details with oil-based paint – this causes a fire hazard. Switch off electricity at the mains or fuse box before tampering with light fittings.

SURFACE TREATMENTS

Emulsion (Latex) If the paint is peeling, strip back to ensure a good working surface. Otherwise, clean with sugar soap and water before painting. New plaster should be primed.
Gloss If the paintwork is cracked, strip right back to ensure a good working surface. Otherwise, clean with sugar soap and water. New or exposed wood or metal should be primed.
Distemper Use a coarse cloth or a scourer and water to scrub the walls. If the layer of distemper is thick, dampen the wall and scrub off. Use

stabilizing solution to cover any remaining areas.
Textured Paint If you are planning to paint the surface, scrub lightly with a mild solution of sugar soap and water. Use a textured-paint stripper to remove it completely and safely.
Wallpaper Dampen the paper with water and use a scraper to strip. Roughen the surface of painted wallpaper with coarse sandpaper or serrated scraper. Washable papers should be stripped using a serrated scraper. Use a steam stripper for 'difficult' papers.

A fireplace is always a focal point and adds to the style and atmosphere of a room. Often, though, you will find either that fireplaces have been removed or that they were never fitted in the first place. Luckily, there are many suppliers of antique and

reproduction fireplaces, so you should find it easy enough to find a replacement to suit the size of the opening, the period or style of the room, and your own budget. Materials for the surrounds include marble, stone, stripped or new pine, cast-iron and tiling.

Stripping Wallpaper

Whether you intend to paint or paper a wall, it is always a good idea to strip the old paper off first. If you do not the dyes or glues in the existing wallpaper may stain through the new surface, the old paper may soften and lift up, the pattern may show through (in the case of relief textures), or (if you are covering washable, metallic, coated or flocked paper) the new finish may simply not stick to the wall.

There are a variety of methods you can use, depending on the type of paper and how firmly it has adhered to the surface. Certain papers can be stripped dry, by simply peeling away the bottom edge and lifting it off the wall. However, this usually leaves a thin backing paper which can be soaked and then scraped off. Generally, though, for most papers you will need to soak the paper with hot water, score the surface and scrape it off or, for more stubborn washable or relief or painted papers, use a steam stripper. In either case, it is important to work gently and methodically to avoid damaging the underlying plasterwork.

Plain painted walls do not need to be stripped before redecoration (unless they have been covered with distemper, which is incompatible with modern paints). Textured coatings, however, cannot be papered over, and so they will need to be stripped.

Remember that textured coatings and relief papers may well have been applied to cover imperfect plaster. If that is the case, stripping will leave you with a surface that requires further work.

Using a Steam Stripper
Steam strippers are fairly inexpensive to hire and can vastly simplify the process of stripping washable, relief or painted paper. Water is boiled in a tank and the resulting steam is fed through a hose to a perforated plate.

Fill the tank with water, according to the manufacturers' instructions, and, when the steam is ready, hold the plate against the bottom of a length of paper for 30–60 seconds, or until the paper appears damp.

● Do not keep the steam stripper in one position for too long or the plasterwork will be damaged.

Materials and Equipment
● broad stripping knife
● serrated scraper, knife or abrasive paper for scoring
● steam stripper
● bucket of hot water
● sponge or brush
● rubber gloves and safety glasses

1

2

3

4

5

6

METHOD

1 To strip standard wallpaper, wet thoroughly with a sponge using hot water. Work from the top down, wetting several times, and allow at least five minutes for the water to soak in.

2 Ease the paper off using a broad stripping knife, held at an angle of 30 degrees. Scrape upwards, taking care not to dig into the plaster. The paper should wrinkle and come away. You may also find that you can pull off big strips.

3 To help water soak into washable paper, score the surface with a serrated scraper, knife or abrasive paper.

4 For painted or heavy relief papers, use a steam stripper. Steam rises, so work upwards. Peel off one area of paper with a broad knife while you are steaming the next.

5 Vinyls or easy-strip papers are designed to be peeled off. Using a craft knife, lift the corner of the covering away from its backing.

6 Use your hands to peel the paper away from the wall. If the backing paper comes away as well, strip it off by soaking and scraping. If it remains intact, however, you can simply paper over it.

Removing Textured Coatings

Removing textured paints is laborious and messy. The best way is to paint on a special textured paint remover and, once the coating has softened, scrape it off. Alternatively, you can use a steam stripper. Wash the wall down afterwards, and make sure to wear protective gloves and glasses. Never be tempted to sand a textured coating.

Woodwork and Metalwork

Unlike painted walls, painted woodwork is often better stripped before you redecorate: built-up layers of oil-based paint will prevent your newly decorated woodwork from looking crisp and even. However, if the woodwork is in good condition you can simply clean and degrease it, then lightly sand it down to provide a key for painting.

Metalwork – window frames, for example – can be treated in exactly the same way. If there is rust you should clean this off with an emery cloth or a wire brush.

Wooden floors often require special attention. Boards may need replacing, levelling or fixing down. Also, it is important to fill gaps and sink nail-heads if you are planning to sand, varnish or stain the floor.

Stripping Woodwork

The three main methods of stripping paint from woodwork are scraping, the use of chemicals, and the application of heat.

If you work with chemicals, make sure to wear protective gloves and glasses. If you use a hot-air stripper, do so with care, especially when stripping window frames: excess heat can cause the glass to crack, and there is a danger of scorching the wood or setting the accumulated paint scrapings ablaze.

Heat Stripping

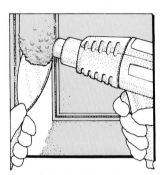

Use a hot-air stripper to soften paint. Move it to and fro, scraping away paint either with a scraper for flat areas or with a shave hook for mouldings.

Chemical Stripping

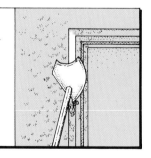

Dab on liquid stripper with a brush. When the paint has softened and bubbled, scrape it off using a shave hook on mouldings (pulling towards you) or a broad scraper on flat areas (pushing away from you).

This is the best method of stripping window frames but it can be expensive, messy and time-consuming.

Sanding

On flat surfaces you can strip paint with an orbital sander, but it can be extremely dusty and messy. For mouldings, use a flexible abrasive block for the job.

1 *Sanded wood-strip floor.*
2 *A stripped wooden fireplace.*
3 *To look their best wood floors require careful preparation.*
4 *Mouldings add period style to a built-in corner cupboard.*

SURFACE TREATMENTS

New Wood Use cellulose filler for cracks and holes. Cover knots with shellac knotting. Smooth the surface with a fine abrasive paper.
Old Wood Make sure that there is no sign of rot, and fill cracks and holes. Smooth with a fine abrasive paper.
Painted Wood If the surface is in good condition, clean with sugar soap and water. Rub down with a medium-grade flexible sanding block or abrasive paper to provide a key for the new paint. Cracked paint should be stripped.
Varnished Wood Use varnish stripper in order to get back to bare wood.

Stained Wood Wood bleach can be used to remove stain. If the surface is to be painted, rub with a medium-grade flexible sanding block or abrasive paper. Wood stain protected by varnish must be removed as above.
Painted Metal Clean with sugar soap and water if in good condition. Otherwise, use a wire brush to remove flaking paint, and treat rust with a primer containing rust inhibitor.
Aluminium/Copper Clean with white spirit and apply enamel without primer or undercoat. Use flour-grade paper to remove signs of corrosion and scratches.

Replacing a Floorboard

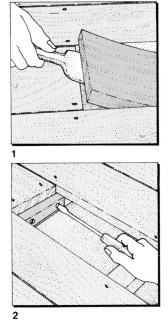

1 Lever up the damaged board with a bolster chisel (brick chisel). If you cannot lift a whole board, cut out a short piece. First drill a starting hole and then cut across the board with a padsaw (keyhole saw) alongside, but not cutting into, a joist, pipe or cable.

Loosen nails by slipping a strip of wood under the board and pressing down hard on the end. Repeat the process, jamming the wood strip up as far as it will go, until the board is free.

2 Screw a short wooden batten to the side of the joist, flush with the underside of the floorboards. Cut the replacement board and nail to batten.

Adding Door Mouldings

Flush doors, cupboard fronts and kitchen units can be dressed up by applying ready-made wooden mouldings to provide decorative detail. There are sets available especially for this purpose, allowing you to create the effect of traditional panelling. These come in sizes to suit standard doors, and are available both curved and straight; the corners are mitred. To attach them, drill very fine holes in the moulding and fix with pins.

Alternatively, you can use ready-made wooden mouldings to make your own picture rail or dado rail, fixing it in position with masonry nails or screws.

Successful Decorating
PREPARATION

METHOD

1 Punch all nail-heads below the surface of the boards, using a nail punch and a claw hammer.

2 Fit coarse-grade paper onto the belt sander, following the operating instructions.

3 Before switching on, tilt the sander so that the drum is clear of the floor. Tilt up at the beginning and end of each row.

4 Sand backwards and forwards, working diagonally at an angle of 45 degrees. Use coarse abrasive paper and overlap each row by about 7.5cm/3in. Follow this by sanding back and forth in the direction of the grain of the board, using first medium-grade and then fine paper.

5 Use an edging sander for edges, following the grain wherever possible and keeping moving while the machine is switched on.

6 For awkward corners, use a hook scraper or a shave hook. Sand by hand any small patches you may have missed.

● Vacuum the floor several times during the course of the sanding. Allow the dust to settle overnight before final vacuuming. Clean with white spirit or turpentine before applying varnish or stain.

SAFETY *Always* wear a dust mask, ear muffs and goggles. Drape the cord of the sander over your shoulder to ensure that it is kept well out of the path of the machine. Always make sure the machine is switched off and disconnected from the mains when you are changing paper.

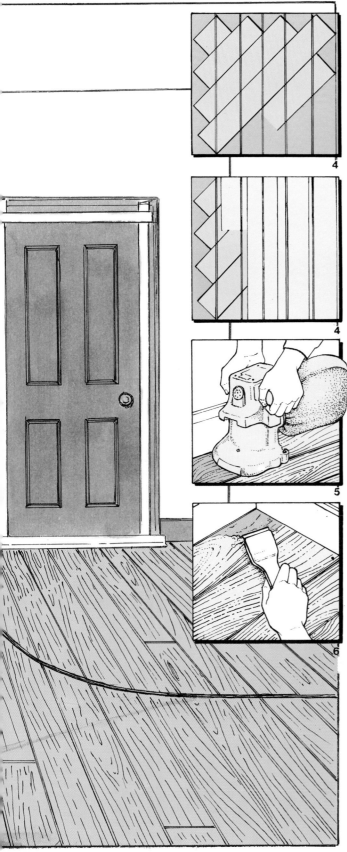

Sanding a Floor

It takes a degree of skill to operate sanding machines, and it is essential that you protect yourself from inhaling dust and observe a number of vital safety precautions.

Preparation

Before sanding, you must prepare the floor suitably. You should make sure you have prepared for the work before you hire a sanding machine – otherwise you are paying for all the time that the machine stands idle.

If there are many large gaps between boards, it may be worth lifting all the boards, moving them along and inserting an extra piece at the end. Alternatively, one or two large gaps could be filled with wooden fillets, glued and hammered in place, then planed smooth once the glue has dried. (Small gaps can be filled with wood filler.)

All traces of old polish should be removed with steel wool and white spirit or turpentine so that the sander does not become clogged. Nail down loose boards and punch all nail-heads below the surface.

Finally, prepare the room in general by clearing furniture, taking down curtains and covering light fittings. Tape around the doors to minimize the amount of dust percolating through the house. Open all the windows.

Using Sanding Machines

You will need two types of sander: a large belt sander and an edging (rotary) sander. The belt sander is an upright machine with a dust collecting bag and a revolving drum around which abrasive paper is wrapped. The edging sander is smaller and lighter and has an abrasive sheet attached to a rubber pad. Both types of machine can be hired from specialist shops, which also supply abrasive paper and protective gear.

Ask for a demonstration when you hire or buy the equipment. Follow the instruction booklet when fitting the abrasive paper. Always tilt the drum of a belt sander back from the floor before switching on. Once it is on, lower it gently. You must keep moving when you are using it: if the sander is left running while it is stationary it will gouge holes in the floor. Tilt it up at the start and finish of each row.

Materials and Equipment
● belt sander for the main floor area
● edging (rotary) sander for the edges
● shave hook or hook scraper for awkward areas
● nail punch and hammer
● coarse-, medium- and fine-grade abrasive paper
● protective gear (dust mask, ear muffs, goggles)
● vacuum cleaner

ALL ABOUT PAINT

Paint is cheap, quick and easy to apply, and available in a variety of different finishes and in a host of different colours. Thanks to technological advances, modern paints cover well, protect surfaces from weather and wear, and resist fading and discoloration. For all these reasons – both practical and aesthetic – painting is the single most popular way of decorating interiors.

Basic painting techniques are simple to master and the equipment required is not elaborate. With a little extra skill, you can open up a whole new dimension of decorative possibilities using special effects such as sponging, ragging and stencilling.

TYPES OF PAINT

Paint consists of pigment (colour) dispersed in a medium (binder), together with a solvent or thinner which evaporates as the paint dries. Some paints may include other materials such as resin or silica to provide special characteristics. The two main types of paint are oil-based and water-based (commonly known as emulsion [latex]). They are incompatible when wet.

It is always a good idea to buy the best paint you can afford. Cheap paint is difficult to apply and looks streaky; you will end up needing to use more of it than with a good-quality paint.

Oil-based Paints

These come in three finishes: gloss, which has a high sheen and is often used on woodwork; semi-gloss or eggshell, which gives a mid-sheen texture and can be used on walls or woodwork; and matt or flat oil paint,

which provides the basis for many special paint effects.

All oil-based paints are soluble in white spirit or turpentine and require an undercoat. They take longer to dry than water-based varieties of paint.

Undercoat

This oil-based paint is designed to provide a good surface for the application of oil-based top coats. It is soluble in white spirit or turpentine.

Water-based Paints

These are also available in different finishes: silk, satin or sheen and matt. A popular choice for walls and ceilings, emulsion (latex) is quick-drying, soluble in water (tools and spills are easy to clean) and needs no undercoat.

Non-drip Paints

Both oil- and water-based paints are available in non-drip versions which are easy

for the beginner to apply. They need no stirring and should not be thinned. Similarly, trays of 'solid emulsion' can be useful for painting ceilings, stairways or wherever it is important to keep splashes to a minimum.

Textured 'Paint'

This thick, permanent coating dries to a textured finish which is very difficult to remove. It is designed to cover up poor surfaces and should be finished with a coat of emulsion.

Masonry Paint

Essentially an external paint, this can be used on interior brickwork for a durable finish.

Enamel Paint

This is an oil-based paint for small areas of wood and metalwork. It is very dense; only one coat is needed. There is also a textured version which separates as it dries to give a 'crazed' finish.

1 *Light green paint with a slight sheen is used to decorate walls and ceiling, creating an airy room.*
2 *A sense of warmth and enclosure is generated by painting all the surfaces in this kitchen the same shade of burnt orange.*

Home-made Paints

You can create your own colours by mixing a small amount of artist's colours (oil or gouache) with the appropriate solvent (white spirit, turpentine or water) and adding the mixture a little at a time to the appropriate paint base.

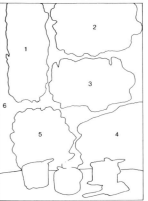

Types of Paint

1 *Gloss*
2 *Floor paint*
3 *Eggshell*
4 *Matt emulsion (latex)*
5 *Vinyl silk (semi-gloss)*
6 *Undercoat*

Applications

	UNDERCOAT	OIL-BASED GLOSS	OIL-BASED EGGSHELL (SEMI-GLOSS)
SURFACES TO USE ON	Use on primed surfaces. Do not use on plastic, copper, brass or stainless steel	Woodwork, metalwork. Can be applied to plastic and copper without using undercoat	Walls, ceilings and woodwork. Ideal for bathrooms and kitchens
EQUIPMENT	Wide paintbrush, roller or spray gun for large areas, small paintbrush for details	Wide paintbrush, roller or spray gun for large areas, small paintbrush for details	Paintbrushes, roller and tray, or spray gun
DILUTING	White spirit or turpentine can be used to thin the paint	White spirit or turpentine can be used to thin the paint	White spirit or turpentine can be used to thin the paint
POSSIBLE PROBLEMS	Can be used as a top coat, but must be covered with matt varnish to avoid marking	Go back over painted surfaces to brush out drips and runs	Patchiness can occur if surface is not thoroughly prepared and completely dry
DRYING TIME	2–6 hours. A second coat can usually be applied after 6–16 hours	4–6 hours. A second coat can usually be applied after 16–24 hours	4–6 hours. A second coat can usually be applied after 16–24 hours
CLEANING	Use white spirit or turpentine to clean brushes immediately after use	Use white spirit or turpentine to clean brushes immediately after use	Use white spirit or turpentine to clean brushes and equipment
NUMBER OF COATS	1 or 2	2	1 or 2
SPECIAL PROPERTIES	It has a high pigment content, and covers well. Chalky texture as top coat	Undercoat is not always necessary. Durable and easy to clean	Smooth finish with dull sheen. Easy to clean and withstands condensation
COLOURS	Limited to a few basic colours	Wide range of colours, some coordinating with water-based ranges	Range of colours

WATER-BASED EMULSION (LATEX)/VINYL	SOLID EMULSION (LATEX)	ENAMEL	TEXTURED PAINT
Walls and ceilings. Vinyl silk/satin can be used as a base coat for paint effects	Walls and ceilings. Do not apply directly onto new/unpainted plasterwork	Metalwork, woodwork. Best for small areas	Walls and ceilings. Particularly useful for covering uneven surfaces
Paintbrushes, roller and tray, or spray gun	Roller for large areas and paintbrush for details. Usually sold in its own tray	Paintbrushes for small areas, roller or spray gun for larger areas	Shaggy (coarse nap) roller and tray
Use water to thin the paint if necessary	Should not be thinned	White spirit or turpentine can be used to thin the paint	Should not be thinned
Oil-based paint and water-based paint are incompatible when wet	Too absorbent to take most paint effects. Not recommended for kitchens and bathrooms	Shows up imperfections of surface, so thorough preparation is necessary	Extremely difficult to remove
2–4 hours. A second coat can usually be applied after 2–4 hours	1–4 hours. A second coat can usually be applied after 1–4 hours	2–4 hours. A second coat can usually be applied after 1–4 hours	1–4 hours
Brushes and other equipment should be cleaned with water and soap	Roller and tray should be cleaned with water and soap	Use white spirit or turpentine to remove paint from brushes	Use white spirit or turpentine to remove paint from roller and tray
1 or 2	2	1 or 2	1 coat, followed by a coat of emulsion (latex) or gloss
No primer required. Dries quickly to a smooth finish	Particularly good for ceilings and stairways because it is non-drip	No primer required. Some brands also contain rust inhibitors. Hard, shiny finish	Much thicker than regular paint. Can be used to create various surface patterns
Wide range of colours	Limited range of colours	Range of colours	Coloured paint is applied to textured surface

Painting Tools and Equipment

The basic tools for most painting jobs are brushes and rollers. Just as you should always buy the best paint you can afford, it makes sense to buy good-quality tools. Maintain them properly during and after use.

Paintbrushes

Brushes can be used with either oil- or water-based paint and are available in a variety of widths for tackling different surfaces. Use wide brushes (10–15cm/4–6in) for walls and ceilings, narrow brushes (2.5cm/1in) for margins and fine trim, and medium brushes (5–7.5cm/2–3in) for bigger areas of woodwork.

Special brushes are produced to make the task of painting awkward areas easier. These include cutting-in brushes, with angled tips for painting edges or window frames, and brushes for painting radiators, where the bristles are fixed at right angles to the handle.

Rollers

Rollers are designed for use with water-based paint. Their principal advantage is that they enable large areas to be painted quickly and evenly. Some rollers can be fitted with handle extensions for painting ceilings or other areas which are difficult to reach. Choose a roller where the sleeve detaches from the frame to make cleaning much easier.

There are three main types of roller: short pile (short nap), shaggy pile (coarse nap) and foam. Both foam and short pile rollers work best on smooth surfaces, but short pile rollers will produce a better finish. Shaggy pile rollers are designed to cover textured surfaces. There are also special rollers designed to apply textured coatings. These have relief sleeves which deposit the paint in a pattern.

Paint Pads

As with rollers, paint pads are best used with water-based paint. They consist of a square or oblong pile-covered foam pad attached to a handle. Use pads to cover large surfaces.

Paint Containers

If you are using a brush, you can paint straight from the paint tin, but it is better to use a special paint container. These have handles, which make them more portable than tins; moreover, should you accidentally spoil the paint with dust picked up on the brush, you will waste only what is in the container.

Paint Trays

Rollers must be used with paint trays. The tray has a reservoir which holds a small amount of paint and a slope to facilitate the even application of the paint onto the roller.

Paint Guards

Plastic or metal guards are protective shields which can be placed against a window, wall or floor when you are painting frames or woodwork. Alternatively, you can use a piece of stiff cardboard or mask out the surrounding area with tape.

Care of Brushes and Rollers

Never overload tools with paint. As soon as you have finished, clean your tools by washing them in the appropriate solvent. Use white spirit, turpentine or a commercial brush cleaner for oil-based paints; cold water for water-based paints. Rinse brushes and rollers thoroughly, leave to dry and store flat. Never stand brushes or rollers upright.

● A loaded brush can be left for up to two hours without cleaning if it is covered tightly with foil or plastic kitchen wrap to prevent the paint from drying out.

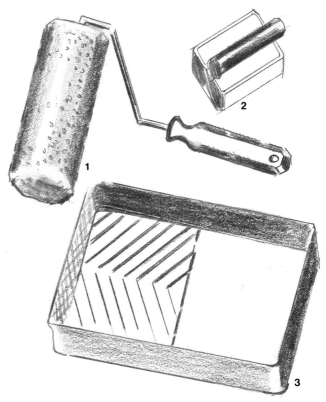

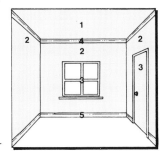

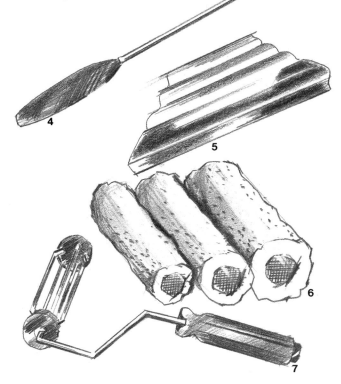

A cornice in a contrasting colour makes a subtle break between walls and ceiling.

Brushes and Equipment

Paintbrushes and other basic equipment can be bought from home decorating stores.

1 Roller for textured coating
2 Paint pad
3 Paint tray
4 Radiator brush
5 Paint guard
6 Regular roller, sheepskin roller and synthetic thick-pile roller
7 Roller frame
8 Medium paintbrush (5cm/2in)
9 Large paintbrush (10cm/4in)
10 Medium paintbrush (7.5cm/3in)
11 Narrow paintbrush (2.5cm/1in)
12 Cutting-in brush
13 Paint container

Order of Painting a Room

Paint a room in the following order. First, paint the ceiling, working away from the main source of natural light. Then come the walls, and after them paint the window frames and doors. Next paint any mouldings and picture rails, and finish by painting the skirting boards (baseboards).

Painting Walls and Ceilings

The most important principle when painting walls and ceilings is to work to a system. The aim is to cover the area evenly, avoiding visible 'joins' where paint overlaps. Work quickly so that the edges of the painted area will not dry before the adjoining area is covered. If you have to stop halfway through, try to do so at a natural break such as a corner.

Order of Painting a Wall

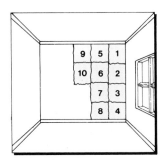

Work away from sources of natural light, especially if you are using a light-coloured paint over a light-coloured ground, or applying a second coat of any colour. Start in the top right-hand corner and proceed from right to left. (If you are left-handed, work in the opposite direction.)

If you are using a brush, work in sections 60cm/2ft square, as shown: complete one vertical strip before moving onto the next, and start each strip at the top. If you are using a roller, work in 60cm/2ft strips.

Painting Platform
Of course, you can paint a ceiling from a stepladder, but there is the disadvantage that you have to climb down frequently to move it along. Alternatively, if the ceiling is not too high, you can simply fit an extension handle to a roller.

Order of Painting a Ceiling

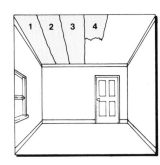

Work in strips about 60cm/2ft wide, away from the source of natural light. First cut-in edges using a narrow brush. Paint one complete strip, then work back in a new row to the end where you started.

However, it is much easier and much less tiring to paint a ceiling when standing on a platform. Set up a pair of stepladders or trestles and lay a sturdy plank or scaffold board across; ensure that the structure is secure before using it.

Cutting-in Using a Small Brush

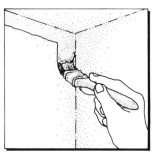

Before painting any section with a brush or roller, paint the edges along, for example, ceiling lines, skirting boards (baseboards), internal corners, window frames and door frames with a narrow brush or a cutting-in brush. Work a little way ahead of the main paintwork – although not too far, or the edges will dry before they are overlapped.

● At all costs, avoid standing on a chair to paint a ceiling.

Applying the Paint

Whether you are using a wide brush, roller or pad, apply the paint in random directions, working out from the corners where the edges have been painted, overlapping and criss-crossing the strokes. When the paint runs out or you complete a section, finish with a light upward stroke to remove brush or roller marks.

WALLS AND CEILINGS
Paint Coverage per Litre (Internal usage only)

Paint Finish	Smooth Plaster or Paper Base	Rough Plaster or Paper Base	Masonry
Undercoat	15m²	12m²	—
All Purpose Primer	7–8m²	7–8m²	—
Matt Emulsion (Latex)	14m²	11m²	14m²
Silk Emulsion (Latex)	13m²	10m²	13m²
Flat Paint	16m²	14m²	16m²
Eggshell	16m²	14m²	16m²
High Gloss	17m²	15m²	17m²
Non-drip Gloss	12m²	9m²	12m²

Multiply by 10 to get the coverage in square feet per US quart.

Stairwell Platform

To paint awkward areas such as stairwells, construct a platform using a stepladder and a straight ladder. Set up the stepladder on the landing, well back from the top step. Lean the straight ladder against the head wall of the staircase, with the bottom resting against a lower stair. The ends of the ladder should be wrapped to protect the wall. Then lay a strong plank or scaffold board across. If the ladders are more than 1.5m/5ft apart, use two boards, one on top of the other for support.

1 *Pale terracotta on a small country stairwell has the soft look of bare plaster.*
2 *Two areas of wall treated in a different manner: pale yellow in a matt finish above the dado rail, and a deeper yellow scumbled below.*

Painting Details

Painting Decorative Mouldings

Cornices (Crown moldings) and ceiling roses (medallions), whether they are the original plasterwork or reproductions made of polystyrene, plaster or anaglypta, should be painted with emulsion (latex) or water-based paint. You will need to exercise some care, especially in the case of intricate mouldings, in order to prevent the design from becoming clogged and obscured with paint. If the cornice is to be the same colour as the ceiling, paint the ceiling first, then the cornice, and finally the walls. If the cornice is to be a different colour, paint it after the walls. If you are going to paper the walls, the cornice should certainly be painted first. The best method is to apply the paint in thin coats with a narrow (2.5cm/1in) brush. Allow each coat to dry before you start on the next.

Some mouldings can look very attractive if elements of the design – usually the recessed parts – are picked out in a second colour. Paint the raised areas first and then fill in the second colour using an artists' brush.

Painting Awkward Areas

The areas behind radiators and pipework are difficult to reach with ordinary brushes. Special crevice or radiator brushes can be very useful in such situations. For painting behind a radiator, an alternative is to use a small roller fitted with an extension handle.

Painting Doors and Windows

If you follow the correct sequence for different types of windows and doors you will ensure a professional result, with all areas being covered evenly and without the formation of hard ridges.

As far as possible, remove fixtures such as handles, knobs, doorplates and window-latches before you begin to paint.

1 An unusual archway with stained glass panels has been painted white to contrast with the sea-green walls.
2 Painting details such as architraves and skirting boards (baseboards) in a deeper shade of the wall colour serves to add graphic interest.

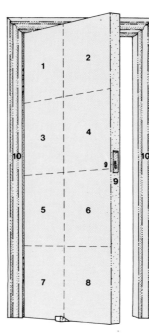

Painting a Flush Door

Painting a Panel Door

Keep the door ajar with a wedge to prevent it from moving. Paint in sections 45cm/18in square (about half the width of the door), working from the top down, completing each horizontal strip before you start on the next. Always paint to a wet edge in order to avoid hard, dried lines.

As for a flush door, wedge it open. Then paint in the following order:
1 Mouldings
2 Recessed panels
3 Centred uprights
4 Horizontals (paint top to bottom, following the grain)
5 Outer uprights
6 Door edge
7 Frame

Painting Sash Windows

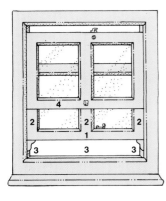

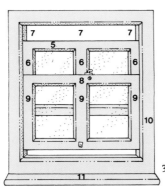

Avoid getting paint onto the sash cords – otherwise they will stiffen and crack. Reverse the position of the sashes to paint as much as possible of the outer sash, the bottom of the inner sash and the inside edges. Then move the sashes back to their original position and paint the rest of the outer frame, inner frame edges and lastly the frame and sill. The most sensible sequence for painting a sash window is as follows:

1 Meeting rail

Painting a Casement Window

First of all paint those windows that open, and start early enough in the day for there to be time for the windows to dry before night falls. The painting sequence of a window should follow the grain of the wood. All casement windows, whether they open or not, should be

2 Outer-sash vertical bars, as far as possible
3 The area beneath the inner sash and the lower runners
4 Lower cross-rail of inner sash and its underside
5 Upper cross-rail of the outer sash
6 Remainder of the outer-sash vertical bars
7 Soffit and top runners
8 Upper cross-rail of the inner sash
9 Inner-sash vertical bars
10 Frame
11 Window sill

painted in the following correct order:
1 Glazing putty
2 Glazing bars
3 Top and bottom rail
4 Outer uprights, or 'stiles'
5 Hinge edge
6 Centred frame, if there is an adjoining window
7 Frame (top and bottom, then sides)
8 Sill

WOOD AND METAL
Paint Coverage per Litre (Internal usage only)

Paint Finish	Smooth Planed Wood	Rough Sawn Wood	Radiators and Metalwork
Undercoat	16m²	15m²	16m²
All Purpose Primer	7–8m²	7–8m²	7–8m²
Eggshell	16m²	—	16m
High Gloss	17m²	14m²	17m²
Enamel Paint	—	—	17m²

Multiply by 10 to get the coverage in square feet per US quart.

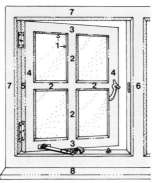

3 *The subtle modulation of different greys creates an atmosphere of elegance and tranquillity. The walls above and below the dado are spattered for an unobtrusive but textural finish, and the desk chair has been sponged.*

METHOD

1 Stir paint thoroughly. Decant paint into paint container, and dip paint brush up to one-third the depth of the bristles. Do not overload the brush, or the paint will drip. Press the brush gently against the side of the container to remove excess paint.

2 If the grain is vertical, paint two or three vertical strips, parallel with each other, leaving between them gaps just narrower than the brush-width. Hold a narrow brush like a pencil.

3 Without reloading the brush, brush out the vertical strokes horizontally across the grain to fill gaps and smooth the paint.

4 Finish with light upward strokes, using a nearly dry brush. Work over the entire section you have just painted.

5 Use a paint guard or shield to protect a glass panelled door or a window. Alternatively, protect the glass with masking tape which you should remove before the paint is fully dry. In either case, allow the paint to cover the glass by about 3mm/⅛in so that the edges between wood and glass are sealed.

6 To paint a skirting board (baseboard), hold a piece of cardboard along the bottom edge so that the brush does not pick up dirt from the floor. Protect fitted carpet with dustsheets.

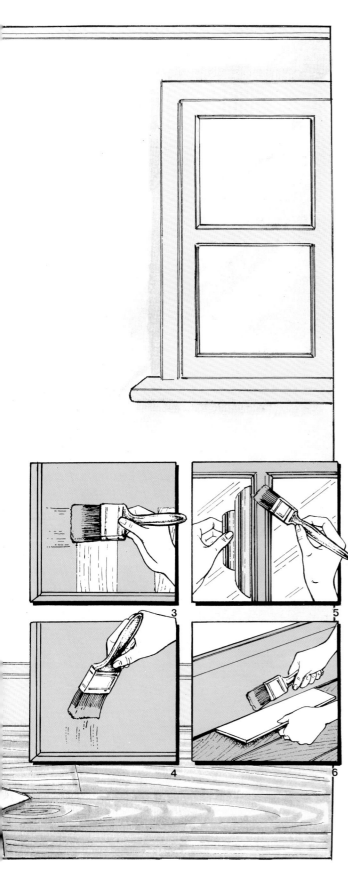

Painting Woodwork

All woodwork should be painted using an oil-based paint, in either a gloss or eggshell (semi-gloss) finish. This type of paint is more durable than emulsion (latex) and gives a thick protective coat which resists scuffs and knocks. All surfaces should be clean, dry and prepared for painting.

The basic principle of painting woodwork, whether it is a door or a picture rail, is to apply the paint *with* the grain, brush out *against* the grain, and lay off *with* the grain. Work in the correct sequence when painting details such as doors and window frames (see pages 178–9).

● Before painting a door, remember to clean the top edge with a rag. Also clean out the keyhole and door-handle slot to remove loose dirt that could be picked up by the tips of the bristles.

Materials and Equipment
● oil-based paint, gloss or eggshell (semi-gloss)
● narrow (2.5cm/1in) brush for fine detail; medium (7.5cm/3in) brush for panels; angled cutting-in brush for frames
● paint container
● paint guard or masking tape for protecting other surfaces
● solvent – e.g., white spirit or turpentine
● rag for cleaning spills

Painting a Wooden Staircase
Wooden staircases comprise a number of upright and horizontal elements which are best painted in a particular sequence. Prepare for painting by removing any stair carpet or covering. Clean the stairs thoroughly.

Work with thin coats of paint to avoid drips and use a selection of brushes of different widths, according to the area you are tackling.

First paint the hand-rail (or varnish it if you prefer). Then paint the newel post and balusters (uprights). Finally, working from the top of the stairs down, paint the stair treads (horizontal parts), risers (vertical parts) and strings (the area of skirting board beside the steps).

Safety Dispose of all paint- or solvent-soaked rags very carefully in order to avoid the risk of fire.

● If you intend to paper a room, paint the woodwork first, overlapping by about 1cm/½in onto the walls. This margin will ensure that slight gaps do not show.

● It is best to paint each particular area of woodwork – for example a window frame – in one painting session. If you stop halfway, the paint will form an ugly edge when it dries, which is very difficult to remove.

PAINT EFFECTS

Traditional methods of painted decoration are enjoying a renewed popularity today, bringing a sense of richness to the interior. Many special paint techniques were originally inspired by the desire to reproduce the look of a particular material. In the past, when marble, fine woods, wallpapers and fabrics were extremely expensive and hard to come by, craftsmen applied their skills to creating excellent simulations.

In addition, decorators learned how to exploit the qualities of different paints to add a dimension of depth to a surface. Layers of transparent washes or glazes, distressed or unevenly applied, can build up a subtle texture that is impossible to achieve with flat colour.

Although certain highly imitative paint effects do require artistic skill for a professional result, most do not. With practice, experiment and a sound understanding of the properties of paints, it is possible to create distinctive decoration at a fraction of the cost of wallpapering, panelling or fabric coverings.

TYPES OF EFFECT

For the sake of clarity, each paint technique in the following section is described individually. It is important to remember, however, that effects can also be combined. Most professional decorators decide how they want the surface to appear and then use a combination of methods to achieve it.

Experiment is essential. Test your ideas on hardboard (masonite) panels or stiff paper before you tackle a wall. The most difficult aspect of using any special paint effect is achieving consistency over a large area; practise until you can work rhythmically and evenly. It is also worth bearing in mind that, although many effects require special tools, good substitutes can often, for the sake of economy, be adapted from household items.

Non-distressed Effects

There are a number of ways to increase the decorative potential of painted surfaces without using a special distressing or illusionist technique. Plain-painted walls and ceilings can be highlighted by picking out woodwork or plasterwork details in a contrasting or toning shade. Alternatively, decoration can be applied in the form of stencilled patterns painted onto walls, floors or furniture as borders, friezes or single motifs.

You can add depth and intensity to a single-colour scheme by applying several weak layers of wash or glaze (diluted 1:9, paint to solvent) over a base or ground colour. This method, known as 'colour washing', produces a finish of great luminosity and warmth.

Distressed Effects

Distressed, or broken-colour, effects represent a whole family of related techniques, most of which are defined by the tools used to create them. In all cases, layers of dilute wash or glaze are applied over an opaque background.

There are two methods of achieving the textured finish. The first – additive – is to apply the wash or glaze unevenly using a particular tool – such as a sponge, rag, comb, brush or whatever – so that patches are left where the base colour shows through. The second – subtractive – is to apply the wash or glaze in a continuous layer and then 'distress' it with the tool, revealing areas of base colour. In either case the texture of the finish will depend on the tool you have used: each implement leaves its own characteristic mark. (See pages 184–5.)

Illusionist Effects

Techniques such as woodgraining, marbling and tortoise-shelling are essentially designed to simulate a natural material. Many of these effects are based on broken-colour techniques, with a distressed background being modified or decorated in such a way as to resemble the natural patterns and textures of stone, wood or whatever. Although it is impossible to achieve a highly realistic result without a high degree of artistic skill, more abstract patterning can be equally effective and is much easier. (See pages 188–9.)

Glazes and Washes

All special paint techniques depend on the use of glazes and washes. A glaze is a thinned or diluted oil-based paint; a wash is a thinned water-based paint. The correct ratio of paint to solvent is generally 1:3, but experiment is important. Glazes or washes diluted to a greater degree have more transparency and dry more quickly. Most effects can be

1 Details picked out in a silver oil-based artists' colour give a look of richness to this cornice (crown molding).

2 Skilfully blended tones and the hint of a floral border make the wall look deceptively translucent and shimmering.

achieved using either a glaze or a wash. A glaze produces a more luminous and sumptuous finish; washes are fresh and soft-looking.

Another consideration is the texture of the paint: matt, mid-sheen or gloss for oil-based glazes, and matt or mid-sheen for washes.

Remember that oil- and water-based paints are incompatible when wet.

Making a Glaze
You can buy ready-made glaze, but the following are recipes; all can be tinted using artists' oil colours.
● Transparent oil glaze, thinned 1:1 with white spirit or turpentine
● White undercoat, flat oil or eggshell, thinned 1:3 with white spirit or turpentine
● Undercoat or flat oil thinned 1:1 with

transparent oil glaze and then mixed 1:1 with white spirit or turpentine
● Linseed oil thinned 1:3 with turpentine

Making a Wash
Thin emulsion (latex) paint 1:3 with water and, if need be, tint to the desired shade using artists' gouache. Allow each coat of paint to dry before applying the next.

Brushes and Equipment
1 Natural sponge
2 Feather
3 Sword liner
4 Mottler
5 Dragging brush
6 Badger softener
7 Stencilling brush
8 Small artists' brush
9 Fitch
10 Lining brush
11 Dusting brush
12 Overgrainer
13 Stippling brush

Distressed or Broken-colour Effects

The two basic methods of creating broken colour are the additive and subtractive techniques. Many effects, notably sponging, ragging and rag-rolling, can be achieved using either. Others, such as spattering, are inherently additive; while stippling, dragging and cissing, for example, are subtractive.

Additive Techniques

A glaze or wash is applied in a broken film over a dry base coat using a tool such as a sponge or rag. This is the simpler of the two methods, since the drying time of the glaze or wash is not critical. It is best to work in 60cm/2ft vertical strips, taking care not to overlap the prints. Once the glaze or wash has dried, a further one, perhaps in a different colour, can be applied on top.

Subtractive Techniques

A glaze is applied over a dry base coat and then distressed using the tool of your choice while still wet. This method is easier if two people work together – one applying the glaze and the other distressing it. Glazes are more suitable for subtractive methods because they do not dry as quickly as washes.

Base Coats

Choose the colour of the base or ground coat carefully. The background will be modified where the glaze or wash covers it, while in the broken or open areas the colour will of course show through.

Texture is a further important consideration. Matt or mid-sheen is often the best choice – gloss can be obtrusive.

Oil- or water-based ground coats can be used with either glazes or washes, depending on the effect required. Layers of glaze over oil-based paint give a rich lacquer-like finish; a glaze over emulsion (latex) will intensify colour. In the same way, a wash over an emulsion base coat can enhance a soft watercolour look or give a crisp fresh effect; putting a wash over an oil-based undercoat is also effective. In all cases, the base coat must be thoroughly dry before you set to work with your glaze or wash.

Varnish

It is not necessary to seal a surface unless it will be subject to wear – for example, a door or window frame or a kitchen or bathroom wall. Use one to two coats of polyurethane, leaving 5–6 hours between each coat for the varnish to dry.

Varnish enhances and enriches colours but also tends to yellow with age. It is available in matt, mid-sheen or gloss textures; matt is the least noticeable.

Sponging

1

2

Sponging involves the use of a sponge either to dab on a layer of colour (sponging on) or to lift off patches of wet glaze or wash (sponging off). The nature of the print left by the sponge is all-important, and so it is best to use a genuine marine sponge.

First do some test prints on paper. Light colours on a dilute glaze or wash will be subtle and soft; darker shades will give a bolder pattern. If you want to use two or three colours, make each layer fairly sparse and build up from light to dark. Sponging will camouflage a poor surface and can be used as a way of blending.

1 First wet sponge and wring it out. Dip into paint; test print. Dab on colour over dry base coat.

2 Leave first coat to dry. Apply second colour, overlapping prints.

Ragging

Ragging is similar to sponging, and is useful for covering imperfections. It can be either additive or subtractive. Different cloths give different effects, but in most cases the result is fairly insistent and emphatic, so light colours are generally better than strong deep ones. Cloths can be used either dry or wet – wet gives a softer pattern than dry.

Apply colour using a bunched rag. Vary the direction and the way the cloth is bunched. When the cloth is saturated, change for a clean one.

Dragging

Stippling

Combing

Making a Comb

Dragging is a subtractive technique. A dry brush is pulled through wet glaze to produce a fine, rather sophisticated striped effect reminiscent of fabric covering. Dragging is best employed on flat surfaces. It is as effective on woodwork, creating the suggestion of graininess, as on plaster walls. Wallpaper brushes make acceptable alternatives to dragging brushes, which can be expensive.

Glaze works better than wash for dragging. Practise beforehand on a sheet of hardboard (masonite) until you can get the lines steady. Drag through the wet glaze with a large dry brush.

Safety Oil-based paints are highly inflammable. Paint- and solvent-soaked rags can spontaneously ignite if left bunched up in a bag or a confined space. Let them dry thoroughly before you dispose of them.

Stippling is a subtractive technique which produces a delicate, flecked texture. It is particularly effective if a pale glaze or wash is applied over a ground coat of a slightly lighter colour.

Stippling can be tiring to do over large areas. Special stippling brushes are expensive, but you can make do with alternatives: flat-faced brushes such as broomheads, scrubbing brushes, textured rollers and so on. All brushes and rollers should be cleaned regularly in order to prevent the build up of paint.

Apply glaze over base coat and, while still wet, strike the surface with a flat-faced brush, lifting off flecks of colour with the brush.

● Many broken-colour methods are messy. Protect surrounding surfaces, wear rubber gloves and keep a rag on hand to mop up spills and splashes.

Combing is much like dragging. It consists of distressing a wet surface with a comb to create various patterns. The base coat should be robust enough to withstand the combing action. The patterns produced depend on the number and size of teeth in the comb. Although decorators' combs are commercially available, it is easy to make your own. The finish is bold and forthright and suits lengths of woodwork and floors.

Apply glaze to dry base coat. Draw comb over the wet surface to create the pattern.

Cissing

Cissing is, as it were, the reverse of spattering. Apply a glaze or wash to a dry base coat. While the glaze is still wet, spatter on solvent – water, white spirit, or turpentine, depending on the type of paint used. Work on a horizontal surface.

Cut out a design from a piece of rigid plastic, such as the side of an ice cream carton. Vary the spacing and size of the teeth to create.

Spattering

One of the simplest of all broken-colour methods, spattering is an additive technique that involves flecking a surface with dots of colour. The pattern and texture of the finish will depend on the tool: use a stiff brush such as a stencil brush or even a toothbrush. Run your fingers over wet bristles or strike the handle of the brush to release a fine spray. Practise first until you are able to achieve a uniform effect.

● If you accidentally sponge, rag or spatter on a too-thick blob of paint, let it dry and then go over it again with a sponge or cloth dipped in the base colour so as to even out the effect.

Rag-rolling a Wall

Rag-rolling is a variation of a ragging technique in which a cloth is rolled down over a surface to create a finish that displays a great sense of movement and liveliness. As with ragging, the effect is dramatic, resembling the texture of crushed velvet or crumpled silk, and suits formal applications such as in dining rooms. Because the finish could easily become too insistent, it is best to use, rather than bold contrasts, shades of pale colour offset with plain woodwork. Rag-rolling is inherently rhythmic, and for this reason it can be a very effective way of decorating furniture.

Although the finish can be achieved by rag-rolling *on* using a cloth dipped in glaze to apply a layer of broken colour, it is much more subtle to rag-roll *off* – distressing a wet surface using a clean cloth. Because of the need to work quickly before the surface has a chance to dry, it is easier to use oil-based glazes rather than the swifter drying washes. It is also simpler to enlist the help of a partner so that one person can apply the glaze while the other follows closely behind distressing it.

Practice is essential to achieve a fluid movement down over the wall. It is better, if there are two of you, not to be tempted to swap roles from time to time: if a single person does all the distressing, the pressure and the print will be consistent.

Experiment by folding the cloth in different ways, and try out different dilutions of glaze to get the effect you want. The cloth should be rolled in a variety of directions so that the finish does not look mechanical.

Using the Cloth

As in ragging, the type of cloth will determine the texture of the finish. Soft cotton is a good choice for rag-rolling – the closer the weave, the crisper the print. Whichever you choose, you must have a good supply of clean cloths, as you must take a fresh one frequently when each becomes sodden with glaze. Cloths can be used dry or dipped in solvent; wet cloths give a softer effect and do not clog up as readily.

Materials and Equipment
- oil- or water-based paint for the base coat
- oil- or water-based paint for making glaze or wash
- appropriate solvent: white spirit or turpentine for oil-based paints, water for emulsion (latex)
- artists' colours for tinting glaze or wash, if required
- paint container
- wide paintbrushes
- rubber gloves
- supply of clean cloths
- polyurethane varnish

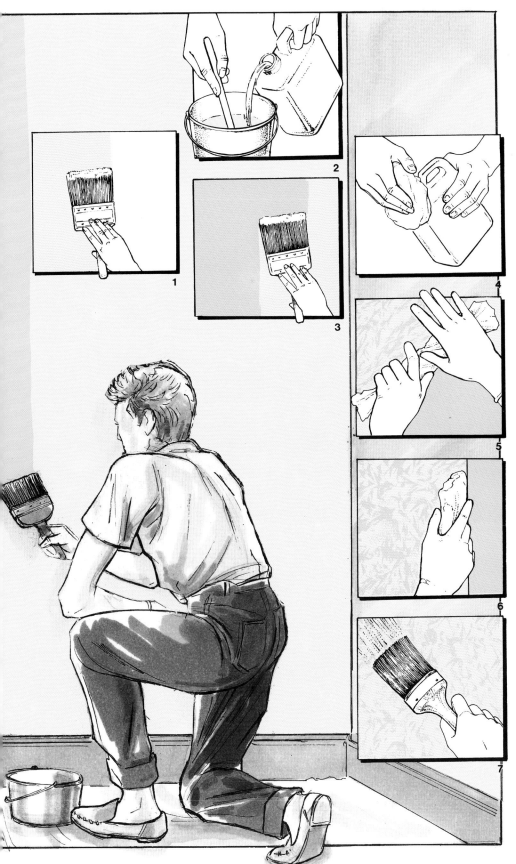

METHOD

1 Apply base coat using a wide brush. Allow to dry overnight.
2 Make a glaze or wash by diluting paint with appropriate solvent in ratio between 1:1 and 1:3 of paint to solvent; experiment to get the right dilution. Tint with artists' colours if desired.
3 One person should then apply the glaze, working in vertical strips 60cm/2ft wide, so that paint is worked while it is still reasonably wet.
4 Soak rag in solvent if you want to achieve a soft effect.
5 The second person should then form the rag into a sausage shape and roll it down over the wet glaze. Vary the direction and bunching of the rag to keep the prints irregular. Be careful not to skid across the surface. The more you dab at the paint, the softer the effect you will create.
   Change rags as they become soaked with paint.
6 Complete an entire wall at a time in order to avoid hard edges. Dab into corners using the end of the rolled-up cloth.
7 Surfaces that need protection, such as kitchen walls, should be coated with polyurethane varnish.

● Let discarded cloths dry out thoroughly before disposing of them – they are highly inflammable, particularly when stored in a confined space.

Illusionist Methods

For the beginner, it is best initially to attempt illusionist effects on a small scale, or to divide up a bigger area into workable sections such as panels or blocks. A good way to start is to study a piece of the material you want to represent and to practise copying the pattern and texture onto hardboard (masonite) or lining paper. You can retain the colours, scale and application of the original or you can opt for a more abstract and freer approach. Bear in mind, though, that you are unlikely to attain realism: that is very much in the province of the professional.

Although most of the effects described here can be achieved using water-based paints, for real depth and translucency it is better to use oil-based glazes.

Marbling

Unless you are marbling a black surface, it is easiest to work from light to dark. Apply several layers of a dirty-white glaze tinted with small amounts of raw umber or black. Distress each layer while it is still wet, using a rag or brush. While the surface is still workable, ciss it with white spirit. Choose a darker colour for the veining, and paint on fine lines with an artists' brush; while these are still wet, smudge the lines gently with a cloth or feather. Varnish to protect the painted surface.

Tortoise-shelling

Apply a base coat of yellow oil-based paint thinned 3:1 with white spirit or turpentine. When this is dry, paint on a layer of varnish, tinted brown and thinned 2:1

varnish to white spirit or turpentine. Distress the varnish with an artists' brush, working diagonally. Apply dots of varnish between the marks, and add squiggles of burnt umber and black oil paint following the same diagonals. Smudge gently with a dry brush and protect the surface with varnish.

Antiquing

Antiquing is the process of artificially ageing a surface. On walls this can be achieved by applying a wash or glaze tinted with a small amount of raw or burnt umber, so that the ground colour is softened and deepened. An aged white can be made in the same way.

To age woodwork, apply a light wash or glaze and rub off the excess; then sand down the surface so that the grain shows up in contrast.

Woodgraining

1

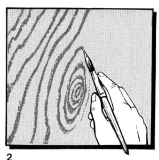

2

Woodgraining can be bold and decorative or it can restore a subtle suggestion of graininess. For a realistic effect, it is important to look at samples of the type of wood you wish to suggest and to practise copying its patterns of grain.

The basis of the technique is dragging. For the glaze, choose a colour slightly darker than the ground coat and drag with a dry brush to make parallel lines.

1 Distress the dragged surface while it is still wet by softening the lines with a dusting brush.

1

2

2 Draw the grain pattern on in chalk. Paint the grain in a deeper shade of glaze using an artists' brush. Print on 'knots', if desired, using cork or bunched blotting paper.

Remember that woodgraining is an effect that attempts to imitate nature, so avoid monotonous lines.

3

5

6

1 *Marbling decorates a hallway.*
2 *Rich tortoise-shelling*
3 *Bleaching, marbling and combing.*
4 *Aged walls decorated with painted cracks.*
5 *A combination of marbling and painted murals.*
6 *Supremely skilful trompe l'oeil.*

4

Distemper

One way to give walls a sense of depth and age is to paint them with distemper, which dries to give a soft, chalky finish. Distemper is no longer commercially available, but you can make your own. Bear in mind, however, that distemper is not compatible with modern paints: if you later decide you want to paint a distempered wall you will first have to strip it.

Recipe for Distemper

1 Mix decorators' glue according to the manufacturer's instructions. Leave to set – it should cool to a jelly.

2 Half-fill a small bucket with cold water and add a 3kg/11lb bag of whiting. The whiting should rise to the surface. Let it soak for an hour and then stir.

3 Reheat the glue until it is runny. Add it to the whiting mixture, stirring constantly. To tint, add powder-colour dissolved in cold water to the whiting mixture before you add the glue.

4 Use the distemper full-strength or, for a wash, diluted with water.

● An alternative to distemper, but which creates a similar effect, is thinned flat oil-based paint.

189

Stencilling

Stencilling is an extremely versatile technique and, with careful planning and a little practice, is quick and easy to do. Almost any surface, as long as it is not glossy or shiny, can be stencilled, including walls, floors, furniture and fabric.

A huge range of effects can be created, depending on the scale and design of the motif – from fresh and charming floral prints or traditional patterns to crisp, geometric designs. Stencilled borders or friezes can stand in for architectural detail where this is lacking; all-over stencilling adds a richness of pattern; handmade designs give interiors a personal touch.

Stencil Motifs
Pre-cut stencil kits are widely available and come in a variety of designs, but it is easy and satisfying to make your own. Inspiration can come from the patterns that already exist in the room – you can borrow motifs from curtain or upholstery fabric, repeat a detail of a cornice (crown moulding), or copy a pattern from a ceramic or rug. Geometric motifs are easier for the beginner, but with practice you can attain to simple freehand shapes.

After you have drawn out your design, experiment with different colour combinations, taking into account the colour of the background. Pin up colour sketches where you intend to stencil to assess how the tones work together.

Planning Patterns
The basic motif can be displayed on its own, as the central feature of a surface such as a table top or cupboard door, or it can be repeated in a continuous pattern, or in a line as a border or frieze. All of these applications require thorough planning to get the spacing right and you may need to make adjustments to the scale of the stencil for it to be effective.

Materials
The traditional method is to cut stencils from oiled stencil card, but using modern transparent acetate can make life easier. Because acetate is see-through, registration is much less necessary; also it can be wiped clean and keeps for longer. But film is more expensive than card and is sometimes fiddly to use.

There is a wide range of stencil paints available. Japan paints (oil-based) or acrylic paints (water-based) are the best, as they are very fast-drying, but emulsion (latex) is also a good choice for walls. Spray painting is a reasonable but inferior alternative to painting with a paint brush.

For furniture and floors use gloss or coloured wood stain, and then varnish to seal; for fabric use special fast-drying fabric paints.

Registration Marks
Because you will need to cut separate stencils for each colour, you must ensure that all of the overlays line up.

On acetate, it is a good idea to draw in the key elements of the rest of the design in dotted lines on each overlay, as an aid to registration. Alternatively, draw crosses at the four corners of each overlay. If you are using stencil card, lay the cut-outs over each other and punch through them with a nail to give a registration hole at each corner.

Making a Stencil
1 Draw or trace your design, then break down the pattern to incorporate bridges – uncut areas linking the openings to prevent the stencil from collapsing. Scale the pattern up or down if necessary, using either a photocopier or a grid system.
2 If using acetate, place the drawing under the film, secure with masking tape over the top. If using card, turn the drawing over and transfer to the card using carbon paper.
3 Cut out small areas before larger ones, so that you do not find yourself trying to cut fiddly details out of an

Equipment Checklist
- tracing paper for sketching or tracing outlines
- drawing paper or graph paper
- pencils, drawing pens, markers
- ruler, compass, setsquare (T-square), plumb line
- acetate or oiled stencil card
- cutting knife
- cutting mat
- masking tape
- stencil brushes
- stencil paint
- solvent
- varnish, if stencilling floor or furniture
- cleaning rags and paper towel
- old saucers or foil containers

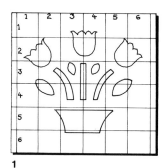

1

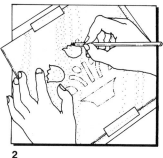

2

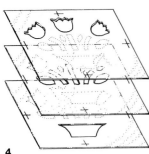

3

4

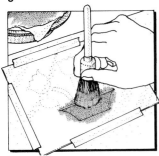

5

6

intolerably weakened stencil.
Use a scalpel or craft knife,
and cut towards you; for
curves, turn the stencil, not
the knife. Mistakes can be
repaired using transparent
adhesive tape.

4 Cut a separate stencil for
each colour. Using dotted
lines, sketch in the key
elements of the rest of the
design on each overlay. Make
registration marks at the
edges or corners.

5 Use paint sparingly to
prevent seepage. Work most
of the paint off onto dry paper
towel, then dab brush on
scrap paper until no blotches
appear and the brush is
almost dry.

6 Apply paint gradually,
working inward from the
outer edges. Use the brush
lightly in circular movements.
To check progress, gently lift
the stencil. Complete one
colour at a time and allow to
dry before proceeding.

Eliminating Bridges

To eliminate bridges, break
down the pattern into two or
more stencils which can be
superimposed to form a
complete design.

● Work as cleanly as
possible. Avoid getting paint
under the stencil or on your
hands. Drips can be mopped
up with tissue moistened
with solvent. Keep
background colour on hand
to touch up any mistakes.

Turning Corners

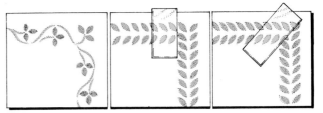

You can adapt a pattern so
that the corner appears as an
intentional part of the design.

The simplest method, if
you cannot adapt the pattern,
is to block the corner. Stop
where the inside edge of the
new border will go. Mask with
acetate what you have just
stencilled, then continue
stencilling at right angles.

Borders

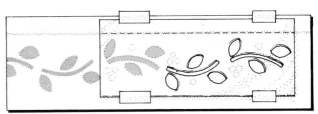

Using a spirit level
(carpenter's level), draw a
horizontal chalk line on the
wall. Make a corresponding
line on the stencil for
registration. Fix the stencil in
the right position with
masking tape while you apply
the colour.

To turn a corner, gently
bend the stencil round, using
acetate to mask off where it
meets the other wall.

For a professional result,
mitre the corner. Draw a
diagonal line into the corner.
Mask along the line on the
side at right angles to the one
that you are stencilling.
Stencil up to the line and
then, when the paint is dry,
move the mask to the other
side of the line and stencil
down the other side.

Fabric Stencilling

The best fabric for stencilling
is flat and even-weaved, such
as pure cotton; avoid fabric
with a pile, such as velvet or
knitted jersey. Wash and iron
the fabric first and then pin it
to a smooth surface. Apply
the paint through the stencil
to the straight grain of the
fabric, working in manageable
sections. Once dry, heat-seal
with a warm iron.

Painting a Child's Mural

Although mural painting sounds as if it must demand artistic expertise, if you take a careful step-by-step approach you will find that attractive and successful results are well within your reach. Very complex scenes, as well as *trompe l'oeil* – the height of decorative painting, aiming literally to 'deceive the eye' – do require great skill. But simpler figurative or geometric designs are easy to do and make particularly cheerful solutions for children's rooms.

Preparing the Surface
The wall should be in good condition: smooth, clean and nonabsorbent. Prepare by painting on an even base colour. Gloss does not make a suitable base for mural painting; emulsion (latex) is acceptable, but matt or midsheen oil-based paint is best.

Transferring the Design
The method shown here involves drawing a grid over the original picture, constructing to scale a larger grid on the wall, and then transferring the design square by square. The size of the grid's squares over those of your original illustration will depend on the complexity of the design. If it is very intricate, you will need a grid of 1cm/½in squares; if it is simple, the grid can have up to 5cm/2in squares.

An alternative method is to use a slide as your reference: project the image onto the wall and draw around the outlines. In either case, however, you will have to establish the horizontal and vertical outlines of the mural by using a plumb line and spirit level.

Materials
Emulsion (latex) paint or interior resin-based paint is the best choice for the beginner. You can use up leftovers from previous decorating jobs, sampler pots, and artists' colours for small areas and for tinting emulsion. You do not have to buy all the colours you need: basic shades can be mixed together to make intermediate tones. Remember to mix up enough for all the areas that are to be done in a particular colour – it is difficult to duplicate a shade if you have to remix.

Equipment Checklist
- drawing materials
- ruler and setsquare (T-square)
- chalk or charcoal
- plumb line and spirit level (carpenter's level)
- paint
- paint containers
- selection of brushes
- solvent
- stepladder, if necessary
- felt-tip pen for outlining
- clear matt polyurethane

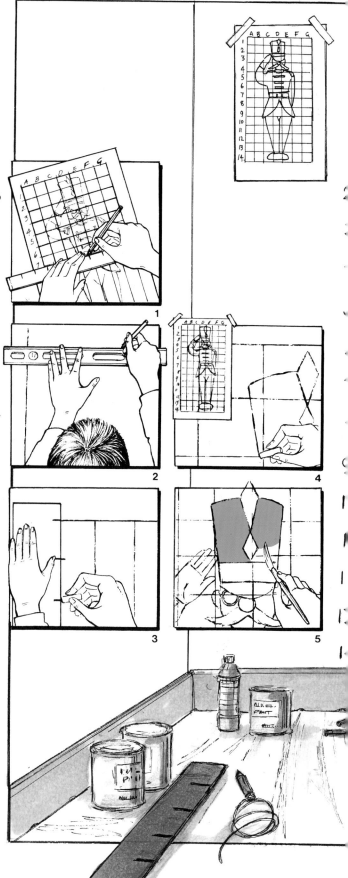

METHOD

1 Draw grid over original picture using ruler and setsquare. Label the grid with numbers and letters.

2 Transfer the outer lines onto the wall, using a plumb line for the verticals and a spirit level (carpenter's level) for the horizontals. Draw in lines with light-coloured chalk or charcoal.

3 Draw grid on wall, using a strip of card marked with grid squares. Use chalk or charcoal.

4 Mark the design on the wall, transferring it one square at a time from your design. Pin the original to the wall so you can refer to it constantly. Use a cloth to rub out incorrect lines.

5 Paint in areas of colour, working if possible from the top down. Complete larger areas first, one colour at a time, then paint details. Do not paint a second area adjoining a first until the paint on the first has dried. Some colours may need two coats. Highlights or special effects, such as stippling or shading, should be added last.

6 For a sharp crisp finish, outline in black, using a fine brush and ink or a felt-tip marker. Test the ink first to make sure it will not run when the varnish is applied.

7 Allow the mural to dry thoroughly, then wipe off the chalked grid lines using a damp cloth.

8 Seal with matt polyurethane varnish or, if you used emulsion (latex) paint, emulsion glaze.

● If you make a mistake, paint over the area with the background colour and leave it to dry. Then paint over again in the correct colour(s).

193

WALLCOVERINGS

As well as the many different paint effects, there are many other wall and ceiling coverings which you can use to create an interesting foundation for a decorative scheme. Wallpapers, paper-backed fabric and hessian (burlap), tiles, wood panelling and mirrors can all be applied relatively easily to a surface, adding a textural dimension often lacking in painted finishes.

WALLPAPERS

Printed Papers
The range of printed wallpapers is immense – not only in terms of colour and pattern but also in terms of cost, quality and practicability. In general, the cheaper papers tend to be thin and difficult to hang; also, they do not last long. Higher-quality papers are thicker and better-printed. At the extreme end of the market, there are very expensive hand-printed papers, including reproductions of antique designs printed from the original blocks.

Aside from plain white lining paper, which is designed to provide an even surface for decorating, the special attraction of wallpaper lies in the pattern. The range of designs available has enlarged considerably in recent years: it includes traditional varieties, such as Regency stripes and floral motifs, as well as cheerful figurative prints for children's rooms and sophisticated modern geometrics. Many papers are coordinated with fabrics and wall tiles and some are available with contrasting or complementary friezes.

All printed papers are treated to repel moisture and promote maintenance, but the degree of protection varies. 'Spongeable' papers can be wiped down; 'washable' papers, coated with plastic film, can be washed with water. Vinyls – wallpapers coated with thick plastic film – can actually be scrubbed; they are designed for use in kitchens and bathrooms.

Textured Papers
The chief advantage of textured papers is that they are useful for covering irregular surfaces. These relief papers are generally embossed with wood and pulp, and are designed to be painted. Other types include the once-fashionable flock paper with a cut-pile surface and relief simulations of panelling or plasterwork.

Other Paper-backed Coverings
Today you can obtain hessian (burlap), grasses and other natural fibres with paper backing, allowing you to hang them like ordinary wallpaper. Often in neutral shades, these provide a subtle textural interest but tend to be difficult to clean and not very robust.

Order of Papering a Room

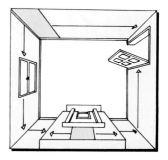

There is a correct order for papering a room if you are to disguise any slight overlaps which may occur. For papers with small or random patterns, it is usual to start in the corner adjacent to the window wall and work away from the source of natural light towards the door, so that overlaps do not cast shadows and are thus less immediately noticeable.

ESTIMATING THE NUMBER OF ROLLS

British Wallpaper

Wall Height	Distance Around Room (including doors and windows)												
	30ft 9.1m	34ft 10.4m	38ft 11.6m	42ft 12.8m	46ft 14.0m	50ft 15.2m	54ft 16.4m	58ft 17.7m	62ft 18.9m	66ft 20.1m	70ft 21.3m	74ft 22.6m	78ft 23.9m
8ft/2.45m	5	5	6	7	7	8	9	9	10	10	11	12	12
9ft/2.75m	6	6	7	7	8	9	9	10	10	11	12	12	13
10ft/3.05m	6	7	8	8	9	10	10	11	12	13	13	14	15

Calculations based on roll measuring 20½in × 34ft/52cm × 10.3m

American Wallpaper

Wall Height	Distance Around Room (including doors and windows)												
	32ft 9.7m	36ft 11.0m	40ft 12.2m	44ft 13.4m	48ft 14.6m	52ft 15.8m	56ft 17.1m	60ft 18.3m	64ft 19.5m	68ft 20.7m	72ft 21.9m	76ft 23.2m	80ft 24.4m
8ft/2.45m	8	9	10	11	12	13	14	15	16	17	18	19	20
9ft/2.75m	9	10	11	12	14	15	16	17	18	19	20	21	22
10ft/3.05m	10	11	12	14	15	16	17	19	20	21	22	23	25

Calculations based on roll measuring 18in (when trimmed) × 24ft/45.7cm × 7.3m

Wallpapers

1, 2 Metallic
   3 Borders
   4 Relief
   5 Flock
   6 Border
   7 Linen
   8 Flock
   9 Suedette
  10 Woodchip
  11 Leatherette
  12 Hessian (burlap)
  13 Silk
  14 Coarse woven
  15 Patterned
  16 Trompe l'oeil
  17 Moiré
  18 Patterned
  19 William Morris design
  20 Paint effects
  21 Victorian design
  22 Bamboo trellis
  23 Large floral
  24 Borders
  25 Small floral
  26 Festoons
  27 Bows
28, 29 Large floral
  30 Borders

Hanging Wallpaper

When you buy your wallpaper ensure that an extra roll with the same batch number will be available. Otherwise, if you need to buy more you may end up with a roll bearing a different batch number and the shades of colour may vary. Wallpaper should be hung on a sound, even, dry surface. Very poor surfaces may need replastering; alternatively, you may just have to line or cross-line with lining paper.

Establishing a Vertical

Once you have decided on a starting position, you need to establish a vertical so that the lengths of paper are correctly aligned.

Measure out from the corner of the wall a distance that is 1cm/½in less than the full width of the paper, and mark it top, middle and bottom.

Hang a plumb line from the top of the wall aligning with the mark nearest the corner and mark along it at intervals. Join up the marks using a straightedge. This pencilled line is the vertical you will use for aligning the first length of paper. The same process must be repeated each time a corner is turned.

Pasting

Some wallpapers are available pre-pasted, but if you are pasting the paper yourself you will need a trestle table or a folding pasting table on which to lay out lengths of paper. To avoid getting paste on the table and the consequent risk of spoiling the next length of paper, some decorators let the paper overhang the table by 2cm/1in, but it can be difficult to paste edges if they have no support. Keep a clean sponge and water on hand, and wipe away any paste which does get onto the table.

Most papers need to be left for a while to allow the paste to soak in. Papers with definite patterns should be pasted and hung one length at a time, so that soaking times do not vary – a length left for too long will stretch irregularly and may not match the previous one.

Materials and Equipment

- rolls of wallpaper: buy enough for the job, and record the batch number
- wallpaper paste, as recommended by the manufacturer
- pasting table
- plumb line and bob
- pencil
- straightedge
- stepladder
- paperhanging shears
- sharp-pointed scissors for trimming
- pasting brush and bucket
- paperhanging brush
- sponge

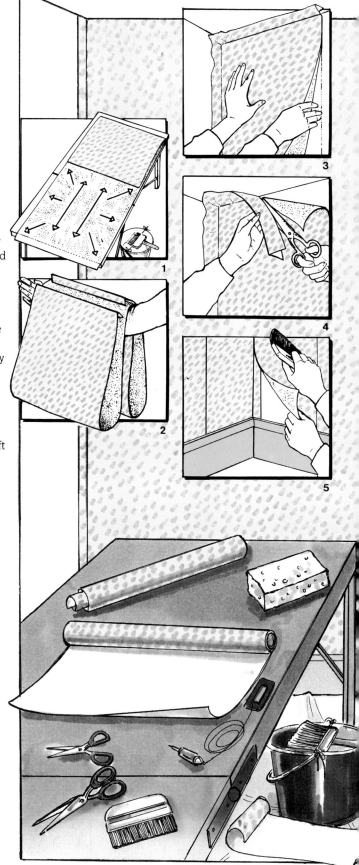

METHOD

1 Apply paste down centre and work outwards. Fold pasted end in and paste second half.

2 Fold paper ends-to-middle and carry to the wall draped over your arm. Turn over ends of paper.

3 Position first length against pencilled vertical, overlapping the ceiling by 5cm/2in and running to about 1cm/½in from the adjacent wall. Brush from the centre out.

4 Score along the ceiling line with the back of the scissors, peel back paper and cut along crease. Brush paper back in place and repeat at skirting level.

5 To turn an internal corner, measure the distance to the corner at the top, middle and bottom of the wall, adding 1cm/½in to the widest distance to allow for overlap. Cut and paste in position. Measure width of offcut from corner and mark vertically this distance from the corner onto the side wall. Paste the offcut, aligning the uncut edge with the vertical line so that the cut edge covers the overlap.

6 To turn an external corner, measure the distance to the corner at the top, middle and bottom, adding 2.5cm/1in to the widest distance to allow for turn. Paste in position but do not brush down. Mark a vertical (using a plumb line) 2.5cm/1in less than the width of the remaining piece on the adjacent wall. Hang offcut to vertical line, and brush overlap down.

7 To paper around a doorway, cut away any excess before pasting and make a diagonal cut into the corners of the door frame. Score around the door frame, peel the paper back and trim. Brush in towards the angle.

197

Wallpapering Ceilings and Details

Papering a Ceiling

The basic method is the same as that for papering walls. Work away from the light, marking a line across the ceiling the width of the paper, less 1cm/½in for overlap. Cut a length of paper, allowing 10cm/4in excess (5cm/2in at each end). Paste and loop the paper into accordion-like folds. Position the paper according to the line and brush down from one end, supporting the folds with a roll of wallpaper. Score and trim overlaps.

Papering a ceiling is very difficult for a beginner working alone. It is far better to get a helper to support the paper while you work.

Papering Around a Switch

To paper around a flush plate, first make sure you turn the electricity off at the mains supply or fuse box. Hang the paper down to the switch and cut diagonally from the middle to each corner.

Partially unscrew the switch plate and pull away from the wall. Trim off excess paper, leaving 3–4mm/⅛in to brush behind the plate. Screw the plate back in place and restore electricity.

To paper around a circular switch make star-shaped cuts out to the edge of the switch, score around the edge and trim off the surplus paper. This method can also be used to paper around ceiling roses (medallions).

● Try to catch bubbles early on by looking sideways at each length before positioning the next piece. Peel the paper back to the bubble and brush out. If the paste has dried, use a sharp knife to cut a cross through the bubble. Peel back the four flaps and paste.

Papering an Archway

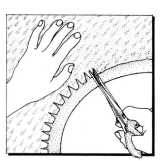

Paper the facing wall first, allowing an extra 2.5cm/1in of paper around the inside of the arch. Cut v-shaped pieces out of this hem so that you are left with a 'saw-tooth' effect. Turn in the 'teeth' so that they lie flat on the inside of the arch. Then measure the width of the arch and cut two lengths of paper, one to run up each side so that they meet at the centre top.

SAFETY Always turn the electricity off at the mains (or fusebox) before unscrewing light switches or sockets (outlets). Never brush metallic or foil wallcoverings behind switches or sockets.

Fitting Around a Fireplace

Cut off excess paper. Make a diagonal cut to the corner and score a line along the top. Snip into the paper to fit around mouldings. Peel back the paper and cut along the scored lines.

Patching Damaged Paper

Tear off the damaged paper, ensuring that the paper left around the hole is firmly stuck down. Select a piece of matching paper; if the paper has a pattern, hold it over the hole and adjust its position until the pattern fits into place. Tear a patch roughly to size, and peel off a narrow 3mm/¹⁄₁₀in strip from the back around the edges. Paste in place, aligning the pattern.

1 *Wallpaper in a muted stripe makes a sympathetic background for a period room. The paper is continued below the dado rail, and care has been taken to match the stripes exactly.*

Borders and Friezes

Borders and friezes can be applied to any sound surface (not over heavily embossed paper). Use a pencil line as a guide for position and cut a length of border to fit across the entire length of wall. Paste the border and loop it up so that it is easier for you to position correctly. Brush out, letting out the loops as you work along.

Corners – for example, around a door or window frame – should be mitred. Paste the borders in place, overlapping the ends where they meet, and then draw a diagonal line across the corner, using a straightedge. Cut along the line, through both layers, using a sharp knife. Remove the excess pieces and smooth the others back into place.

● Mark the exact position of screw holes by inserting a matchstick or toothpick in each, leaving 0.5cm/¼in protruding. This will pierce the paper as it is brushed on.

Matching Patterns

Wallpapers with definite patterns are either 'straight' (aligned horizontally) or 'drop' (aligned diagonally). Because lengths of paper are laid side by side across the wall (butt-jointed) and not overlapped, the patterns must match along each length of paper.

Cut the first length of paper about 10cm/4in longer than the depth of the wall; this allows a margin of 5cm/2in at both top and bottom for trimming. Before cutting the second length, match the pattern with the first, again allowing a 10cm/4in excess. Number each length consecutively as it is cut and mark which end is the top.

To avoid wastage when cutting 'drop' patterns, it may be necessary to cut alternately from two rolls at once. Even so, wastage is unavoidable.

Special Effects

You can create your own wallpaper by using thick writing paper, marbled paper or even photocopies of interesting prints to line a wall. This is best attempted on a small area and the surface should be sealed with a coat of polyurethane (which will yellow with age). An alternative is to stencil your own design on plain wallpaper and seal.

Large Patterns

If the paper has a large pattern, it should be centred on a focal point, such as a chimney breast, or on a wall which is the focus of attention in the room.

From the starting point, work in sequence around the room. Whichever way you go, plan to finish in the least important corner or at a doorway, since it will almost certainly be impossible to match the pattern on the last length. If your wallpaper has a large pattern, ensure that the first length features a complete motif near the top of the wall so that broken motifs are near the floor.

2 Borders lend distinction to a papered room, particularly if the paper has been applied to the ceiling as well as the walls. Here, a paper with a tiny sprig motif has been enhanced by a bold border fixed around the window and defining the bath alcove.

Tiling and Cladding

A variety of hard materials can be used to cover walls and other built-in surfaces. Many of these improve insulation and most are easy to maintain as well as being highly decorative.

Ceramic Tiles

The most popular form of hard wallcovering, ceramic tiles are available today in a huge range of colours, patterns, finishes and sizes, from expensive handmade originals to mass-produced types. Cost varies accordingly.

Tiles are generally glazed, but unglazed and textured varieties are available, too. Most tiles have squared or bevelled edges, but you can buy them with one or two rounded sides for use as edging; also, special coping tiles are made for covering joints (for example, around a bathtub). Some tiles incorporate spacing lugs (pegs) to ensure the joint lines between all the tiles are uniform in thickness.

Tiles are ideal for bathrooms or kitchens, or wherever surfaces need to be wiped down regularly. All tiles are fixed with ceramic tile adhesive and are easy to hang. But, although they have tremendous practical advantages, there is no reason why tiles should look utilitarian, or be used purely for utilitarian purposes.

Manufacturers produce tiles as an element of an entire decorative range, so that you can coordinate their motifs with curtain fabrics and/or wallpaper, or simply achieve a precise colour match.

Plain tiled walls can be enlivened by a contrasting or patterned border, by cheerful coloured grouting, or by insetting occasional handmade or antique tiles. Simple patterns can be created by alternating colours or by laying tiles in a diagonal or herringbone design.

Mirrors

Mirror tiles and sheets of mirror are both effective ways of maximizing light and space in a small area such as a bathroom. Mirror tiles are cheaper and easier to install than sheets of mirror. Both require a flat surface; a large expanse of mirror may need to be mounted professionally. And both need to be kept clean to look their best.

Wood Panelling

This is a traditional way of adding richness and warmth to a room. Today the most common type is tongue-and-groove panelling, mounted on battens (furring strips). As well as its textural qualities, wood is a good insulator and is long-lasting, but it is not a cheap way of covering a wall. However, panelling can be very effective in limited

applications – for example, up to half-height as a dado (wainscot), or to cover the side of a bath. It can also be varnished, stained or painted.

A less expensive way of achieving a similar effect can be gained by using manufactured boards, such as plywood, blockboard or hardboard (masonite) faced with veneer. Cork, too, can be used as a wall covering, although it does not wear as well as wood. Available in rolls or tiles, it can be protected by coating with polyurethane varnish. Some cork tiles are supplied with a protective coating already applied to their surface for greater durability.

Preparation for Tiling

Before you start, make sure all the surfaces are sound, level and dry. Small cracks and irregularities can be filled with a commercially available filler; a really bad surface will need replastering or lining with plasterboard (drywall). If the walls are papered, you will have to strip them; a painted finish can be simply sanded down to give a key.

Tiles can easily be laid over existing tiles as long as these are sound and firmly fixed.

Bathroom treatments *red and white border (1); 'crazy' tiling inset with mirror (2); diagonal pattern in white (3); redwood panelling (4).*

Wall Tiles and Cladding

1 *Glazed mosaic*
2 *Hand-pressed terracotta*
3 *Glazed Mexican*
4 *Dutch style*
5 *Wood-effect laminate*
6 *Glazed Mexican*
7 *Relief border*
8 *High glaze*
9 *Paint effect laminate*
10 *Dutch style*
11 *Patterned*
12 *Hand-pressed terracotta*
13 *Glazed Mexican*
14, 15 *Checkerboard with floral border*
16 *Glazed relief with border*
17 *Tongue-and-groove pine cladding*
18 *Relief border*
19 *Cork*
20 *Glazed terracotta*
21 *Glazed mosaic*
22 *Glazed Mexican*
23 *Relief pattern*

Tiling a Bathroom

Tiling is a particularly good solution for bathroom surfaces. However, most bathrooms present a number of challenges such as recesses, sills, ledges and pipework. The first step is to decide where you want to tile. In a small room, it often looks better to extend the tiling all the way up to the wall rather than stop at half or three-quarter height.

Making a Tile Gauge
The next step is to plan the position of the tiles. The best way to start is to make a tile gauge: mark tile-widths along a length of wooden batten and use this to judge where tiles are going to have to be cut to fit around a window, sink or other obstruction. Try to avoid gaps that are less than half a tile wide.

Starting Position
Using a spirit level, establish a horizontal line no more than one tile width up from the floor, and temporarily nail a wooden batten below it. Work out how many tiles will fit along the wall, leaving large enough gaps at either end. Using a plumb line, draw a vertical line down the wall to mark where the first whole tile will go. Fix the whole tiles first; when the adhesive has dried, the gaps can be filled with cut pieces.

Materials and Equipment
- tiles – most straight-edged, some with rounded edges
- combined adhesive and grout (water-resistant if necessary)
- notched spreader or trowel for applying adhesive
- tile gauge, made from length of wooden batten
- battens (furring strips)
- pencil, metal rule and spirit level (carpenter's level)
- spacers, if tiles are not bevelled or have no spacing lugs (pegs)
- pincer-action tile cutter
- tile saw
- pincers or pliers
- tile file, sandpaper or carborundum stone
- grout, coloured if desired
- squeegee or sponge
- rubber latex sealant

METHOD
1 Use a small trowel to apply adhesive. Work at an angle of about 45 degrees and in patches 1m/3ft square. Using a notched spreader pull the adhesive into ridges to ensure good suction. Do not cover your pencilled line. Place the bottom edge of the tile against the wooden batten and lower into place ensuring that its vertical edge is aligned with the vertical line marked on the wall. Press firmly. Position next tile. If tiles have no lugs, insert spacers. Finish one horizontal row before starting on the next. When the whole area of adhesive is covered, check straightness with a spirit level. Sponge off excess adhesive. Allow to dry.

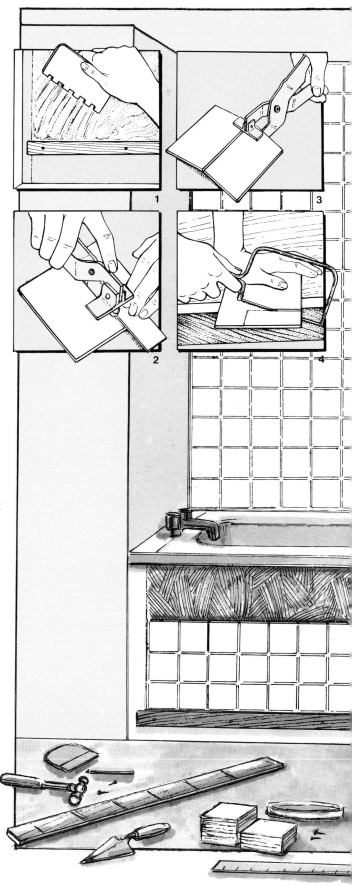

5

6

7

2 To fill gaps, measure the area to be filled with a metal rule. Draw line on tile to mark where it should be cut, and score through glaze using the wheel on a pincer-action cutter.

3 Break the tiles using the pincer-action cutter. When handles are brought together over the scored mark, the tile breaks cleanly.

4 To cut awkward shapes, score a line deeply through the glaze. Then cut the tile with a tile saw. Work slowly and gently. Alternatively, use pliers or pincers to 'nibble' the shape away bit by bit.

5 Smooth the rough edge of a cut tile with a suitable file held at an angle of 45 degrees. Work downwards, away from the glaze. Alternatively, use a small carborundum stone.

6 For joints between surfaces, such as at ledges or sills, fix tiles on vertical surfaces first and then lay tiles with rounded edges along the horizontal surface to create a finished joint. Many tiles have squared, glazed edges which form an equally finished joint. Special edging strips (plastic beading, or moulding) are also available.

7 Allow 12 hours for adhesive to dry before removing the batten and tiling the bottom row. Allow a further 24 hours before removing the spacers and beginning to grout. Mix grout with water to a creamy consistency. Rub into joints using a squeegee or damp sponge and wipe off surplus with a damp cloth. For a really professional look, run a rounded stick along the grout lines to point up.

Tiling Details

Cutting a Hole in a Tile

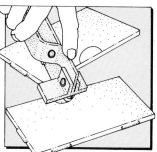

To accommodate a pipe or similar obstacle, first measure the hole and make a pattern, or template, out of thick cardboard. Use this pattern to score the circle on the tile, and then score a straight line to bisect it. Snap the tile in half and cut out each semicircle with a tile saw or tile cutters.

Fixing Sheets of Mosaic

Tiny squares of mosaic or mirror tiles are available in sheet form, with a paper backing. These are easy to fix – each tile comes with its own pad of adhesive already applied and grouting is not required. You must ensure, however, that the wall surface is even and flat. If necessary, the wall should be lined with a 1cm/½in-thick sheet of plywood or chipboard (particleboard) screwed in the right position.

2 *Fragments of broken tiles, both plain and patterned, set randomly in a crazy border, make an original design between bands of deep blue hand-glazed tiles.*

1 *Brilliant white grouting lines make an effective contrast to the deep green tiles on the work surface. Different tiles, with a softer, Provencal-style pattern, have been chosen for the wall area below the kitchen cabinets. Tiling is a particularly practical choice for kitchen surfaces.*

Tiling a Recess

To tile a window recess or a ledge around a bathtub, lay the tiles on the horizontal surface first before you tile the sides and top. Plan the tiling so that the cut tiles are at the rear and the whole tiles are at the front. Use tiles with glazed edges for a border.

Grouting Effects

You can make a feature of grouting by adding dye either to grout powder or to ready-mixed grout. To change the colour of existing grouting, make sure the lines are clean and dry and follow the manufacturer's instructions.

Cladding

Wood Panelling

The most popular form of wood panelling is tongue-and-groove, which is usually fixed to battens (furring strips) nailed to the wall. Boards can be laid horizontally or vertically, depending on the look you want to create. Note that you can never panel over damp walls.

Store the boards for a few days in the room where they will be used to allow their moisture content to adjust. Boards not left to adjust properly could shrink and pull apart after fitting. Panelling should be stopped slightly short of the ceiling to allow airflow and expansion.

3 *Pine panelling encloses a tiny lavatory; the warmth and texture of the surface contrasts with the polished brass fixtures.*

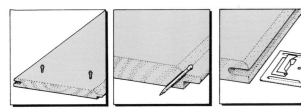

Fixing Methods

There are three basic ways of fixing boards to battens (furring strips). The simplest is face-nailing, where nails are driven through the face of the board. The nail head can be sunk with a nail punch and the hole filled, or it can be left flush with the surface.

Secret-nailing takes longer but the result is invisible. The nail is hammered diagonally through the tongue of the board and is covered when the groove of the next board slots into place.

There are also special metal clips which can be used to fix boards. These fit onto the groove of a board and are nailed to the batten.

To fix the first board, you will need a starting clip. Nail this into the corner and then cut off the groove of the first board and slide the end onto the spikes of the clip.

Fixing the Panels

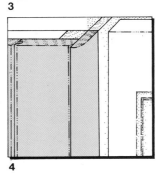

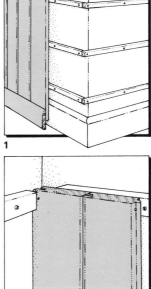

1 Battens should run at right angles to the direction of the boards. They should be fixed directly to the wall using masonry nails or screws and wall plugs, spacing the battens by about 0.5m/20in. The new panelling can then be nailed on, with a new skirting board (baseboard) fitted at the bottom.

2 The method of fixing shown here is secret-nailing. Start by butting a groove end into the corner. Then nail at an angle through the tongue. Tap the groove of the next board over the tongue, protecting with an offcut if necessary.

3 For internal or external corners, the tongued edge of the last board is cut off to butt against or overlap the grooved end of the next board. For a professional look, the corner can be finished off with a decorative moulding to hide the nails.

4 Remove architraves or window frames and add battens around the opening, leaving a margin so that a strip of moulding can be applied to cover the battens and the edge of the end board to finish.

Light switches can be framed in the same way. Alternatively, employ an electrician to bring them out flush with the panelling by putting packing behind the plate covering. Do not attempt this yourself.

205

Fabric Finishes

Fabric-lined rooms are luxurious. There are paper-backed materials, which are applied like wallpaper, but more excitingly fabrics can be draped, gathered or shirred to create a soft, intimate atmosphere. Alternatively you can stretch fabric over wooden battens to give an upholstered look. All of these effects are particularly good at disguising poor surfaces and correcting proportional defects in a room.

Although covering walls in fabric is an extravagant way of using material, you do not

1 *In this bedroom, a simple wooden frame has been constructed and covered in shirred fabric to give the impression of a four-poster bed.*

need to opt for the most expensive. Inexpensive lightweight cottons, such as muslin or cheesecloth, are ideal for shirring or gathering.

Simple Drapery
Lengths of material draped over poles or rods can make decorative frames for beds, alcoves, mirrors, windows and doors.

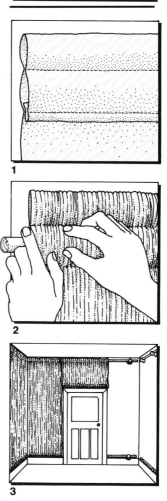
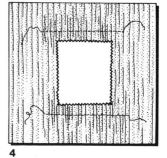

Gathered Wall Coverings
Choose a fabric which is light enough to gather up easily. Calculate the amount required by first measuring the height and width of the wall. Allow 1½–2 times the width for gathering, and add 10cm/4in to the height for hems. Then divide the fabric width (less selvedges) into the total width and multiply the number of widths by the total height to find the length of fabric you require.

1 Make casings at the top and bottom of each fabric length. Fold 5cm/2in of fabric over to the wrong side and machine stitch 2.5cm/1in below the fold. Then turn the hem under and machine-stitch in position.

2 Gather fabric by inserting rod, dowel or curtain wire into the casings at top and bottom. Rods, dowels or wires should extend to the full width of the area. Fix rods or dowels to wall with wardrobe (closet) or curtain rod brackets; wires can be tacked in position.

3 Short panels may be required over doors and around windows.

4 To hang fabric over an obstacle – such as a light switch – first mark the area and cut to within 1cm/½in. Then trim the edges and work a row of gathering stitches top and bottom. Unscrew the switch plate, pull up gathers to fit and fix plate back.

Making a Tented Ceiling

This method of tenting is suitable for square or nearly square rooms.

1 Decide where to position the tenting – level with a door frame, window frame or picture rail, for example. Draw a line around the room at this point and fix wooden battens at the required height. Mark the central point of the ceiling with a dot.

2 Make a paper pattern by cutting out a large triangle, with a base measuring the distance between two corners and two equal sides which are the distance between the central dot and a corner. Cut the triangle in half and insert a rectangular piece between the two halves. The rectangular piece should be the width of the base of each half triangle.

Cut out four fabric pieces according to the pattern, adding seam allowances.

3 Stitch pieces together. Press seams open and finish off, for example, by pinking. Make a casing around the central opening, insert drawstring and pull tight. Stitch two rows of gathering around the perimeter and pleat up fabric until it is the width of the battens. Suspend tenting from cup hook securely screwed into a ceiling joist at the central point. Fix the perimeter to battens and trim with braid or ribbon to finish.

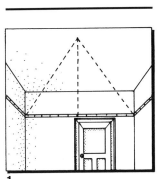

1

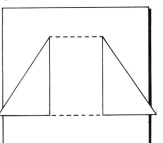

2

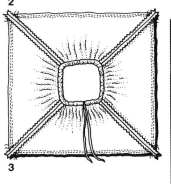

3

2 *Lined furnishing fabric has been fixed and draped to create a dramatic headboard for this bed. A similar effect can be used behind sofas positioned against walls.*

Joining Fabric Wall Coverings

Some fabrics, such as hessian (burlap), are available paper-backed. They can be hung and butt-jointed like wallpaper. Unbacked 'furnishing' hessian can be stuck by applying wallpaper paste to the wall. To join, overlap edges by about 2.5cm/1in then cut through the double thickness, down the whole length, using a sharp craft knife or scalpel held against a metal straightedge. Peel back both strips and remove the excess. Smooth back into place with a brush.

SAFETY Always turn the electricity off at the mains (or fuse box) before unscrewing light fittings.

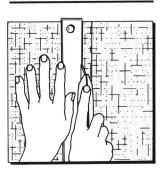

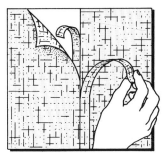

Covering Walls with Fabric

Although fabric can be stuck directly to walls (paste should be applied to the wall, not the fabric), the result can look flat. For a softer, more upholstered effect, fabric should be fixed by stretching it over a framework of wooden battens to provide an even surface. For a really professional finish line the walls first with a layer of polyester wadding (batting) stapled in position.

Calculating Fabric Quantities

Measure the height and width of the area you want to cover. Divide the total width by the width of the fabric (less selvedges) and multiply by the height, plus 5cm/2in.

Plain or randomly patterned fabrics are easiest to work with. Fabrics with definite patterns need to be matched across the wall, and so to get them right you will have to accept that there will be more wastage.

Positioning Wooden Battens

Horizontal battens will be needed at the top and bottom of the wall; vertical ones should be spaced evenly, taking into account windows, doors and other obstacles. If you intend to hang pictures or mirrors on the finished walls, establish where they will go and fix the battens in these places.

Trimming

Fabric can be fixed so that the joins between panels are invisible. But alternatively you can also make a feature of the joins, by covering the staples with contrasting or coordinating trim. Ribbon, braid or fabric-covered strips will give a smart, tailored appearance and introduce graphic interest to a room lacking architectural detail.

Fabric-fixing System

As an alternative to using wooden battens there is a product which enables fabric to be clipped in position without stapling or gluing. This consists of metal or plastic track which you mount around the wall. Previously seamed fabric is stretched and gripped in place by the track. This system enables fabric to be taken down easily for cleaning.

Materials and Equipment

- fabric, cut in lengths
- polyester wadding (batting), if desired
- wooden battens
- screwdriver
- countersunk screws
- hammer
- tacks
- staple gun and staples
- pencil
- straightedge
- braid, ribbon or other trim
- cardboard strips for invisible joins, if desired
- glue

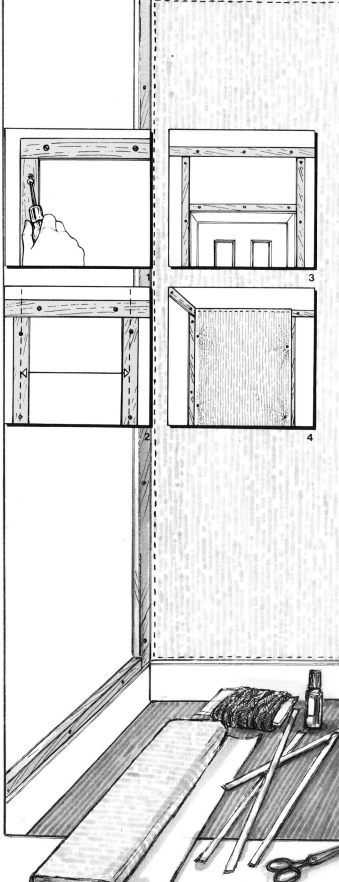

METHOD

1 Fix horizontal wooden battens first. The bottom batten can be fixed just above the floor or skirting board (baseboard). Screw in place with countersunk screws.

2 Space vertical battens one fabric width apart, less selvedges (see arrow). Pencil lines on wall where the fabric joins will go and centre battens on these lines.

3 Frame obstacles such as doorways, windows, switches and sockets (outlets). The fabric will be stapled to the outer edge of the battens.

4 Position first fabric panel and tack temporarily, driving tacks in halfway. Staple top edge. Pull fabric taut and staple bottom, then sides, removing tacks.

5 Make invisible joins by placing the second panel wrong-side up over the first. Insert a thin cardboard strip the length of the panel and staple in position.

6 Pull the panel to right side, leaving 2.5cm/1in turned over.

7 Finish off by covering bare staples with braid, ribbon or fabric strips glued in place.

FLOORS

Always on view and taking up a large proportion of the surface area in any room, the floor has a great impact on the decorative scheme in terms of colour, texture, pattern and style. But a floor must also fulfil certain practical requirements – requirements that vary from room to room and household to household. It may be required to wear well; be warm, safe or non-slip; be easy to maintain, resilient or sound- or heat-insulating. In addition to these considerations, new floors and floor coverings represent a large investment of either time or money or, usually, both. Whatever you choose may well have to outlast several changes of the rest of the room's decorative treatments.

From wall-to-wall carpeting to quarry tiles, wood strip to sheet vinyl, there is a great variety of types and styles of floor covering from which to choose. Careful assessment and sound research is necessary if you are to find the solution that suits your tastes and needs.

Combinations of different types of floor surface can be very effective: coir matting with kelims; slate with stone; polished floorboards with area rugs. And, because of the practical demands of different areas, it is unlikely that you will want to extend the same type of flooring throughout your home. For these reasons it is important not to consider each room in isolation: the view from area to area and details such as the junctions between different floor coverings will contribute to the success of the overall result.

WOOD FLOORS

A wood floor is a classic surface that wears well, improves with age and complements modern as well as period decoration. Costs vary: renovating existing floorboards is one of the cheapest flooring solutions; installing new parquet can be expensive.

Wood floors come in different forms: boards (of varying widths), ready-made strip or parquet, mosaic tiles or panels, and blocks. Many types of wood, both hardwoods and softwoods, are suitable; a local supplier can advise on different varieties. Also sheets or boards of manmade woods, such as hardboard (masonite), chipboard (particleboard) and plywood, can be used to create stylish and economical floors.

Boards

Existing floorboards can be prepared and sanded, and then finished off by sealing, bleaching or painting.

To install a new wood floor, it is important to select the right type and quality. Common varieties include pine, beech, mahogany, oak, walnut, maple and elm, but there are other, more exotic, species as well. Different widths of board are available, depending on the type.

Wood for flooring must be properly dried and seasoned. The moisture content should suit the conditions of the room where the boards will be laid (6–8 per cent moisture content if there is underfloor heating; 10–14 per cent if there is central heating), as otherwise shrinking or swelling may occur. Ideally, wood should be left unwrapped in the room where it is going to be fitted for at least two days.

When laying a new floor, you must establish first where cables and pipes run to avoid nailing through them. Boards can be nailed to joists; tongue-and-groove boards can be slotted together and secret-nailed to joists or to a wooden subfloor.

Ready-made Wood Floors

Manufactured wood floors are available in different woods – usually either in a hardwood or in a softwood with a hardwood veneer – and in different colours. They can be laid in simple patterns. Most are presealed and designed to interlock.

Strip or parquet floors should be laid on level plywood or hardboard (masonite) subfloors; wood block and mosaic on concrete screed, ply or chipboard (particleboard). Fixing is either by adhesive or by interlocking and secret-nailing.

Painting Floorboards

If floorboards are not attractive enough simply to be sealed, you can paint them. Make sure the surface is dry and clean, apply several coats of undercoat to act as a primer, and then apply a topcoat of oil-based gloss, eggshell or special floor paint. Deck or marine paint can also be used, and is very durable, but it is hard to apply and takes a long time to dry. In addition, it is available only in a limited range of colours.

Simple patterns can be created by alternating colours, by stencilling a border, or by scoring a design into the floor with a knife so that colours do not run.

Manufactured Boards

Although these cheap, manufactured boards are essentially designed to make an even surface for wood, tiles or other covering, they can also be used in their own right. They are not particularly resilient, however, and are badly affected by water.

Hardboard (masonite) can be painted or sealed to promote durability. Lay it smooth side up, beginning at the mid-point of the room, and fit a border around the edges to finish.

Tongue-and-groove chipboard (particleboard) can be fixed with adhesive and secured with nails around the edges of the room.

Plywood is available in tongue-and-groove boards or in squares, and can be painted, stained, or varnished to a high gloss.

Finishes

Apart from presealed manufactured floors, all new and renovated wood must be treated in some way to prevent the surface from degrading. The simplest method is to seal it with several coats of transparent wood sealer – but bear in mind that polyurethane tends to yellow with age. An alternative is to apply several layers of wax polish.

To lighten dark floors you can bleach wood using a solution of household bleach and water. Rinse off well. A similar 'limed' effect can be created by using a whitewash or white oil-based paint.

Floors can also be stained. As well as natural colours, a wide variety of bright stains is available today. Work quickly, using a soft cloth to rub the stain into the grain.

1 *A gleaming polished wood floor.*
2 *Duck-egg blue floorboards.*
3 *Trompe l'oeil oriental rug painted on a wooden floor plays a visual trick.*

Liming Floorboards

For liming, you can use special limed wax, white paint thinned with white spirit or turpentine, or gesso; mix the gesso so that it is reasonably runny. You will need a supply of clean, dry cloths. Limed boards should be sealed with a two-part varnish for durability.

1 Paint the gesso along the length of the board, working 90cm/3ft at a time. Work board-by-board to avoid unsightly lines.
2 Wipe the paint off with a clean rag, pulling strokes along the length of the board and leaving paint in the cracks. Leave to dry.

1

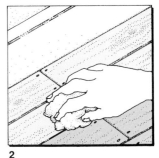

2

Laying Wooden Mosaic Tiles

Wooden mosaic tiles are manufactured panels made up of blocks of wood in a basket weave pattern. Solid or veneered, they are designed to be easy for the amateur to lay.

After you have bought the tiles, unwrap them and leave them for at least two days in the room where you plan to lay them. This allows the wood to 'condition', or adjust to the temperature and humidity of the room.

Mosaic tiles can be laid in any room – they are designed to be multi-purpose – but it is essential that the surface is properly prepared: it must be clean, dry and level. For best results on floorboards, cover them with hardboard (masonite).

Most mosaic tiles are already sanded and sealed. If you buy unfinished tiles, sand them after laying. After 1 or 2 weeks, apply three or more coats of the appropriate sealant to protect.

Establishing a Starting Point
Tiles are laid from the mid-point outward, so the first task is to find the central point of the room. Stretch a chalked string from the mid-points of two opposite walls and snap it to transfer a chalked line to the floor.

Repeat this with the other two opposite walls, and you have established the central point of the room – the point

where the two lines cross. Dry lay the first tile here, and then dry lay further tiles along each chalk line until you reach the edges.

If there is a small gap (less than half the width of a tile) left at the margin, adjust the starting point. Remember to leave a margin of 1cm/½in around the perimeter of the room as an expansion gap.

● It is advisable to have a bowl of warm water and a rag to hand, so you can clean off adhesive that gets on the tiles or on your hands.
● Keep any extra tiles. In time, some of the floor tiles may become damaged and it might be necessary to replace them. This can be done relatively easily by cutting around the damaged tiles and lifting them using a chisel. Scrape off any adhesive from the hole and glue new tiles in position.

Materials and Equipment
● mosaic tiles
● adhesive
● notched spreader
● string and chalk
● wooden batten
● trimming knife
● tenon saw
● cardboard
● hammer and panel pins (brads)
● wood moulding or cork strips
● sander, if necessary
● sealant, if necessary

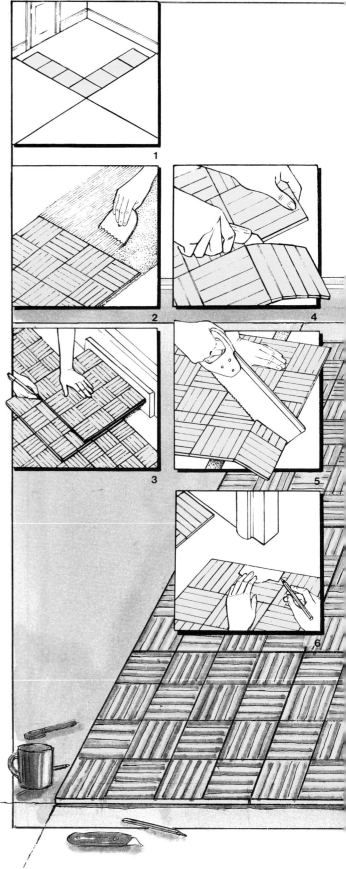

METHOD

1 Establish a starting point by using chalked lines as guides (see main text). Dry lay tiles.

2 Using a trowel or notched spreader, apply adhesive to the floor and lay tiles from centre outwards.

3 To fill gaps, place a whole tile squarely over the last one in the row. Then place another tile over the top, butting it up against a 1cm/½in wooden batten (to allow for the expansion gap) held against the skirting board (baseboard). Using the opposite edge of this top tile as your guide, mark a cutting line on the central tile of the 'sandwich'.

4 Try to arrange the tiles so that at least some trimming is along the edges of the 'fingers' of the wood. This means you have only to cut through the backing with a trimming knife.

5 When you have to cut through the wood, use a tenon saw and cut face upwards.

6 To fit around a doorway, cut away part of the architrave and slide a complete tile underneath. Otherwise make a template or pattern out of cardboard and transfer the shape onto the tile. Cut with a padsaw (keyhole saw).

7 To fit tiles around a pipe, cut through the backing to separate the fingers of wood that will be affected. Mark the shape on cardboard and cut out.

8 The expansion gap is a margin of about 1cm/½in around the perimeter of the room which gives the wood space to expand. It can be covered by nailing wooden mouldings to the skirting board with panel pins. Mitre the joins at the corners.

9 Alternatively, fill the gap with cork strip. Secure with adhesive.

213

Sheet Flooring

Manmade materials such as vinyl, rubber and linoleum are available in sheets up to 4m (13ft) in width and also in tile form. The particular advantage of sheet flooring is that a large area can be laid with the minimum of seams. Sheet flooring is useful also in small areas such as bathrooms where you may have to cut difficult shapes.

Vinyl
Vinyl – polyvinyl chloride (PVC) – is waterproof and resistant to chemicals. Quality varies: there are cheap thin types which can be cold and hard, as well as more expensive warmer cushioned vinyls which include a higher percentage of PVC. Vinyl comes in a wide range of colours, patterns and textures. There are modern, clean-looking geometric designs, heavier-weight industrial types flecked with quartz crystals, and simulations of tiles or natural materials with relief surfaces.

Linoleum
Slightly thicker than vinyl, linoleum is strong and similarly resistant to chemicals. It consists of a baked compound of natural materials pressed onto a jute, hessian (burlap) or fibreglass backing sheet.

Linoleum makes a tough flooring for kitchens, bathrooms and hallways. It is available in a range of colours and patterns, including marbled or stippled effects. It is also easy to cut, so it can be used to make original floor designs. Shapes can be cut from a contrasting linoleum and inlaid to define areas.

Rubber
'Borrowed' from industry, rubber flooring has a utilitarian, 'hi-tech' look that suits modern interiors. It is very tough: non-slip, soundproof and resistant to burns, it comes in a range of plain colours and some patterns. Many types are textured with round studs.

Care and Maintenance
Vinyl flooring can be damaged by burns or grit. Keep it clean with warm soapy water, rinsing off thoroughly. At all costs, avoid using harsh detergents, white spirit, turpentine or wax polish. Linoleum is likewise easily damaged by strong detergents. Keep it clean by sweeping and washing; shine with an emulsion polish or a recommended linoleum dressing. Make sure that water is not allowed to seep under the linoleum – this will cause it to rot.

Rubber is very resilient, but there is a tendency for grime to build up on textured types – around studs, for example. Wash with mild detergent; avoid strong chemicals.

Laying Sheet Flooring

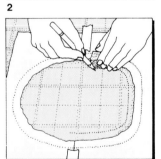

1

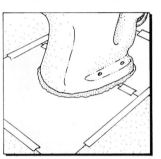

2

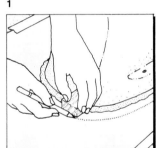

3

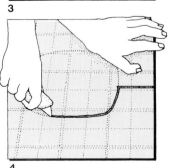

4

The easiest way to lay sheet flooring in a small area, such as a bathroom or utility room, is to make a paper pattern or template for the whole floor. Stiff paper is best.

This method relies on the use of a scriber, a wooden block 4cm/1½in wide. When the paper is laid, trim 1cm/½in around the edges and around obstacles. Place one edge of the scriber against the skirting board (baseboard) and trace a pencil line onto the paper all around the room.

Then place the paper template on top of the sheet flooring and tape it in place. Place one edge of the scriber against the pencil line on the template and draw a pencil line onto the sheet flooring, this time using the 'outer' edge of the scriber as a guide. The flooring can then be cut.

Cutting Around a Lavatory
1 Cut a paper template (in two halves for easy fitting) and lay it roughly around the obstacle. Stick it to the floor with tape.
2 Press the scribing block against the base of the obstacle and trace the outline onto the paper.
3 Lay the paper pattern over the flooring and transfer the outline, using the scribing block and pencil.
4 Cut the flooring along this line, making a cut at the back for access.

Rubber flooring complements a 1950s retro look.

A 'tiled' floor created the easy way – with sheet flooring.

WHAT TYPE OF SHEET FLOORING TO USE AND WHERE?

	Fitting	Suitability	Durability
SOLID VINYL	Fairly straightforward to lay. It is flexible and is suitable for any dry, flat surface. Should be warmed before laying as it becomes brittle in cold temperatures.	Ideal for kitchens and heavy-use areas such as hallways and utility rooms. Not usually suitable for bedrooms, living rooms or stairs.	Resilient and practical. Waterproof, resistant to oil and fat, but not burns and abrasive substances. Do not use harsh domestic detergents.
CUSHIONED VINYL	Fairly straightforward to lay. Easier to manipulate than solid vinyl flooring.	Like solid vinyl, not usually fitted in bedrooms or living rooms. Ideal in kitchens and bathrooms. Suitable for utility rooms, hallways and conservatories.	Similar qualities to solid vinyl. Good for soundproofing and warm underfoot.
LINOLEUM	More complicated to lay than vinyl. Lay on dry, level floor, preferably chipboard (particleboard) or hardboard (masonite).	Can be used in most rooms. Ideal for hallways and utility rooms, but not stairs.	Tough, good resistance to household chemicals, but will rot if water gets underneath.
RUBBER	Lay on subfloor or concrete. Most types need to be stuck down with adhesive.	Excellent for heavy-use areas. Good for bathrooms and utility rooms. Not suitable for kitchens.	Very tough. Non-slip, resistant to water, and is good for soundproofing.

Laying Sheet Vinyl Flooring

Most types of sheet flooring, including sheet vinyl, are available in large widths, so it is possible to cover fairly extensive areas without seams. If you do need to use more than one width, avoid laying the flooring so that a join bisects a doorway. Ideally, lay sheets parallel to a window so that seams are less visible.

Patterned vinyl looks better if the pattern is aligned with the doorway – few rooms have walls which are perfectly square to each other.

Vinyl can be loose-laid (i.e., not stuck to the floor). In particular, cushioned-back vinyl has an interlayer, which makes it very stable, but 'lay-flat' vinyl can bubble up or lift in the middle. The answer to this problem is to trim for a snug fit (not a really tight fit, because this is more likely to encourage buckling). Also, before laying the vinyl, reverse the roll and leave it in a warm room for at least two days to make it supple.

Flatten out any kinks. Once the vinyl has been laid – allowing 5cm/2in overlap at each edge – brush with a soft broom to eliminate any air bubbles which might be trapped underneath.

Other types of vinyl need to be stuck, either around the edges or all over. To stick vinyl all over, roll the sheet back and do half a room at a time. Follow manufacturers' recommendations.

● A large room may need more than one width of vinyl. Always use lengths cut from the same roll. If you are laying a large sheet of vinyl, enlist a friend to help you,

Materials and Equipment
● roll of sheet vinyl
● sharp knife
● sharp scissors
● adhesive, if necessary
● straightedge and measuring tape
● chalk or pencil
● soft broom
● wood block

METHOD

1 Lay the vinyl out roughly, making diagonal cuts in each corner. Remove excess from edges, using a sharp knife and leaving a 5cm/2in overlap all around. Brush with a soft broom to remove air from beneath.
2 To fit an internal corner, lift the sheet and make a diagonal cut across the corner with scissors. Press the vinyl back into the angle.
3 To fit an external corner, such as at an alcove or doorway, cut downward, ending up diagonally in the corner. Trim excess, leaving 5cm/2in overlapping the wall to allow for mistakes.

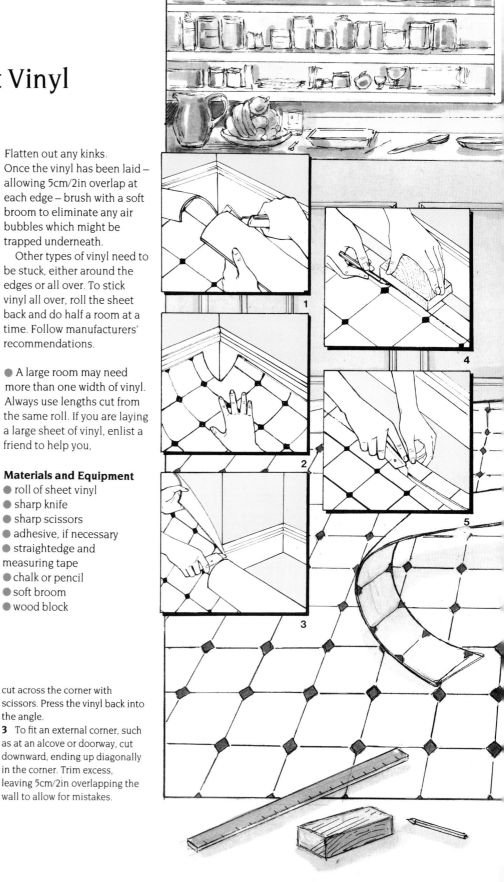

4 Fit the vinyl against the longest wall first. Pull the flooring away from the wall, keeping the alignment. Take a softwood block and place it over the gap, overlapping onto the vinyl. Draw the block and a pencil along the flooring, with the block pressed against the skirting board (baseboard), to make a trimming line.

5 Pull the vinyl away from the wall and trim. Slide back to fit. To trim thin flexible vinyl, press it into the angle of the floor and wall and crease the edge with a wood block. Make the cut along the crease with a knife, guided by a straightedge.

6 Next, trim the other edges. Measure a distance of 20cm/8in from the wall and mark the vinyl. Pull the vinyl back from the wall and make a second mark, measuring back 20cm/8in from the first mark towards the edge of the sheet. Slide the vinyl back to the wall. Make sure the adjacent edge is straight. Make a wood block the width of the distance between the second mark and the end of the sheet and use this to guide a pencil marking the contour of the wall.

7 To fit flooring around a doorway, make a paper template or pattern to the shape of the mouldings and then transfer this shape to the vinyl. Alternatively use a profile gauge.

8 To join lengths, overlap the edges of both pieces, aligning the pattern. Cut through both thicknesses, using a straightedge. Remove the surplus strips and stick the edges of the pieces to the floor using double-sided tape (use adhesive instead if the vinyl is to be stuck down).

217

Successful Decorating
FLOORS

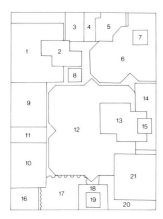

Floor Tiles

  1 Glazed Spanish
  2 Slate
  3,4 Vinyl
  5 Linoleum
  6 Terracotta
  7,8 Glazed Mexican
  9,10 Distressed slate
  11 Slate
  12 Marble
  13 Plain glazed
  14 Quarry
  15 Glazed Mexican
  16 Vinyl wood strips
  17 Glazed mosaic
  18 Plain glazed
  19 Glazed Mexican
  20 Cork
  21 Terrazzo

Tiling

Floor tiles come in every conceivable form: hard, soft, warm, cold, light, heavy, easy to lay, difficult to lay . . . Sizes, colours, patterns and textures likewise vary widely.

It is important when using heavier rigid tiles or slabs (such as ceramic and quarry tiles, marble, slate or terrazzo) that they are laid on a floor that can bear their weight and which is absolutely level. Floorboards should be covered with hardboard (masonite) or plywood; concrete should be covered with cement or sand screed. You may have to call in a surveyor or engineer to check if a floor can bear the load, particularly in upstairs rooms and hallways.

TYPES OF TILES

Ceramic Tiles
Made from baked clay, ceramic tiles are very hard and strong. Popular colours are the natural shades of yellow through brown, but other colours are available as well. Textures vary from smooth and shiny to knobbly; there are also patterned, hand-painted and unglazed varieties of tiles.

Ceramic tiles are heavy, cold, noisy and hard – an object dropped on them is more than likely to break.

Lay the tiles on level floors such as screeded concrete or plywood-covered floorboards.

Quarry Tiles
Normally square or rectangular, quarry tiles come in a range of warm, natural shades. They are made from unrefined alumina clay high in silica (quartz). Because they are water- and grease-resistant, they make practical floors for kitchens and hallways, although they are hard, cold and noisy. Lay on screeded concrete.

Brick Tiles
Bricks for indoor use (paviors) are hard-wearing, water- and grease-resistant, and warmer than either ceramic or quarry tiles. They can be laid only on ground floors, in a mortar bed. They come in a range of colours, including not only the standard red, brown and yellow, but also blue, purple and green. They often look best in a rustic setting or when linking interior rooms to the garden – for example, as a hall or kitchen floor.

Marble Tiles
The most practical way of using marble is to lay it in thin sheets or tiles, because marble slabs are very expensive and very difficult to work with. Tiles should be laid in cement on concrete or on a perfectly level strong wooden floor.

Like other hard tiles, however, marble is cold, heavy and noisy.

Slate Tiles
Suitable for ground floors only, slate slabs are very heavy, expensive, unwieldy, cold and noisy; they must be laid in cement on concrete. Despite all these disadvantages, slate is a very beautiful material, typically in shades of grey and with a rippled surface. It can be effectively combined with other materials – marble, wood, etc. – and is impervious and durable.

Stone Tiles
Stone floors have a mellow, ageless quality that suits contemporary settings as well as period ones. A variety of types of natural stone can be used for flooring. These include granite, sandstone, York stone and limestone, either in slabs or, more economically, cast with cement. Some types will stain easily.

Terrazzo
Terrazzo consists of marble or granite chips set in thin tiles or slabs with concrete or cement. Smooth, tough and elegantly flecked with colour, terrazzo must be laid on screed. It can be expensive.

Mosaic Tiles
Made of various materials, including marble, clay and glass silica, mosaic tiles are nowadays available with a peel-off backing to facilitate laying (which must be on smooth screeded floors).

Cork Tiles
Made from pressed and baked natural cork, these tiles make a warm, comfortable, quiet and durable floor. Make sure you buy flooring-grade tiles; lay them on a smooth floor, using adhesive. Cork must be properly sealed.

Vinyl, Rubber and Linoleum Tiles
These materials are available in tiles as well as sheet form. Because they are softer, cheaper, quieter and warmer than most hard tiles, they are a popular choice for utility areas such as kitchens and bathrooms. They are also extremely easy for the amateur to lay.

Quarry tiles integrated with painted floorboards tease the eye. It is, however, a very practical and stylish solution.

Laying Ceramic Tiles

Ceramic tiles are ideal for kitchens and bathrooms, but they are heavy, and so you first have to check that the floor can bear the weight.

Because the tiles are hard and rigid, they must be laid on a flat, stable surface that is also clean and dry. Also, the floor must be well ventilated. Strengthen wooden floors by first covering with sheets of plywood at least 1cm/½in thick, laid in staggered rows and fixed with screws at 30cm/12in intervals. Ceramic tiles can be laid straight onto concrete, assuming it is level.

Calculating Quantity
To work out how many tiles you need, measure the length and width of the room using the dimensions of the tile (adding on the width of a join) as the unit of measurement. Round up both distances to the nearest tile-width and then multiply the two figures together to give the total number of tiles you need.

Alternatively, you can work out the floor area and then divide by the area a pack of tiles will cover, thereby establishing the total number of packs you will need. (Many tiles come in packs which state the coverage.) Which-ever method you use, remember to allow for extras in case of damage. For a com-plicated area it may be best to draw up a scale plan.

Finding a Starting Point
First establish the mid-point of the room (see page 212).

Dry lay the tiles from the middle to the wall and from this point out to the furthest corner from the door. Arrange the tiles so that at least half a tile width is left around the edge, then lay a wooden batten along the last row of tiles and nail temporarily. Lay another batten across the adjacent wall, at an angle of 90 degrees. The point where the battens meet is your starting point for tiling.

● Make a tile gauge using a length of wooden batten marked with the tile widths and spaces.

● Remember that tiling will raise the level of the floor. You may have to plane off the bottoms of doors.

Materials and Equipment
● ceramic tiles
● recommended adhesive
● trowel
● notched spreader
● string and chalk
● spirit level (carpenter's level)
● wooden battens
● hammer and nails
● spacers or pieces of stiff cardboard
● heavy-duty tile-cutter
● squeegee or sponge
● grout
● clean cloths
● rubber gloves

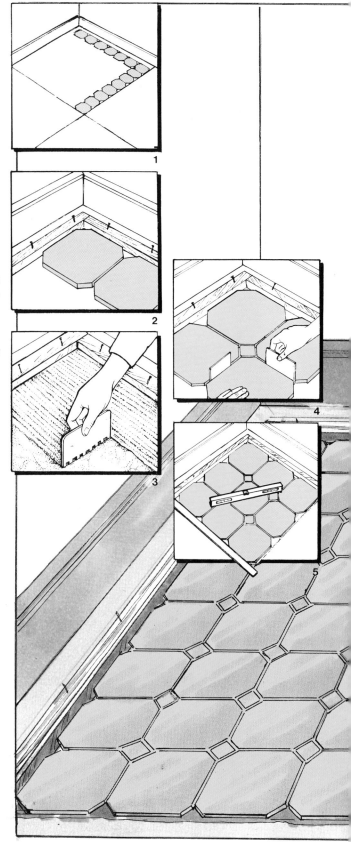

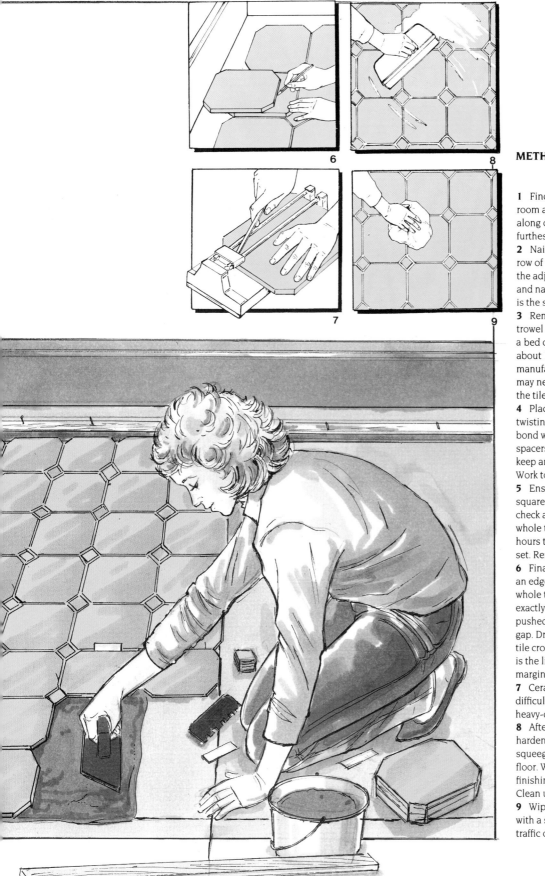

METHOD

1 Find the mid-point of the room and dry lay tiles out from it, along one wall to the corner furthest from the door.

2 Nail a batten along the last row of tiles. Lay a batten along the adjacent wall at 90 degrees and nail. Where the battens meet is the starting point.

3 Remove the tiles. Using a trowel and notched spreader, lay a bed of adhesive over an area about 1m/1yd square. Follow manufacturers' instructions: you may need to apply adhesive to the tiles as well as the floor.

4 Place tiles in position, twisting slightly to improve the bond with the adhesive. Insert spacers or pieces of cardboard to keep an even gap for grouting. Work towards the door.

5 Ensure that tiles are level and square – use a spirit level to check as you go along. Lay all whole tiles first and leave for 24 hours to allow the adhesive to set. Remove battens.

6 Finally, lay edge tiles. To cut an edge tile, lay it over the last whole tile in the row, covering it exactly. Place another tile on top, pushed against the wall over the gap. Draw a line where the top tile crossed the one below. This is the line for cutting. Allow a margin for grouting.

7 Ceramic tiles are thick and difficult to cut. Hire or buy a heavy-duty tile-cutter.

8 After the adhesive has hardened (about 24 hours), use a squeegee or sponge to grout the floor. Work into the joins, finishing flush with the tiles. Clean up joins with a cloth.

9 Wipe off excess grout. Buff with a soft dry cloth. Avoid heavy traffic on the floor for 48 hours.

Successful Decorating
FLOORS

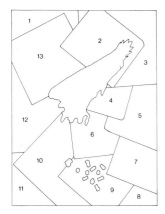

Carpets

1   Cord
2   Deep shag pile
3   Twist pile
4   Velvet
5   Coarse loop
6   Patterned velvet
7   Deep pile velvet
8   Rubber underlay
9   Coarse berber loop
10 Berber twist pile
11 Velvet
12 Cord
13 Patterned velvet

Carpet

Carpet is warm, comfortable and easy to clean and it comes in a wide range of colours, textures and patterns. Price also varies, according to the fibre or fibres used, the method of manufacture and the general performance.

Different grades of carpet are suitable for different locations, from light-use types for bedrooms to heavy-duty varieties for stairs. Durability is a function of the density and weight of the pile, with short, dense-pile carpets being the hardest-wearing type.

Carpets generally have either a woven or a foam backing. Laying woven-backed carpet is a professional job, but laying foam-backed carpet can be done by the amateur. An alternative to orthodox carpet is supplied by carpet tiles, which can be loose-laid or stuck down.

Carpet terminology can be confusing. As well as the fibre composition, carpets can be classified according to the method of manufacture and the type of pile. However, the most important indication of quality is the type and amount of fibre used.

Types

As well as the natural carpet fibre, wool, a number of synthetics are used to make carpets. Most modern carpets use mixtures – either of wool with an artificial fibre such as nylon, or of several synthetic materials.

Wool is expensive, but luxurious; it is often mixed with a percentage of nylon to promote durability – 80:20 wool to nylon is an all-purpose grade. Nylon is very durable and is often used in mixes. Good-quality nylon can be expensive. Acrylic is similar to wool in appearance but is more difficult to clean. Polyester is cheap and is often used to make shag-pile carpet. Viscose rayon is again cheap, but it gives a poor performance overall. Polypropylene is cheap, durable and water-repellent. It is used in mixtures.

Method of Manufacture

In woven carpets the pile and the backing are made together. Types of pile include smooth, uncut-loop, low-loop, long-loop and mixtures of cut and looped pile for sculpted effects. In tufted carpets fibres are inserted individually into a prepared backing which is then sealed with adhesive to hold the tufts in place. The pile may be cut, looped, or both. With non-woven carpets fibres can be bonded onto backing with adhesive; needlepunched and fixed with adhesive; or electrostatically flocked to the backing.

Carpet Terms

Axminster is a type of woven carpet, where the pile is inserted in tufts into the weave, allowing many different colours to be used. The pile is cut, but may be short and smooth, long and shaggy, stubbly or sculpted.
Berber is a term for fleeced carpets with a nubbly pile.
Body carpet is carpet produced in narrow widths less than 1.8m/6ft for use on stairs, halls, and so on.
Broadloom is carpet produced in widths over 1.8m/6ft, commonly 2.75m/9ft and 3.7m/12ft.
Brussels weave is a term referring to dense uncut looped pile.
Carpet tiles are squares of carpet with sealed edges, available in different sizes, colours, patterns and fibres and with different backings, including PVC, rubber and felt. Useful for areas of heavy wear, since damaged squares can be lifted easily and replaced, or tiles can be moved regularly to distribute wear evenly.
Cord is a low-loop woven carpet with a ribbed appearance. It is very durable.
Shag pile is a long-pile carpet with loops of 2.5–5cm/1–2in. It is hazardous on stairs and is prone to tangling.
Wilton is a smooth cut pile carpet. It is woven from continuous yarn, so only limited colours are possible.

A beautiful Axminster carpet, displaying a range of tones.

Types of Underlay

Good-quality underlay is essential for all woven-backed carpets. Foam-backed carpets should be laid on felt paper so the foam does not stick to the floor. Underlay evens out the carpet's upper surface, is a good insulator and protects the carpet from dirt, damp and excess wear.

Foam or rubber underlay is resilient but is not suitable for areas of heavy wear, such as stairs. Avoid laying it over damp floors or underfloor heating. To test good-quality foam, rub it between your fingers and thumb: if it crumbles, it is second-rate.

Felt underlay is made of jute or animal hair, or a mixture. Hair is stronger and wears better. You can also obtain rubberized felt.

Bonded underlay is made from a mixture of wool and synthetics, bonded to rubber.

Laying Carpet

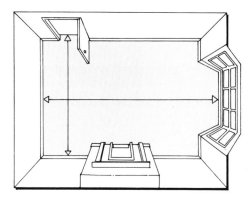

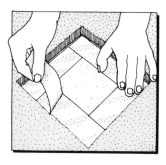

Laying Woven Carpets

Woven carpets should be fitted professionally: a cut in the wrong place would be an expensive mistake. Moreover, carpet will wear out prematurely unless it is tensioned correctly.

The carpet must be laid over thick underlay and secured to the perimeter of the room by gripper rods. At doorways, a metal binder bar is used instead of a gripper rod: the carpet is hooked onto pins and the edge covered with a metal strip.

Measuring for Carpets

Most carpet suppliers will measure rooms, but to do this yourself, measure the length and width of the room, including alcoves, and add an allowance for places where the carpet must extend under doors. Multiply the dimensions together for the number of square metres or feet you must buy.

Narrower carpets are sold in terms of length, rather than of square metres or yards. Measure the length of the room (by the 'length' is meant the opposite direction to that in which the carpet will be laid) and divide the result by the width of each carpet strip. Multiply this by the other dimension and you can easily calculate the length of carpet you need.

To measure for stair carpeting, first measure from the front to the back of a single tread (horizontal part) and multiply by the number of treads. For treads around corners take the longer measurement. Bottom treads are often longer, so take account of this. Next, measure the height of a riser (vertical part) and multiply by the number of the risers. Add in amounts for half-landings or landings, together with an allowance if the carpet is to be moved to distribute wear.

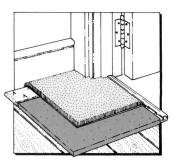

Patching Fitted Carpet

1 Place new piece over damaged area. Cut through both layers at once.

2 Apply adhesive around the edges of both the hole and the patch. Leave to dry.

3 Stick double-sided tape to the underlay or floor. Remove the backing.

4 Place the patch in position and press down firmly. To finish, trim loose fibres.

Laying Carpet Tiles

Carpet tiles are easy to lay. Because they do not need to be fixed down, they can be taken up and moved around to distribute wear; irrevocably damaged tiles can simply be replaced. Carpet tiles need no underlay, but it is important that the surface should be clean, dry and level.

As with ceramic tiles (see page 220), you can calculate how many carpet tiles you will need by measuring the length and width of the room using the width of the tile as the unit, and then multiplying the two figures (rounding up for part tiles). Buy extra tiles in case of damage.

Follow manufacturers' instructions for laying, as techniques vary. Begin by laying from the mid-point of the room (see page 212). Some carpet tiles have an arrow on the back to indicate the direction of the pile. You can either lay all the tiles with the same direction of pile or lay them so that it alternates at right angles to give a checkerboard effect.

Carpet tiles are usually loose-laid, but you can place a strip of double-sided tape around the perimeter of the room to keep the assemblage firmly in place. It is also a good idea to stick the first tile down with tape or adhesive so that it remains in place when the rest are being laid. Push each tile up against the previous one for a snug fit.

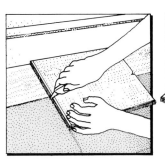 

1 After all the whole tiles have been laid, you must cut edge pieces. Place the tile in position upside-down, butting it against the wall. Nick it at each end using a trimming knife. Measure any irregular gaps carefully and make a template or pattern in order to ensure that you cut the tiles correctly. You could also use a profile gauge.

2 Cut through the tile, holding the knife against a metal straightedge. Turn the tile over and fit it so that the cut edge is against the wall. You can cut rounded shapes using a template.

● If tiles dislodge, such as in a busy hallway lift them up and apply carpet adhesive to the underside.

Laying Foam-backed Carpet

Unless the floor is already covered with hardboard (masonite), the carpet should be laid on a paper underlay that stops short of the walls to allow a margin for double-sided carpet tape. Lay the carpet with the pile running away from the window. Try to avoid seams, but if you find you must join widths secure them with carpet tape and butt the pieces together.

● Carpet tape is available in different widths. When you are fitting a single piece of carpet the narrowest width is sufficient. It can be stuck to both wood and concrete.

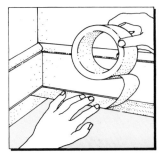 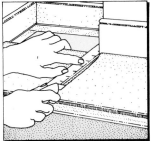 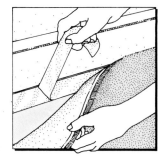

1 Lay the carpet tape around the perimeter of the room. However, at this stage, do not peel off the backing strip. Cut your piece of carpet roughly to size, leaving a 5cm/2in overlap. Make diagonal cuts at the corners to allow the tongues to lap against the base of the wall.

2 To fit carpet around a chimney breast, make freeing cuts in line with the sides of the chimney breast by folding the carpet over a board and cutting through the back. Allow the tongues of carpet to fit into the recess. Trim off excess across the face of the chimney breast.

3 Press the carpet under the base of the skirting board (baseboard) with a bolster chisel (brick chisel) or a similar tool, and trim off excess with a trimming knife. Peel the tape backing off and press the carpet back into position. Finish with a threshold strip in doorways.

Rugs

An interesting rug transforms the floor into a focal point. From fine antique Persian carpets to relatively inexpensive rag or braided mats, there is a design and a price to suit every decorative scheme. As well as the wealth of traditional handmade types, there are also manufactured rugs produced in contemporary designs – an exciting and original way of dressing up a modern room.

The three basic types of rug are: flat-weaves, such as kelims and dhurries; pile rugs (often from the Middle or Far East); and braided, hooked or rag rugs assembled from scraps of different materials. Prices vary according to the age and rarity of the design, composition (with cotton the cheapest and silk the most expensive) and method of production – for example, a good handmade Persian carpet will be very dense, with about 125 knots or tufts per square centimetre (800 per square inch), and therefore very expensive.

Flat-weave Rugs

These rugs are woven and have no pile. They are generally cheaper than pile carpets, and are usually made of cotton or of wool and cotton, although silk is also used. The two main traditional types of flat-weave rugs are kelims and dhurries. Kelims are produced in Turkey and Afghanistan. Patterns are geometric and the vegetable dyes used produce rich, warm colours that mellow beautifully with age. Most kelims are woollen.

Dhurries are Indian flat-weaves, usually made of cotton, although up-market silk versions exist. Designs tend to be modern interpretations of traditional motifs; borders are common. The increasing popularity of these rugs means that they are available in a huge range of colours and patterns. Dhurries are easy to maintain – they can even be reversed – and are fairly cheap.

Serapes are coarse flat-weave rugs from Mexico. They are often fringed, and come in a variety of bright cheerful colours and patterns.

Pile Rugs

Traditional pile rugs are made by knotting tufts of wool (or silk) – the more knots per square centimetre the better the quality. Many of these carpets are very expensive and 'collectable'. Although there are some adequate reproductions, it is hard to match the clear, distinct patterns of originals. Typical designs and colours vary according to the region and the period.

Chinese rugs are thick, often sculpted, and they feature pictorial motifs such as flowers, dragons and

Types of rub: *antique kelim from Persia (**1**); William Morris design (**2**); Turkish carpet (**3**); modern tufted rug (**4**); 1930s pile rug (**5**).*

butterflies. Yellow, pink, black and blue are common colours for Chinese rugs.

Persian carpets, from central Asia, display stylized or geometric motifs in rich reds and blues.

Turkish carpets are likewise produced in rich, glowing colours. Many are prayer rugs, typically with a design showing an arch supported by pillars.

Today, hand- or machine-made pile carpets in graphic, contemporary designs are produced. Although those by 'name' designers and one-offs commissioned from hand-weavers are obviously

expensive, cheaper mass-produced versions can be very reasonable.

Other Types
Flokatis are inexpensive shaggy-pile wool rugs from Greece, usually white or off-white. Ryas are shaggy-pile Finnish rugs in contemporary designs. Numdahs are cheap felt rugs from India which have birds, animals or flowers embroidered on an off-white background.

Braided, Hooked and Rag Rugs
These are cheerful, hand-made rugs produced using

scraps of fabric or wool. Antiques – especially early North American ones – can be expensive, but their modern equivalents are much more reasonable.

Braided rugs are made by plaiting and coiling material. They are usually oval but can be round as well. Hooked rugs consist of a looped pile worked in a pattern or naive design. Rag rugs consist of irregular stripes in bright cheerful colours.

● Care for rugs by moving them regularly to avoid excessive wear or fading in one spot. Clean them by

beating them with a carpet-beater, rather than by vacuuming. Never use strong detergent, steam or excess water to wash out stains. If necessary, have the rug treated by a specialist. Frayed edges can be mended by blanket-stitching, but if the rug is valuable you should seek expert help for any repair work that must be undertaken.

● Secure rugs on hard floors by placing them over rubber or webbed underlay. Underlay will prolong the life of the rug as well as preventing it from sliding underfoot.

6

6 A Portuguese rag rug in shades of rose, apricot and cream reflects the colour scheme in this New York apartment and adds textural interest.

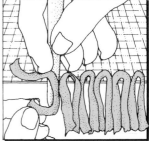

1

Making a Rag Rug
Choose rags made of the same type of material and of the same weight. Wash the pieces and cut them into strips 10cm/4in long and 2.5cm/1in wide.

For the backing you will need a piece of hessian (burlap), cut to the required size, with 5cm/2in allowed all round for finishing. Work with the wrong side facing you.

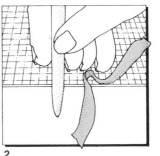

2

To insert the rags in the backing you will need a round-pointed peg.

1 Poke a hole in one corner and push one end of a strip through until it protrudes by just under half.

2 Poke a second hole four threads along (about 1cm/ ½in) and insert the other end of the strip through this hole.

3

3 Poke one end of another strip into the same hole as the last. Make a further hole four threads along and push the other end of this second strip through. Continue working in straight rows, 4cm/ 1½in apart. Check the density after a few rows. Finish edges by applying latex-based adhesive and folding over a double hem.

Matting

Coir matting in an American country living room.

Cheap and practical, matting is woven either from a variety of natural fibres or from coloured plastic strands. It makes a simple cheerful alternative to more expensive surfaces. Some types can be laid wall to wall, most can be used like rugs to cover existing floors.

Natural matting is woven in different patterns, including rib, checkerboard and bullseye. This choice of patterns, together with the warm, earth shades of light biscuit brown, honey gold and dark brown, make matting a sympathetic foil for all kinds of flooring. But the particular attraction of matting lies in its texture.

Because it is comparatively cheap, matting is a good solution for floors in temporary accommodation. In warm climates, scatter mats can be laid over hard floors in bedrooms and living rooms to increase comfort. Wall-to-wall matting makes a good base for rugs, and all types of matting are excellent choices for areas which connect directly with the outdoors – not just for doormats but as the principal flooring in halls and conservatories.

TYPES OF MATTING

Coir
One of the cheapest, most widely available and most popular types of matting, coir is made from coconut fibre. As well as making thick, dense doormats, coir is available in various ribbed weaves, narrow and broadloom, which can be laid like carpet and provide a good all-purpose surface that suits modern as well as traditional interiors.

In addition to the natural honey colour, coir matting comes in a range of other shades, including black; this range, while limited, extends coir's decorative applications. There are also types which include coloured sisal in attractive patterns, but these are more expensive.

The disadvantages of coir are that it can be uncomfortable underfoot and dusty, and it will eventually become slippery on stairs – although there are more expensive types that are backed with latex or vinyl to increase durability.

If you are using coir for a doormat, it is a good idea, if circumstances permit, to stop the hall flooring short of the entrance and to create a well that can be filled entirely with the matting.

If you are using coir for a scatter mat, cut it slightly oversize and allow it to adjust to the conditions for at least 24 hours.

For wall-to-wall laying, choose a broadloom type, stitch lengths together and bind the edges with jute tape; alternatively, butt the edges together and join them with double-sided tape or carpet adhesive. Do not tack the edges down – this will cause bumps and ridges.

Sisal
As durable as coir, sisal is made from the leaves of various types of agave plant. Available in a range of interesting colours, it is sometimes woven into mixtures with coir. The applications and method of laying are similar to coir.

Rush, Seagrass and Maize
Matting made of these various fibres has an ethnic, natural charm and comes in a wide range of fineness of weave and depth of colour, maize matting being the smoothest and palest. These types of matting are readily available and cheap and, unlike rugs, need no underlay. Small sections or strips can be sewn together with twine to make a larger covering. None of these fibres will resist heavy wear, and they can be dusty.

Plastic
Woven plastic matting comes in rectangular pieces or in rolls, and a wide range of bright paintbox colours is available. There is also a type of plastic matting made of honeycomb duckboard; this is more substantial but also more expensive. Plastic matting is cheap, durable and comfortable, but it can be damaged by strong chemicals.

Binding Coir Matting
Bind the edges of coir with hessian (burlap) strips 5cm/ 2in wide. Sew the hessian to the right side of the matting using strong thread and a running stitch. Fold the hessian over to the back and slip-stitch to the matting. Mitre the corners.

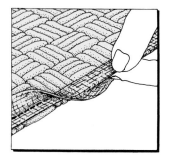

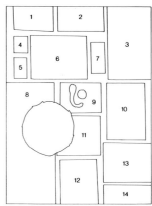

Matting

1 Sisal
2 Herringbone coir
3 Seagrass
4 Ribbed coir
5 Sisal
6 Dyed coconut
7 Tufted coir
8 Bullseye rush
9 Sisal
10 Dyed herringbone coconut
11 Dyed herringbone sisal
12 Dyed coconut
13 Sisal
14 Bleached herringbone coir

WINDOW TREATMENTS

A window is a natural focal point, and so a window treatment can set the whole style of a room. The range of effects you can create is very wide: from the delicacy of lace panels to the crisp, contemporary look of Venetian blinds; from tailored, pleated full-length curtains to soft, billowing festoons; from grand, traditional swags and tails to the natural charm of split-cane blinds.

CURTAINS
Curtain Fabrics

Curtain fabrics come in a variety of fibres and in different weights, finishes, textures, colours and patterns. In general, the shorter the curtain, the lighter the fabric can be; curtains which hang full-length in straight folds need heavier fabric. Simple cased headings and loose gathers and ties work best if the material is lightweight; tailored pleated headings are more successful in a stiffer, thicker fabric.

Cotton is still the principal fibre used in furnishing fabrics; today it is often blended with artificial fibres such as polyester. Cotton prints well, wears well and comes in a wide range of weights, weaves and finishes. In addition to plain weave cotton, you can obtain cotton brocades, lawns, damasks, chintzes, ginghams, sateens, satins, and velvets.

Linen is sturdier than cotton and more loosely woven. A blend of linen and cotton, known as 'linen union', is the most common linen furnishing fabric.

For furnishing use, wool is usually blended with other fibres. Both light wools and tweeds can be used to make curtains, especially if extra warmth is desired.

Other fabrics involved in curtain-making include linings, interlinings and buckram. Cotton sateen, in colours as well as neutral shades, is the most common type of lining material. Thermal lining comes either in a cotton and acrylic blend or in an aluminium-coated form. Black-out lining, which excludes all light, comes in neutral shades. Interlining consists of a layer of padding stitched between the lining and curtain.

Calculating Fabric Amount

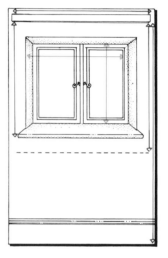

Before measuring, fix the track or pole in position. Use a metal rule to take measurements, as a fabric one can stretch.

Curtain length is a matter of taste. The three standard lengths are to the sill, to the floor or to just below the sill (to the top of a radiator, for example). But curtains can also look luxurious if they are allowed to fall onto the floor in rich, deep folds or flaring like the base of a column.

To establish the length, take the following measurements from the base of the glider or ring: to 5mm/¼in above the sill; to 1cm/⅖in above the floor (or lower if desired); or to 2cm/¾in above a radiator. Add 25cm/9in for hem and heading, plus extra for any pattern repeat. Remember to make allowance for headings which stand up above the track.

A curtain's width is a function of the style of heading used. Measure the length of the track, rod or pole (not the width of the window) and multiply by the required fullness for the heading. Add 15cm/6in for side turnings, and account for any overlap in the middle. It is important not to skimp on fabric width – certain types of heading demand more material than others to work successfully. If you need to economize, choose a simpler style of heading.

1,2 *Either in conjunction with outer curtains or as the sole window treatment, lace is a highly effective fabric. Because it is so delicately patterned and lightweight, it does not need to be gathered tightly – it can simply be hung flat. Lace is also excellent for disguising a dreary view.*

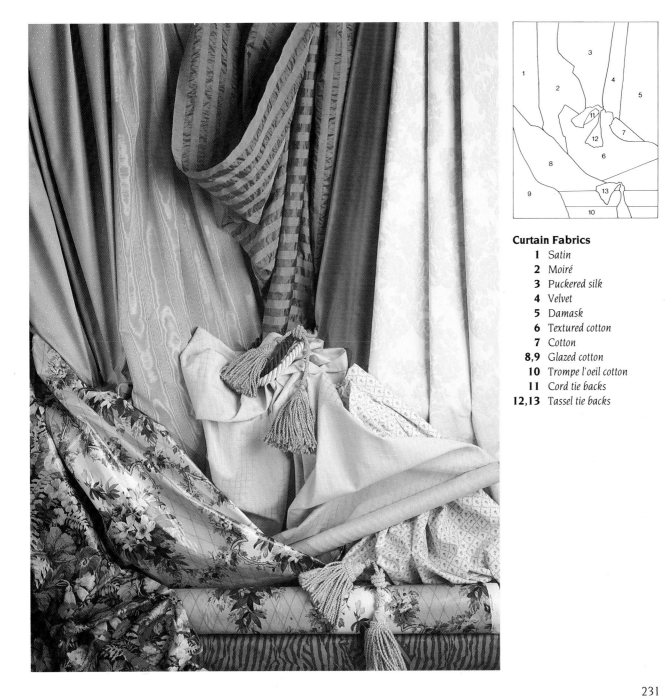

Curtain Fabrics

- **1** Satin
- **2** Moiré
- **3** Puckered silk
- **4** Velvet
- **5** Damask
- **6** Textured cotton
- **7** Cotton
- **8,9** Glazed cotton
- **10** Trompe l'oeil cotton
- **11** Cord tie backs
- **12,13** Tassel tie backs

Curtain Treatments

The practical purposes of curtains are to provide privacy and warmth, to exclude light completely or partially, and to screen unwelcome views. But the type of window treatment you select for a particular location depends also on the window itself, the style and decoration of the room, and the amount you wish to spend on it.

Tailored formal styles extending to the floor suit large windows in living and dining rooms; sill-length curtains in lighter fabric can be chosen for kitchens, bedrooms and bathrooms. In period settings, you can experiment with traditional pelmets (cornices) or elaborate swags and tails.

Headings
The heading defines the style of the curtain. It will determine the fullness of the curtain, how it hangs, and how it is suspended. If the curtain-top is not covered by a pelmet (cornice), the heading will also be a feature in its own right.

Deep, tailored headings which keep the fabric hanging straight in full folds include pencil pleats, box pleats and pinch or triple pleats. Narrower headings, which give a softer, less formal look, include standard gathered headings, smocked headings and cluster pleats.

Today all of these styles can be achieved by the use of special heading tapes sewn to the back of the curtain. Tapes are available in different weights to suit different fabrics. By pulling cords threaded through the tape the fabric is gathered into a particular pattern. Alternatively, the fabric can be gathered by inserting pleater hooks, which serve also to attach the curtain to the track or pole.

Simpler sewn types of heading for lightweight unlined curtains or sheers include cased headings and shaped headings. A cased heading is a sewn channel along the top of the curtain (or at both top and bottom) which enables a wire or rod to be threaded through, shirring the fabric. Also, fabric can be cut and sewn into scallops or castellations which are then threaded through rings or directly onto a pole or rod.

Tracks and Poles
Tracks, which are available in plastic or aluminium, make discreet fittings for curtains, especially if the heading extends a little way over the top. They come with guide hooks into which curtain hooks are slotted, they can be shaped to fit around a bay or bow window, and they can be fitted with a cord set and pulleys so that the curtains can be drawn from one side.

Poles – either of metal or of wood – can be highly decorative. They come with supporting brackets, matching rings or inset runners and hooks. Poles can be mitred to fit around angled windows.

Other means of curtain suspension include fine metal or brass rods for attaching sheer curtains or curtains with cased headings, and plastic-covered sprung wire for the same purpose.

Types of headings and tapes: *gathered heading using standard curtain tape (**1**); pencil pleats (**2**); pinch pleats (**3**); smocked heading (**4**); box pleats (**5**); cartridge pleats (**6**); scalloped heading hung from rings (**7**); cased heading on covered wire (**8**).*

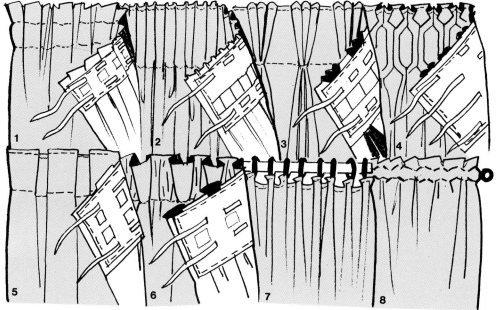

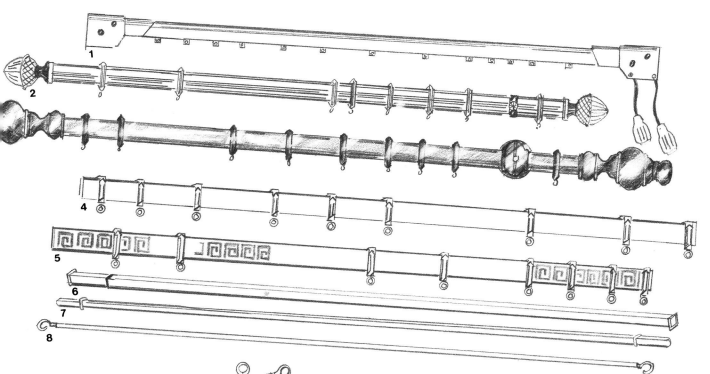

Hooks and Rings

There is a variety of designs of hooks and rings to suit different types of headings, tracks and poles. Hooks and rings are both available in metal and plastic; there are also wooden rings for use with wooden poles. Some designs are unobtrusive; others are meant for display.

Types of tracks and poles: *corded track with pulleys (**1**); metal pole with finials and rings (**2**); wooden pole with finials and rings (**3**); plastic track with glide hooks (**4**); plastic track with motif (**5**); expandable pole (**6**); fine rod for net curtains (**7**); expandable wire with eyes (**8**).*

Putting up a Track

1 Measure the window or recess and mark the desired fixing height at intervals across the window. Join the marks, extending the line to the width of the track. Use a spirit level (carpenter's level) to check that the line is straight and horizontal.

2 With a pencil, mark along the guide line where the brackets will go, spacing them evenly. Drill and plug the holes, screw the brackets in place and clip or slot the track onto the brackets.

● To position the track on the ceiling you must fix the brackets to joists.

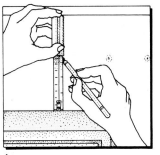

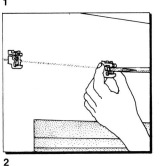

Putting up a Pole

1 Construct a guide line, as for a track. To mark the positions for support brackets, measure in from the ends of the pole (note that the screw hole is often slightly above centre). Drill and plug the holes, and drive in screws, leaving the heads projecting. Fit brackets.

2 Centre the pole on the brackets, leaving one ring outside the brackets at either side. Push the finials into place. Drive a screw into the base of each bracket. The screws bite into the pole, and prevent it from becoming dislodged when the curtains are pulled.

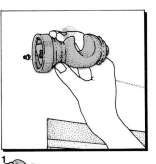

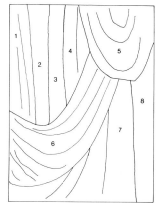

Sheer Fabrics
1 *Loose-knit polyester*
2 *Plain voile*
3 *Patterned nylon*
4 *Silk and polyester mix*
5 *Iridescent polyester*
6 *Crushed polyester*
7 *Cotton Chantilly lace*
8 *Patterned muslin*

Sheers and Unlined Curtains

The typical sheer curtain is the net curtain, long used in conjunction with outer curtains to provide daytime privacy and to filter strong sunlight. Almost any kind of light, semi-transparent fabric can serve the purpose – muslin, lace, voile and lawn are all attractive options. Sheer curtains are often suspended from a rod or wire by means of a cased heading, but they can also be hung from a special track or they can be fixed top and bottom as panels – on French doors, for example.

Making Sheer Curtains

Net and other types of semi-transparent material are available in many different

Lightweight, filmy material draped over a pole frames French windows leading onto a balcony.

widths (90–270cm/36–108in), so you can almost always avoid joins. The sides are usually finished but, if not, hem by 5mm/¼in. The bottom edge too may require hemming: stitch a 5cm/2in double hem (turning the fabric by a total of 10cm/4in).

1 Turn a 5cm/2in double hem at the top and machine-stitch close to the edge of the turning and again 2.5cm/1in above the first seam, so that you form a channel. Machine-stitch both lines in the same direction.
2 Thread plastic-covered wire or a rod through the casing and gather up the curtain. The fabric at the top will form a soft frill.

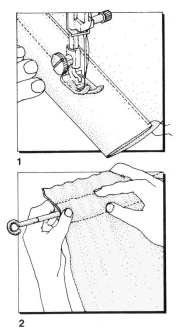

1

2

Making Unlined Curtains

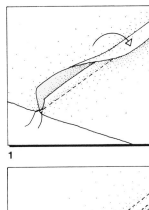

1

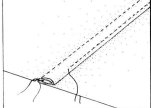

2

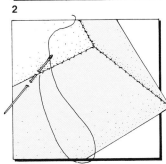

3

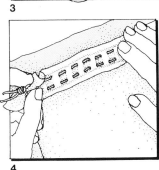

4

1 Join widths with flat fell seams. Machine right sides together, trimming one seam allowance and folding the wider one over the narrower to enclose it.
2 Press and machine-stitch down the seam, close to the edge. If you do not want stitching to show on the right side, use a simple flat seam. Finish by pinking or machine-stitching, and press open.
3 Turn 2.5cm/1in double hems down the sides and 7.5cm/3in double hems at the bottom, mitring the corners (see page 237). Slip-stitch into place.
4 Turn down the top edge of the curtain, and attach heading tape to cover the raw edge. The corner should be angled slightly. At one end of the tape, knot the ends of the cord and turn under. At the other end, free the cords and machine-stitch along the top, bottom and sides, stitching underneath the free cords. Pull the cords so that the fabric draws up to the required width.

● To prevent puckering, remove or snip selvedges. Make sure half-widths of fabric are positioned toward the outer edges of the curtains. To help the curtains hang properly, weight them with special discs or continuous weighted tape sewn inside the hem before you finish stitching it.

Making a Loose-lined Curtain

The easiest method of lining curtains is loose-lining. It is suitable for almost all curtains except those which are made of heavy fabric or those which are very wide.

When you have cut the fabric, pull out a thread across the top of each drop to ensure that you have a straight edge. Check that the pattern aligns at the top of each drop. When cutting out lining fabric, use a setsquare (T-square) and rule to chalk a line across, which you can follow to ensure a straight edge. Lining fabric should be 23cm/9in shorter and 12.5cm/5in narrower than the curtain fabric.

Matching Patterns

Cut out all the fabric lengths (drops) so that the patterns match across the finished curtain. There should be a complete motif at the top of each drop, and both curtains should match.

To join drops, first fold under the seam allowance of one drop and press it. Place this over the seam allowance of the second piece, matching the pattern. Pin in place.

Tack (baste) by stitching across the join, turning the needle through the bottom piece, then stitching across the join again and running through the fold on the top. Turn the top piece back and, with right sides together, machine-stitch along the tacked seam. Remove the tacking, making sure not to pull fabric threads, and iron to finish.

Materials and Equipment
- curtain fabric
- lining fabric
- thread
- heading tape
- ruler and setsquare (T-square)
- tailors' chalk
- pins and needles
- sewing machine
- scissors
- iron (for pressing)
- curtain weights
- curtain hooks

METHOD

1 Join widths of curtain fabric, using flat seams and matching the patterns (see above). Clip seams, press open and repeat for the lining. Mark the mid-points of curtain panels and lining panels with pins or chalk.
2 Place lining and fabric right sides together, with the lining 7.5cm/3in down from the top and side edges aligned. Machine-stitch 1cm/½in seams up to 7.5cm/3in from the bottom of the lining; the surplus fabric will make a pleat at the back. Clip seam turnings.
3 Turn up and press 5cm/2in to the wrong side of the lining and machine-stitch a 2.5cm/1in double hem.

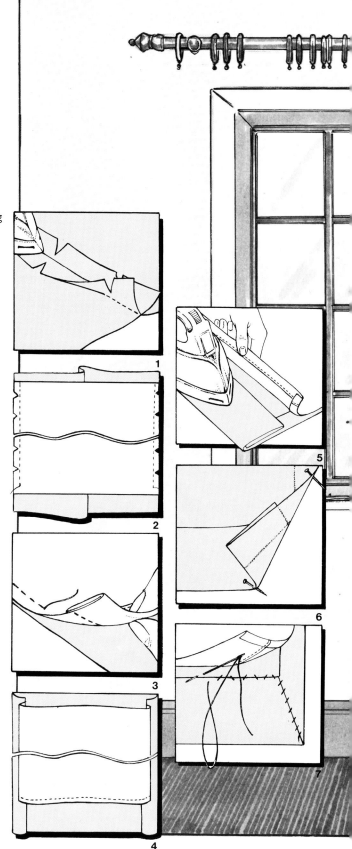

236

4 Turn curtain right-side out and press, matching the mid-points of curtain and lining panels to create equal margins of curtain fabric on each side of the lining face.

5 Press a double 7.5cm/3in hem in place on the curtain fabric. The lining should finish 5cm/2in above the curtain edge.

6 Mitre corners by marking where the turnings converge with pins. Unfold the corner and then fold up diagonally through both of the pins.

7 Refold the side and hem edges so that a mitre is formed across the corner. Slip-stitch the mitre. To weight the curtain, sew weighted tape or discs into the hem. Slip-stitch the hem.

8 Turn down the top edge of the curtain, angling it slightly at each corner. Attach the heading tape to cover the raw edge. Knot the cords at one end of the tape (on the wrong side), but leave the other ends free. Machine-stitch the tape along the sides and ends (turning the ends under) but do not sew over the free cords. Both lines of sewing should be in the same direction.

9 Pull up the cords to gather the curtain. Knot the ends into a bow or use a cord-tidy. Do not cut off the surplus – whenever you want to clean the curtain you will need to untie the knots so that you can pull the curtain flat.

10 Thread the required number of hooks through the pockets in the heading tape, spacing the hooks evenly. Hang the curtain onto the track's hooks or gliders.

11 To set the folds, tie strips of fabric around the curtain at intervals down its length and leave for a couple of days.

237

Linings and Loop Headings

Locked-in Lining

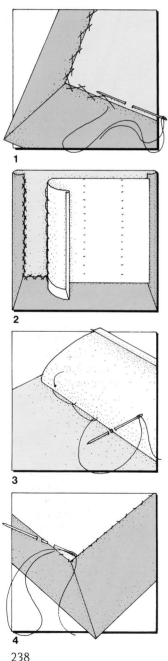

This is the professional way to line curtains. The lining is stitched to the curtain fabric with vertical rows of loose stitches. This results in the fabric hanging better. The technique is particularly recommended for curtains made of heavier material. You need equal amounts of curtain fabric and lining.

1 Turn and press 5cm/2in single-side turnings. Turn up 15cm/6in on the hem and press. Mitre the corners (see page 237) and sew edges in place, using herringbone stitch or slip stitch.

2 Using chalk, mark vertical guide lines on the reverse of the main curtain fabric, 30cm/12in apart. On the lining, trim 2cm/¾in from the top and then turn and press 2cm/¾in to the wrong side at the sides and 5cm/2in at the hem. Place the lining on the curtain fabric, 2cm/¾in down from the top, right-side out and with the mid-points aligning exactly.

3 Work from the middle out, folding back to each line. Make long loose lock stitches down the marked line, picking up only one or two threads from each layer of fabric. Space your stitches by 10cm/4in, and do not pull too tight.

4 Slip-stitch the lining to the turnings of the curtain. Turn down the top edge of the curtain and attach the heading tape (see page 232).

Detachable Lining

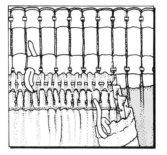

A detachable lining is useful if you need to have the curtains or drapes cleaned regularly or if you like to change them often. Like other types of lining, it will help to screen light more effectively and improve the curtain's insulating properties. However, a detachable lining does not improve the way the curtain hangs.

The curtain and the lining are made separately, the method used being in both cases as for unlined curtains (see page 235). That done, the top edge of the lining is enclosed in special lining tape. Hooks are inserted through buttonholes in the top of the lining tape, looped onto the bottom cord of the main heading tape, and turned over to slot through the glider. Some gliders have special slots for hooks.

Interlining

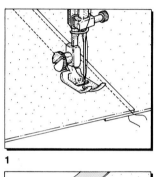

1

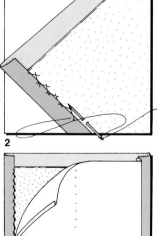

2

3

2

Interlining consists of a soft layer of wadding stitched between the lining and the curtain fabric. Available in different weights, interlining makes curtains warmer, blocks light, and keeps the fabric hanging in soft, rounded folds. You need the same amount of fabric and lining as for locked-in lining. The amount of interlining you need is the same as for a finished, flat curtain.

1 Overlap widths of interlining by 1cm/½in and sew them together either by machine-stitching two parallel rows or by herringboning. Place interlining to the wrong side of the fabric, 7.5cm/3in down from the top and centred. Lock-stitch, spacing rows of stitches at 40cm/16in intervals across the curtain.
2 Turn the edges of the fabric over the interlining at the sides and bottom, and herringbone-stitch in place.
3 Apply the lining to the interlined curtain with lock stitches, but avoid stitching over the same rows. Slip-stitch the lining to the curtain. Turn down the top edge and apply heading tape.

1 Traditional, full-gathered curtains add period style.
2 Stylish pelmets (cornices) can be made using heading tape. A coordinating trim adds decorative detail.

Making a Loop Heading

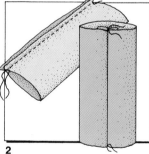

1

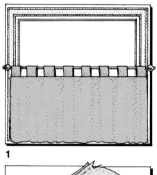

2

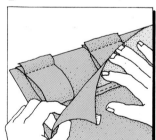

3

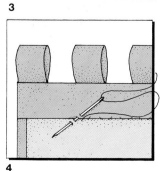

4

A loop heading is suitable for café curtains or for hanging panels of fabric.

1 Make up the curtain in the same way as for an unlined curtain (see page 235), leaving the top edge unfinished, with 1cm/½in extra allowance for turnings.
2 To establish the length of the loops, measure the circumference of the rod or pole and then add 5cm/2in for ease plus 2.5cm/1in for seams. Each loop should be 5–7.5cm/2–3in wide. Cut out, fold in half lengthways and make a 5mm/¼in seam down the long edge. Turn right-side out and press flat, with the seam at centre back.
3 Fold the loops in half widthways, and pin them to the right side of the curtain, raw edges matching. End loops should be 2cm/¾in from the edges, with the rest spaced evenly. Tack (baste) in place 1cm/½in from the top. Cut a strip of curtain fabric 7.5cm/3in deep and the same width as the curtain. Turn 5mm/¼in to the wrong side along the lower edge, press and tack. Place the facing against the top edge of the curtain, with the right sides together. Pin, tack and stitch 1cm/½in in from side and top edges, catching the loops.
4 Trim and turn the facing to the wrong side and press. Slip-stitch the bottom edge. Thread onto the pole.

239

Special Effects

Curtains can be given added impact if you dress them with pelmets (cornices) and fabric tie-backs. Both of these details are practical as well as decorative – pelmets hide the curtain heading and track, while tie-backs hold curtains in place when they are open.

Other effects can be created using fabric; you can drape lengths of material over a decorative pole, or you can make swags and tails, either to frame a window or to add a special flourish.

Pelmets (Cornices)
There are two types of pelmet: flat, shaped ones, usually attached to a pelmet board, and gathered ones (valances) which are headed or gathered like curtains and suspended from a special rail mounted just above the curtain track.

Flat pelmets have three layers: facing fabric (which can coordinate or contrast with the curtain), stiffener and lining. The lower edge can be shaped.

Gathered pelmets have a softer appearance, the folds of fabric flowing elegantly into the curtain drapery. As with flat pelmets, the lower edge can either be left straight or can be curved or castellated to frame the window. Gathered pelmets are made by attaching heading tape to pleat up the fabric in the required pattern.

Making a Pelmet

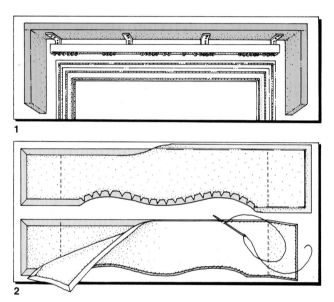

1 Make a flat pelmet from 1cm/½in plywood, 10cm/4in deep, and long enough to extend 5–7.5cm/2–3in at either end of track. Fix it to the wall using brackets.

You will need enough fabric to cover the front and sides of the board. Make a paper pattern of the pelmet shape: either draw one half of the design on folded graph paper which you can then open out to achieve a symmetrical shape or use a ready-made template or pattern. Allow 1cm/½in for the seams.
2 Cut out the pelmet stiffener to the shape of the finished pelmet, and place on the wrong side of the facing fabric, peeling off the backing.

Fold over the edges of the turnings, clip the curves, and press into place.

Press in the seam allowance on the lining, clipping curves, and lay the lining on the pelmet, wrong sides together. Slip-stitch in place. Fix the pelmet to the board with Velcro or with tacks concealed by braid.

Swags and Tails

Swags and tails are essentially draped pelmets (valances) but, unlike flat or gathered pelmets, they can be used on their own – for example, for hall windows, or wherever curtains are not desired. The swag is a draped length of fabric fixed to a board; it hangs in a graceful curve across the top of a window. At either end are pleated tails, which frame the window. A wide window can be dressed using a series of swags, with shorter tails at each tie-point.

Where the tail meets the swag it is usual to add some type of trimming, often a bow or rosette. Swags and tails can also be frilled, fringed or lined in a contrasting fabric and decorated with braid, cords or tassels.

1 A pelmet and half corona, both trimmed with red bows, enhance a cool blue bedroom.
2 Tie-backs play a significant part in unifying this scheme.

Making a Swag

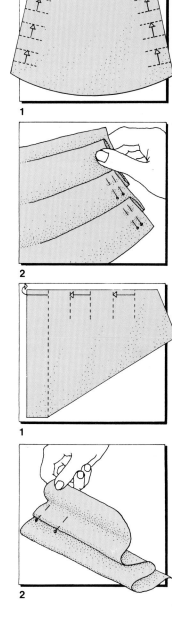

1 Cut out a pattern, as shown in the diagram. Mark pleat lines 10cm/4in apart. Cut out the main piece of fabric and lining following the pattern. (If the curtain fabric is not too heavy, you can use it for lining, too.) Sew the lining to the main fabric down the sides and along the bottom, right sides together. Trim corners, finish seams and turn right-side out.

2 Transfer the pleating points to the main fabric. Starting at the top, pin and then sew in place. Turn under the raw edge at the top and tack to the top edge of the pelmet board.

● Practise first using an old piece of material.

Making Tails

Line the tails in the same fabric, in a contrasting colour or a lining fabric.

1 Cut out the pattern, as shown in the diagram, and mark pleating lines across the top. Cut out the main piece of fabric and lining and sew them together, right sides facing, around the sides and bottom. Trim the corners and turn right-side out.

2 Fold the fabric into the pleats. Pin and sew in place. Turn under the raw edge at the top and tack to the top edge of the board. Reverse the pattern and make the tail at the other side.

Making a Tie-back

Like pelmets, tie-backs can be made of fabric, shaped in various ways and coordinated or contrasted with the curtain fabric. They can also be trimmed (with braid, piping or frills) or plaited. A simple finishing touch, tie-backs are particularly useful for curtains that do not draw.

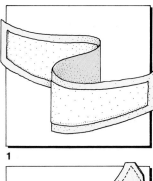

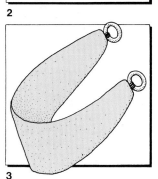

To calculate how long the tie-back should be, hold a tape measure around the curtain, and drape it loosely. Position a hook on the wall, and screw it into place.

Make a pattern of the shape you want. For a symmetrical shape, place the pattern on a double thickness of fabric, with the centre of the pattern aligning with the fold. For each tie-back you will need two pieces of fabric, 1cm/½in larger than the pattern all around.

1 Cut a piece of fusible interfacing to fit the pattern, and iron to the wrong side of one piece of fabric.
2 Place the second piece of fabric over the first, right sides together. Pin, tack (baste) and stitch all round, leaving an opening of about 10cm/4in for turning.
3 Trim the corners and seams and turn the tie-backs right-side out. Slip-stitch the opening and stitch onto each end a curtain ring to loop onto the hook in the wall.

Fabric Blinds and Shades

Fabric blinds make versatile, practical and attractive alternatives to curtains. Unlike curtains, they do not provide much insulation against heat loss, but they are more economical to make since you need much less fabric. Styles range from plain, utilitarian roller blinds or shades to extravagant festoon blinds.

Measuring
The size of blind you require will depend on whether the window is recessed or not. If the window is flat, take width measurements across the frame; if it is recessed, measure between the flanking walls or from the outside of the recess to the other side. On large horizontal windows, a series of blinds looks more balanced and works better than one large one.

Festoon blinds require twice the width of fabric if they have a heading, and 1⅓ times the depth; otherwise, you need merely 1⅓ times the depth.

Roller Blinds and Shades
The most widespread type of fabric blind, the roller blind, consists of a sturdy or stiffened fabric wound onto a usually wooden roller. The roller incorporates a spring so that the blind can be lowered to any position and then released to snap back

into its rolled-up state. A lath is slotted through a casing on the lower edge of the blind to hold it straight.

You can buy roller blinds ready-made or have them made-to-measure. Alternatively, kits are available which consist of a roller, brackets for holding the blind in place, a lath and a cord pull (you use your own fabric); the roller supplied can be sawn shorter if it is too long for the window.

Roman Blinds
Classic and elegant, Roman blinds are less severe-looking than the flat version. The blind is attached at the top to a wooden batten; vertical cords threaded through rings attached to the back of the blind allow it to be pulled up into soft horizontal folds. The bottom of the blind is stiffened with a wooden lath. Roman blinds look best if they are lined. They can be very effective if trimmed with contrasting banding.

Festoon Blinds and Shades
Festoon blinds can be made in different ways, but all types pull up into soft, billowing folds. Depending on the type of fabric and trimming, the festoon can look theatrical or elegant. Trimming with ruffles, flounces or fringing will accentuate the opulent flowing lines and will add simple decorative detail.

One type of festoon blind is a cross between a curtain and a Roman blind. Like a curtain, it is headed, lined, weighted and hung from a track using hooks; like a Roman blind, it is pulled up by means of cords which run through rings sewn on the reverse side. Other festoon blinds have cased headings or are attached to rails.

Suitable Fabrics
For roller blinds, choose any firm closely woven cloth, such as cotton furnishing fabric. Specially stiffened fabrics for roller blinds are available, but you can equally well buy a lightweight cheap fabric and apply spray-on stiffener to it (see right). Avoid fabric that might sag, stretch or bunch up untidily. Plain colours,

small repeat designs and even large prints can all be very effective.

Most types of curtain fabric – including cotton, chintz, sateen and linen union – are suitable for Roman blinds. Fabric with an overt texture can look very attractive, but it is important to select patterns with care – stripes and geometric designs work better when pleated up horizontally than do large, figurative or circular motifs.

Festoon blinds with curtain headings can be made from any type of not too heavy curtain fabric sturdy enough to pleat up well. Lining is recommended. By contrast, festoons with cased headings can be made in lighter, semi-transparent material and left unlined.

Avoid prints that are too busy and fussy. Geometrics, stripes, plain textured weaves and simple floral prints are all good prints to use.

Spray-on Stiffener

Lightweight material, including lace, can be used to make a roller blind if you treat the fabric with stiffener.

You will need to hem the sides by 1cm/½in to prevent fraying. The fabric might shrink after the stiffener has been applied, so allow extra. Test a small area first: spray it with stiffener, leave it to dry, and see what happens. Avoid loose-weave fabrics that might stretch after hanging.

Decorative Edges

To add interest and soften the plain lines of a roller blind, finish it by adding a decorative edge.

First stitch a casing for the wooden lath, about 12.5cm/5in up from the bottom edge of the blind. Stiffen the hem with iron-on fabric facing. Make a paper pattern of the required shape and cut it out. Finish the cut edge. To keep a castellated edge hanging straight, slot a rod through.

4

5

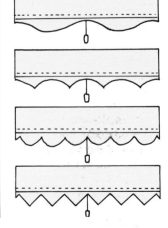

1 Luxurious festoon blinds in a light cream fabric.
2 Floral patterned roller blind makes a cheerful kitchen view.
3 Roman blinds look crisp and elegant in geometric fabrics.
4 The effect of Japanese screens, created by plain Roman blinds.
5 Sheer fabric festoons, for a turn-of-the-century atmosphere.
6 A roller blind painted with a country scene.

6

Making a Roman Blind

Roman blinds can be fitted to either recessed or unrecessed windows. If the window is recessed, you can hang the blind inside or outside: inside the recess, the board can be fixed to the recess ceiling; outside, secure it to the wall using brackets.

them at intervals of 25–30cm/10–12in. Also, you will need cord and a screw eye for each row of tape: to calculate the amount of cord required, measure twice the length of the blind, add the width, and then multiply this figure by the number of rows of tape.

Calculating Amounts

Fix the heading board in position temporarily to measure up. To calculate the length of fabric required, measure from over the top of the board to the sill, adding 15cm/6in to the length for hem and top fixing. Add 7.5cm/3in to the width for the side turnings. The lining should be 10cm/4in shorter and 10cm/4in narrower than the blind fabric.

The blind is pulled up by means of cords running through ringed tapes sewn to the back. The tape is attached in vertical rows, one at each side with others between

Materials and Equipment

- blind fabric
- lining
- ringed blind tape
- cord
- screw eyes (one for each row of tape)
- thread, pins and needles
- scissors
- sewing machine
- wooden batten (5 × 2.5cm/2 × 1in) for the heading board
- wooden batten (2.5 × 0.5cm/1in × ¼in)
- cleat for securing cords
- hammer and tacks, or stapling gun and staples
- angle brackets
- screwdriver

METHOD

1 Trim or snip selvedges to prevent puckering. Join any widths with flat seams; place part-widths to the outside, matching pattern if necessary. Repeat with lining fabric. Mark the mid-points of the lining and blind fabric and, with right sides together, align the top and sides and machine-stitch 1cm/½in side seams. The surplus fabric will form a pleat at the back. Press the seams open.

2 Turn right sides out, matching the mid-points, and press so that the blind fabric forms equal margins at the sides. Turn up the main fabric by 1cm/½in at the bottom, then turn up 10cm/4in to make a hem. Pin in place.

3 Mark guide lines for tape rows. Attach tapes, the first two covering the two side seams and the others spaced evenly between. Rings should align horizontally across the blind; the

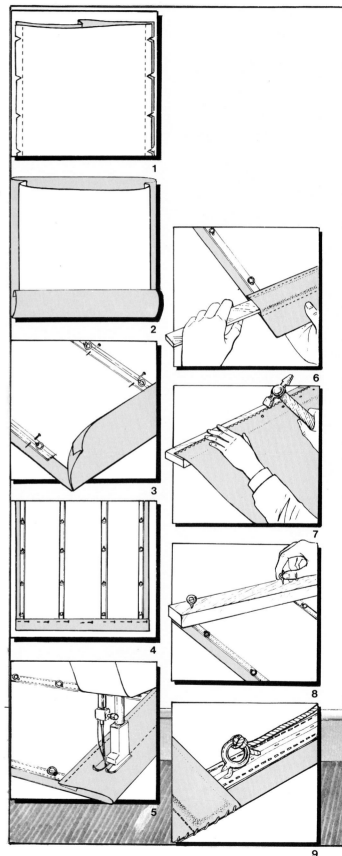

bottom ring should be 1cm/½in from the hem edge. Tuck the tape ends into the hem.

4 Machine-stitch through all thicknesses along both sides of the ringed tape.

5 Machine-stitch twice across the hem, first to catch in the ends of the tape and, again, 4cm/1½in down to form a casing.

6 Trim the smaller batten to make it just shorter than the width of the blinds and slot it into the casing. Slip-stitch the ends so that the batten is enclosed; continue down the ends of the hem to finish.

7 Zigzag-stitch the top edges of the blind together, catching in the raw edges of the tapes. Lay the heading board on a flat surface and position the edge of the blind 2cm/¾in over the wide side of it. Tack or staple at 10cm/4in intervals.

8 Fix screw eyes into the underside of the heading board at the top of each row of tape. Use a larger eye at the right-hand side, because all the cords will converge here.

9 With the blind still laid flat, tie cords to the bottom rings and thread them through each row and through the eyes at the top, working towards the right.

10 Knot the cords together about 5cm/2in from the last eye.

11 Fix the heading board either to the top of the window using angle brackets or directly into the recess ceiling. Trim the cords so that they are level and knot at the bottom. Screw the cleat to the wall near the bottom of the window to secure the cords. Keep the blind drawn up for a couple of days until the pleats in the fabric are firmly established.

Other Types of Blinds and Shades

Blinds come in materials other than fabric: metal, paper, wood and plastic are the notable ones. In style they range from the crisp, graphic quality of Venetian blinds to the soft, diffused effect of slatted wood and split cane. Most of the types discussed here are available in a range of standard widths and lengths; the more expensive, such as Venetian blinds, can be made up to your own specifications.

Prices vary widely. Standard pleated-paper blinds are among the cheapest window treatments of all, whereas Venetian blinds can cost almost as much as lined curtains. Maintenance, too, varies – from easy-care types such as cane blinds to Venetian blinds which are notoriously difficult to clean.

Paper Blinds
Made of tough paper or fibre, these blinds are permanently pleated and, since they pull up into the window reveal, can be combined with curtains. They are cheap and easy to dust, but are available only in a limited range. Balastore blinds are paper blinds with pierced holes.

Cane Blinds
Evocative of Mediterranean terraces, cane blinds – made from whole or split bamboo – roll or pleat up. They do not

screen light completely, but they are effective in conservatories or wherever there is no requirement for privacy but where you want to mute strong sunlight.

Wooden Blinds
Wooden blinds are made of slats of wood in either natural shades or dark green (they can also be sprayed). 'Pinoleum' blinds have thin strips of wood woven with cotton in wide widths, and suit inaccessible windows.

Plastic Blinds
Available in a good colour range, plastic blinds consist of thin strips assembled in roughly the same way as the laths of a wooden blind. Easy to clean, plastic blinds suit kitchens and bathrooms.

Vertical Louvres
These vertical blinds, made of canvas, wood or synthetic-fibre strips, are fixed to the

window. They can be pivoted to allow different degrees of light to filter through, or they can be drawn across. They particularly suit contemporary settings and large picture windows.

1 *Vibrant yellow pleated-paper blinds diffuse light effectively in a modern kitchen.*
2 *Tiered louvred shutters have a traditional appearance.*
3 *Black Venetian blinds screen a utility corner.*

4

5

7

6

Venetian Blinds

Venetian blinds – slatted, adjustable blinds that pull up to the reveal – are available in plastic, metal and wood. The metal variety comes with either standard or fine slats and in a range of colours and finishes, including striped and gradated versions; there are also types pierced with holes. Operation of the blinds is by use of cords or rods. Wooden Venetian blinds are made of cedar or pine.

The great advantage of Venetian blinds is that they can be adjusted to allow varying degrees of light to filter through: fully open, they are almost invisible. Also, they can be used to cover very wide windows and made to any specification. Originally designed for office use, they suit modern interiors, but in neutral colours they can be unobtrusive enough to combine well with curtains in more traditional settings.

Shutters

Internal wooden shutters have a traditional, rustic appearance. They can be fixed to half or full height, and are usually louvred to allow light to filter through.

4 Fine Venetian blinds make a shimmering window treatment.
5 Vertical louvres particularly suit large expanses of window.
6 Bamboo blinds add character to a modern bedroom.
7 Natural wooden louvres.

Glossary

Where meaning differs, the US term is cross-referenced to the British term.

Accent lighting The use of lights such as spots or wallwashers to highlight architectural features, objects or displays.

Acetate (cellulose acetate) Strictly speaking, any of a family of esters used in fabrics, etc. The type used in, for example, stencilling comes in thin, tough transparent sheets.

Advancing colours Colours which, when painted on a surface, seem to make that surface come towards you; they can be used to make a room seem smaller. 'Hot' and 'warm' colours – reds, oranges and yellows – can have this effect.

Alkyds A family of synthetic resins used as binders in oil-based paints.

Anaglypta An extremely heavily embossed wallpaper, used for wall or ceiling decorations.

Antiquing Any of various painting and varnishing techniques used to artificially age a surface.

Background lighting Essentially, the use of artificial lighting sources as a replacement for natural daylight, providing a general level of illumination.

Baseboard See *skirting*.

Batten A wooden or metal strip. In the United States larger battens are referred to as furring strips (*q.v.*).

Bauhaus movement This movement took its name from a workshop (the Bauhaus) founded in 1919 by Walter Gropius. The movement aimed to design articles that were suitable for mass-production and yet were elegant and functional.

Beading Wood or other material supplied in the form of a thin strip and used for edging, ornamentation, etc. See also *moulding*.

Blind nailing See *secret nailing*.

Blistering The formation of air-bubbles in a layer of paint or varnish, or under a wallcovering.

Blockboard A thicker form of plywood (*q.v.*). Two layers of softwood, their grains at right angles, are sandwiched between two outer layers of veneer.

Burlap See *hessian*.

Casement A type of window having, typically, one fixed pane, a small top pane that can be opened, and one large pane that can be opened (usually hinged at the side).

Cavity wall A wall constructed in the form of two outer layers sandwiching a gap of air. Extra insulation can be provided by filling the gap with, e.g., expanded polystyrene beads.

Ceiling rose (medallion) A roughly circular ceiling decoration, usually placed centrally on the ceiling. The rose is often of plaster, and in many cases a lighting fixture may be suspended from it.

Cellulose acetate See *acetate*.

Chipboard (particleboard) A substitute for wooden boards created by bonding together fragments of wood using a synthetic resin. Chipboard can be bought either plain or veneered in wood or plastic laminate.

Cissing A technique analogous to spattering (*q.v.*). Rather than spattering on a wash or glaze, however, you completely cover the base coat and then flick it with specks of the appropriate solvent for effect.

Coir matting Matting made from coconut fibres.

Colour washing Painting on several weak layers of wash or glaze over a base colour in order to produce an extremely luminous colour effect.

Combing A decorative paint technique. Paint on a base coat and, when this has dried, cover it with a glaze. While the glaze is still wet, 'tease' it with a comb.

Corbel A bracket of brick, stone or plaster; usually an internal feature.

Cornice See *pelmet*.

Cornice (crown molding) A decorative band of plaster, wood or other material set horizontally at the junction of a wall and a ceiling or of a wall and a roof.

Crown molding See *cornice*.

Cutting-in brush A paintbrush specially designed for painting along the edges of, for example, ceiling lines and window frames.

Dado (wainscoting) The lower part of a wall whose upper and lower parts have been divided by a horizontal rail (a dado rail). By analogy, the lower part of a wall, if decorated differently from the upper (e.g., with different wallpaper).

Dhurrie Also spelled 'durrie', an Indian flat-weave rug, usually made from cotton, and displaying geometric designs.

Distemper A type of paint made by mixing glue and water with size, whiting etc. Ready-made distemper is now out of commercial production, but you can make it yourself.

Distressed effects Decorative paint techniques that make use of broken colours rather than solid ones. Examples are ragging and sponging (*qq.v.*).

Double glazing The setting of two parallel panes of glass in a window frame to reduce heat loss, external noise, etc. Equivalent to the fitting of a storm window (*q.v.*).

Double hem A hem in which the fabric is turned over not once but twice by the same amount, so that the raw edge is completely enclosed.

Dragging A decorative paint technique for walls and ceilings.

After a coloured base coat has dried you apply a glaze and, while this is still wet, you drag an almost-dry paintbrush across it.

'Drop' pattern A wallpaper pattern in which the repeated images match up diagonally rather than horizontally.

Dry laying Setting down tiles without using adhesive so that you can adjust pattern and positions before starting to fix the tiles into place.

Dry rot Severe form of decay in which, due to the presence of certain fungi, wood (or any other vegetable matter) dries out and crumbles. Dry rot spreads readily.

Drywall See *plasterboard*.

Efflorescence A powdery white substance that can appear on the surface of new brickwork or a newly plastered wall. Soluble salts in the brick or plaster react with moisture and force their way to the surface.

Eggshell (semi-gloss) paint A type of oil-based paint with a mid-sheen finish – halfway between matt and gloss.

Emulsion (latex) paint Water-based paint used principally to cover walls and ceilings.

Enamel paint Very dense oil-based paint used for small areas of woodwork and metal; only a single coat is required.

Faux bois Decorative paint technique which simulates the effect of wooden surfaces.

Fender A low screen that stops burning coals and logs rolling out of an open fire.

Fibreboard Plant (usually wood) fibres compressed to form thin sheets, often used for insulation and as a wallcovering. Compare *wallboard*.

Fibreglass Any material made out of thin, closely matted fibres of glass. Fibreglass blankets are much used for insulation. Sometimes called 'glass wool'.

Flat fell seam The most widely used seam in upholstery and curtain-making, whereby raw edges are completely enclosed.

Flat paint Oil-based paint which is matt (*q.v.*).

Flat seam The simplest way of stitching two pieces of fabric together, but not advisable where a strong finish is required. Compare *flat fell seam*.

Flokati A type of shaggy-pile woollen rug, usually white or off-white, made in Greece.

Frieze A band of plaster, paper or other material usually placed horizontally all around the four walls of a room, often at or above cornice (crown moulding) height.

Furring strips Large battens (*q.v.*) of wood or metal.

Glaze A transparent, or semi-transparent, thinned oil-based paint applied over a base colour, so that one or both are enriched and intensified. A number of decorative techniques – e.g.,

combing (*q.v.*) – depend on the use of glazes.

Gloss paint Oil-based paint that provides a shiny finish. Gloss is used mainly for woodwork and metalwork, for interior and exterior surfaces.

Graining See *woodgraining*.

Grosgrain Heavily ribbed silk (or, nowadays, rayon) tape used as a trim for upholstery or clothes and as banding on fabric-covered walls.

Grout Often called 'grouting', a filling that is inserted between tiles after they have been stuck in place. The grout ensures that the entire area is properly sealed. It can be coloured for graphic decorative effect.

Gypsum board See *plasterboard*.

Hardboard (masonite) A type of board usually used for surfacing. Made from compressed vegetable (usually wood) fibres, it is shiny on one side (the outer side) and textured on the other.

Herringbone stitch A simple type of stitch widely used for fastening hems.

Hessian (burlap) A coarse fabric woven from jute, hemp or similar fibre. It can be used as a wallcovering and is available with a paper backing.

Hygrovents Porous earthenware tubes inserted in walls to attract water, which then evaporates away through them.

Insulating board A type of board applied to ceilings and walls in order to reduce noise penetration and improve heat insulation.

Kelim A type of flat-weave rug, usually woollen and in rich earth colours, made in Turkey and Afghanistan.

Key (1) A surface of suitable roughness for the application of a coat of paint, plaster or whatever. (2) A substance applied in order to create such a surface.

Lacquer (1) A hard, glossy coating. (2) The substance used to produce such a coating, consisting of natural or synthetic resins dissolved in a volatile liquid; as the solvent evaporates it leaves the coating behind.

Lambrequin A deep valance (*q.v.*) that frames a window, extending some distance at either side.

Latex paint See *emulsion paint*.

Load-bearing wall A structural wall supporting a load (usually the wall above). Before you remove or alter a wall of this type you must install a lintel to carry the load. Compare *partition wall*.

Local lighting See *task lighting*.

Lock stitch This is used to hold the lining and interlining of a curtain loosely to the main fabric.

Mahlstick Often called a 'maulstick', a stick used by artists to help steady the hand.

Glossary

Marbling A decorative paint technique designed to simulate the appearance or general effect of a marbled surface.

Masking tape Sticky tape that can be peeled off easily without lifting off the surface beneath it. It can be used to provide a straight crisp edge when you are painting a flat surface, or to protect the glass when you are painting a window frame.

Masonite See *hardboard*.

Matt paint Water- or oil-based paint whose finish shows little or no sheen.

Maulstick See *mahlstick*.

Medallion See *ceiling rose*.

Mitre More correctly, 'mitre joint', a joint whereby two pieces of wood, plastic or other material are joined by cutting bevels at complementary angles at the end of each piece.

Monochromatic colour scheme A colour scheme in which all the colours used are variants of a single colour.

Moulding (1) A narrow piece of wood or other material used as a decorative edging; essentially, a synonym for beading (*q.v.*). (2) A decorative element, usually on a wall or ceiling (often where a wall joins a ceiling), commonly made out of plaster or similar material. See also *cornice*.

Mural A picture or pattern painted directly onto a wall. The term is often used today to mean also anything that gives the general impression of being a true mural – such as the self-adhesive 'mural panels' you can buy in some stores.

Numdah A type of cheap embroidered rug made in India.

Ogee A moulding with an S-shaped cross-section.

Paint pad A rectangular pile-covered foam pad attached to a handle and used to apply paint (usually emulsion) swiftly and smoothly to large surfaces.

Parquet A form of wooden floor covering, usually polished. Traditionally, laying parquet involved the use of small pieces of wood. Today parquet is available in tile form.

Particleboard See *chipboard*.

Partition wall An internal wall that divides up areas but does not carry any direct load. Compare *load-bearing wall*.

Pelmet (cornice) A decorative surround, usually made of fabric or wood, which covers a curtain heading, and adds definition to window treatments.

Plasterboard (drywall, gypsum board) Board used for surfacing walls and ceilings. It consists of standard-sized sheets of plaster sandwiched between external paper coverings.

Plywood A type of board made by gluing together several thin layers of wood. Often used to make sub-floors.

Polyesters A family of plastics with diverse uses. Polyester fibres are used (usually blended with natural fibres) in fabrics, while resinous forms are used in varnishes and certain paints.

Polystyrene A plastic used in both solid and expanded forms for wall or ceiling tiles, packaging, etc. The expanded form is used also for insulation and as a stuffing for cheap furniture. Should you be thinking of buying polystyrene-stuffed furniture, first check that it does not constitute a fire hazard.

Polyurethane (1) A synthetic resin used in the manufacture of paints and varnishes. (2) Synonymous with any transparent synthetic wood varnish, usually but not necessarily containing polyurethane. These yellow with age. (3) A foam used in cheap upholstery. Unless specially treated it is highly inflammable, and furniture containing it is banned in several countries.

Polyvinyl chloride See *vinyl*.

Primer A first coat of paint applied to a surface in order to provide a good key for subsequent coats, to seal and protect the surface, and to prevent it from absorbing the outer coats.

PVC See *vinyl*.

Ragging A decorative paint technique whereby you dip clothes into washes or glazes (*q.v.*) and use the crumpled fabric to make prints on a surface. In much the same way, you can completely cover a base colour with a wash or glaze and then selectively reveal the base colour using crumpled fabric.

Rag-rolling A variant of ragging (*q.v.*) whereby you roll a cloth down over a surface. Either roll a cloth dipped in glaze over a background colour or use a clean cloth to distress a wet surface.

Receding colours Colours that, when applied to a surface, make it appear to recede from you. Receding colours – the 'cool' colours such as blue and grey – can be used to make a small room seem larger.

Room divider Any unit – such as a bookcase, set of shelves or screen – that can be used to divide a larger room into much smaller areas.

Rose (medallion) See *ceiling rose*.

Rya A type of shaggy-pile rug made in Finland.

Screed (1) A layer of material (e.g., concrete or cement mortar) used to even off the surface of a floor prior to the application of a hard or heavy type of flooring. (2) As a verb: to bring a material flush with the surface around it.

Secret nailing Also known as 'blind nailing', a technique of driving nails into wooden boards so that their heads are underneath the surface and are hidden by an adjoining board.

Selvedge On a piece of fabric, a finished border that will not fray.

Semi-gloss paint See *eggshell paint*.

Serape A coarse flat-weave Mexican cloak, often fringed, used as a rug.

Shirring (1) Gathering or puckering a piece of fabric into rows, using elastic or stitching. (2) Adorning a wall with panels of shirred fabric.

Sisal matting Matting made using fibres derived from the leaves of various types of agave plant.

Skirting (baseboard) A border, usually of wood but sometimes of plaster or plastic, covering the base of a wall where it meets the floor. Can conceal wiring.

Slip stitch A type of stitch used for joining two folded edges or to hold a folded edge to a flat edge – e.g., a curtain hem.

Soffit The underside of, for example, an arch, door or window frame.

Spattering Simple distressed paint effect achieved by dipping the bristles of a stiff brush in paint and flicking it at a surface.

Sponging Decorative paint technique using a sea sponge or equivalent either to dab a top coat (or coats) of a wash or glaze over a base coat or to remove selected areas of an overlying wash or glaze.

Stencilling A way of decorating surfaces by dabbing paint through a motif (or motifs) cut

out of acetate or similar medium onto a surface.

Stippling Creating a 'speckled' effect using one of two similar techniques. Either cover a base coat with a glaze or wash and, while it is still wet, strike it with a flat-faced brush, so that flecks of the base colour are revealed, or simply apply speckles by dipping a brush into a glaze or wash and then stab with it at the base coat.

Storm window An extra window fitted externally to reduce heat loss, noise, etc.

Straightedge A metal or wooden strip one of whose surfaces can be used to draw an exactly straight line.

Sugar soap An alkaline preparation, available in crystal form to be mixed with water, which is used to clean and degrease painted surfaces.

Swag A loop of draped fabric, suspended across the top of a window, either as a pelmet (*q.v.*) or on its own as a window treatment. A wide window may have a series of swags.

Tails Lengths of pleated fabric attached to either end of a swag (*q.v.*), framing a window.

Task lighting Lighting placed to perform a particular function. Task lighting can be anything from a bedside lamp to a strip light in a kitchen. Also called 'local' lighting.

Template A cut-out pattern (perhaps in card) used so that

the same line can be reproduced many times over.

Tie-back A length of fabric, cord or similar attached to a window frame and used to loop back a curtain.

Tongue-and-groove panelling A type of panelling that is easy to assemble. Each board has on one side a tongue and on the other a groove into which a tongue can fit.

Tortoise-shelling Paint technique that seeks to imitate – or at least give the overall effect of – natural tortoise-shell.

Trompe l'oeil A type of highly realistic decorative painting which aims to 'deceive the eye'; for example, balusters painted at the base of a wall.

Undercoat A type of paint or stain applied to a surface to provide a good key for the final top coat.

Valance A frill of fabric. Valances can be used to cover curtain fittings (i.e., as a fabric pelmet (*q.v.*) or to trim the base of a chair or bed.

Veneer A thin sheet of material fastened to the surface of a board or plank. Veneers are typically of wood – often of valuable wood – but synthetic materials of many kinds are also used.

Vermiculite Any of various minerals largely made up of hydrated magnesium, aluminium and iron silicates. Expanded by heat, they are much used for

insulation (often in granular form).

Vinyl (polyvinyl chloride, PVC) A thermoplastic found in many applications: floorings, tiles, fabrics, etc. However, the exact properties of any vinyl-based product depend on the nature of the 'plasticizer' – the material used in conjunction with the PVC.

Vinyl wallpapers Wallpapers that have a plastic coating so that they can be scrubbed. They are especially suitable for kitchens, bathrooms and children's rooms.

Wainscoting An additional surface, usually of wood, applied to the lower part of a wall to a height of perhaps 1m/3ft 3in.

Wallboard Board made out of compressed plant (usually wood) fibres or plaster sandwiched between paper and used as a surface for walls and ceilings and in insulation. Compare *fibreboard*, *plasterboard*.

Wet rot Caused by various types of fungi, a condition in which wood decays. The surface of the wood feels 'clammy'.

Whiting Powdered and cleansed white chalk used, for example, in distemper and whitewash.

Woodgraining A painting technique which seeks to imitate – or at least to give the overall effect of – the grain of wood.

Woodworm Condition in which wood is invaded by the common furniture beetle.

INDEX

252

ACKNOWLEDGEMENTS

EWA in the acknowledgements is an abbreviation of Elizabeth Whiting & Associates. The publisher thanks the following photographers and organizations for their kind permission to reproduce the photographs in this book:

1–2 1 Dennis Krukowski (designer David Webster), 2 Dennis Krukowski/Conran Octopus (Mary Jean and John Winkler); 4–5 Ken Kirkwood/*Homes and Gardens*/Syndication International; 8–9 Bill Stites; 10–11 EWA; 30–31 Jan Baldwin/*Homes and Gardens*/Syndication International; 32–33 1 Dennis Krukowski (designer David Webster), 2 Simon Brown/Conran Octopus (Graham Carr), 3 Jean-Paul Bonhommet, 4 Roland Beaufre/Agence Top (designer Jacques Granges); 34–35 1 Ianthe Ruthven, 2 Dennis Krukowski (designer Tonin MacCallum), 3 Bill Stites/Conran Octopus (Mary Gilliatt), 4, 5 Jean-Paul Bonhommet, 36–37 Dennis Krukowski/Conran Octopus (designer John Paul Beaujard); 38–39 1 Karen Bussolini (stencils by John Canning), 2 Roland Beaufre/Agence Top (Suzy Frankfurt), 3 Bill Stites/Conran Octopus (designer Mary Gilliatt), 4 Karen Bussolini (paint by John Canning), 5 Roland Beaufre/Agence Top (designer Henri Garelli), 6 Jean-Paul Bonhommet; 40–41 1 Lars Hallen, 2 Jean-Paul Bonhommet, 3 Jack Parsons for *Sante*

Tonin MacCallum); 150–151 1 Clive Helm/EWA, 2 Rodney Hyett/EWA, 3, 4 Jean-Paul Bonhommet; 152–153 1, 2 Jean-Paul Bonhommet; 154–155 Simon Brown/Conran Octopus (architect Trevor Horne); 156–157 John Hollingshead; 158–159 1 John Hollingshead, 2–3 Jean-Paul Bonhommet; 160–161 1 Michael Dunne/EWA, 2 John Hollingshead, 3 Jean-Paul Bonhommet; 162–163 Shona Wood/Conran Octopus (Polly Powell); 166–167 1 Michael Newton, 2 Garry Chowanetz/EWA, 3 Simon Brown/Conran Octopus (designers Jerry Hewitt and Angela Hewitt-Woods), 4 Shona Wood/Conran Octopus (Helen Preston); 170–171 1 Camera Press, 2 Michael Dunne/EWA, 3 Michael Newton/Conran Octopus; 174–175 John Hollingshead/UK, *Family Circle*; 176–177 1 Spike Powell/EWA, 2 Simon Brown/Conran Octopus (architect Ian Hutchinson); 178–179 1, 2 John Hollingshead, 3 Simon Brown/Conran Octopus (architect Ian Hutchinson); 182–183 1 Simon Brown/Conran Octopus (artist Elyane de la Rochette), 2 Dennis Krukowski/Conran Octopus (designer John Paul Beaujard); 184–185 1 Jessica Strang, 2 Shona Wood/Conran Octopus (designer Anthony Paine), 3 Simon Brown/Conran Octopus (Paul Hodgkinson—design by Simon Design Consultants), 4 Shona Wood/Conran Octopus (Michael Snyder); 188–189 Roland Beaufre/Agence Top (designer Madeleine Castaing), 2 Michael Dunne/EWA, 3 Karen Bussolini (paint by John Canning), 4 Simon Brown/Conran Octopus (paint by John Ebdon), 5 Ianthe Ruthven, 6 Jean-Paul Bonhommet; 190–191 1 Karen Bussolini (stencils by John Canning), 2, 3 David Cripps/EWA, 4 Spike Powell/EWA; 194–195 Michael Newton/Conran Octopus; 198–199 1 Dennis Krukowski (designer Tonin MacCallum), 2 Pascal Hinous/Agence Top; 200–201 1 Andreas von Einsiedel/EWA, 2 Jean-Paul Bonhommet, 3 Simon Brown/Conran Octopus (Paul Hodgkinson—design by Simon Design Consultants), 4 Karen Bussolini (architects Andrew Robinson & Marsden Moran), 5 Michael Newton/Conran Octopus; 204–205 1 Tom Lorimer/EWA, 2 Michael Dunne/EWA, 3 Annet Held; 206–207 1 Ken Kirkwood/Conran Octopus (designer George Powers), 2 Andreas von Einsiedel/EWA; 210–211 1 Ornella Sancassani/*Abitare*, 2 Lars Hallen, 3 Karen Bussolini; 215–216 1 John Vaughan, 2 Ralph Bogertman/*Decorating Remodeling*; 218–219 1 Michael Newton/Conran Octopus, 2 Dennis Krukowski (designer David Webster); 222–223 1 Michael Newton/Conran Octopus, 2 Roland Beaufre/Agence Top, 226–227 1, 2 David Black, 3 P J Gates, 4 Helen Yardley, 5 Jean-Paul Bonhommet, 6 Omberto Gigli; 228–229 1 Dennis Krukowski/Conran Octopus (Mary Jean & John Winkler), 2 Michael Newton/Conran Octopus; 230–231 1 Annet Held, 2 Jean-Paul Bonhommet, 3 Michael Newton/Conran Octopus; 232–233 1 Michael Dunne/EWA, 2 Jean-Paul Bonhommet; 1 234–235 1 Michael Newton/Conran Octopus, 2 Pascal Chevalier/Agence Top (designer Henri Garelli); 238–239 1 Brian Harrison/*Ideal Home*/Syndication International, 2 Ian Kalinowski/*Options*/Syndication International; 240–241 1 Michael Dunne/EWA, 2 Spike Powell/EWA; 242–243 1 Jean-Paul Bonhommet, 2 Di Lewis/EWA, 3 Shona Wood/Conran Octopus (Helen Preston), 4 Antoine Rozès, 5 Roland Beaufre/Agence Top (Suzy Frankfurt), 6 Dennis Krukowski (designer Beverly Ellsley); 246–247 1 John Hollingshead/*Homes and Gardens*/Syndication International, 2 Dulux, 3 Rodney Hyett/EWA, 4 John Hollingshead/*Homes & Gardens*/Syndication International, 5 Jean-Paul Bonhommet, 6 Tim Street-Porter/EWA, 7 Rodney Hyett/EWA.

The publisher would also like to thank the following for their assistance: ICI Paint Division, Wexham Road, Slough SL2 5DS; Crown Decorative Products, Darwen, Lancs; The Flowersmith, 34 Shelton Street, London WC2.

Material for photography was supplied by the following companies:

p.171 Types of Paint
1,3,4,5 Crown Decorative Products; 2 International Paint
p.195 Wallpapers
1,2 John Oliver; 3,24,30 Designers Guild; 4,10 Crown Decorative Products; 5,8 Nairnflock; 6,20 Osborne & Little; 7,12 Tektura; 9,11,13,14,19,29 Arthur Sanderson & Sons; 15,18 Habitat; 16,21,22,23,26,27,28 Warner & Sons; 17 Jane Churchill; 25 Laura Ashley
p.201 Wall Tiles and Cladding
1,21 Boydens; 2,3,6,8,12,13,20,22 Fired Earth; 4,7,10,11,14,15,16,18,23 World's End Tiles; 5,9 Formica; 17 Barkers; 19 Wicanders
p.218 Floor Tiles
1,2,12,14 World's End Tiles; 3,4,16 Amtico; 5 Forbo-Nairn; 6,7,8,9,10,11,13,15,18,19 Fired Earth; 17 Boydens; 20 Wicanders; 21 Reed-Harris
p.222 Carpets
1,12 Tretford Carpets; 2,5,7,9 Allied Carpets; 3,4,6,10,11,13 Brintons; 8 The Gates Rubber Company
p.229 Matting
1,2,4,5,6,9,10,11,12,13,14 David Douglas; 3,8 Habitat
p.231 Curtain Fabrics
1,2,6,9, Arthur Sanderson & Sons; 3 Osborne & Little; 4,5,8,10 Warner & Sons; 7,11,12,13 Laura Ashley
p.234 Sheer Fabrics
1 Ado International; 2,4,5,6 Paris Voile; 3 John Aird & Co.; 7,8 Warner & Sons

Author's Acknowledgements

I have so many people to thank for this book: Elizabeth Wilhide gave so much of her time, help and energy in a particularly generous way. Hilary Arnold, who conceived the project in its present form, makes working with Conran Octopus a great pleasure, not just I think for me, but for everyone. Polly Powell kept me on the straight and narrow as gracefully as possible and became a new friend, and I have always to thank Alison Cathie and Ray Roberts for their strong support. I could not even begin to encompass my various projects without the efficiency, care and thoughtfulness of Amelia Anderson and Mary Rooke, who are both so talented in design in their own way. Nor could we have illustrated the book so well without the inspiration, intuition and sheer hard work of my art editor, Karen Bowen, editorial assistant, Jane Harcus and picture researcher, Shona Wood.

Barbara Pierce, Alathea Michie, David and Bobby Margolis were also very generous with their suggestions, enthusiasm and patience in various ways. And I particularly want to record my gratitude to Felicity Bryan and Bob Levine who have been so caring, and so very supportive.

The Publisher would like to thank the following companies for supplying fabric and wallpaper samples for the jacket photography:
Laura Ashley, Coloroll, Jane Churchill, Designers Guild, Heal's, John Lewis, Osborne & Little, Sanderson's, Sandpiper Papers (Mary Gilliatt's Edwardian Garden Collection), and Warner and Sons Ltd.